PELICAN BOOKS

HISTORICAL INTERPRETATION 2

Advisory Editor: J. H. Plumb

John J. Bagley, Reader in History in the Department of Adult Education and Extra Mural Studies of the University of Liverpool, graduated in 1930. Since then, apart from war-time service with the R.A.F., he has been teaching and studying history, first as a schoolmaster and secondly as a university teacher.

In the 1940s John Bagley published a history of Up Holland Grammar School and a biography of Margaret of Anjou. Then, out of his special interest in the history of the north-western counties, came his *History of Lancashire with Maps and Pictures*. His *Life in Medieval England* is still in print, and *Henry VIII and his Times* has been published in America and Mexico, as well as in this country. More recently, in collaboration with his son, Mr Bagley has written books on Poor Law and Education for a historical series. Penguin Books published the first volume of *Historical Interpretation* in 1965, and *A Documentary History of England* (J. J. Bagley and P. B. Rowley) in 1966.

For nearly twenty years Mr Bagley edited the *Transactions of the Historic Society of Lancashire and Cheshire*. Currently, he is editing a *History of Cheshire* for the Cheshire Community Council, and a series entitled *Medieval Life*, also published in America.

HISTORICAL INTERPRETATION

2

Sources of English History
1540 to the Present Day

J. J. BAGLEY

PENGUIN BOOKS

Penguin Books Ltd, Harmondsworth, Middlesex, England
Penguin Books Inc., 7110 Ambassador Road, Baltimore, Maryland 21207, U.S.A.
Penguin Books Australia Ltd, Ringwood, Victoria, Australia

———

First published 1971

———

Copyright © J. J. Bagley, 1971

———

Made and printed in Great Britain
by Cox & Wyman Ltd, London, Reading and Fakenham
Set in Monotype Bembo

CONTENTS

FOREWORD

This book is a continuation of an earlier Pelican Book, *Historical Interpretation: Sources of English Medieval History, 1066–1540*. The records of the activities and thoughts of Englishmen both at home and abroad are far more numerous for post-Tudor than for pre-Tudor times. Therefore, this second volume has even less chance than its predecessor had of being comprehensive. All I have been able to do is to describe and illustrate with examples the main types of written and printed records upon which is based our knowledge of the political, social, and economic history of England and Wales during the last four centuries, and to include in the bibliographies the more obvious texts and collections of documents.

The historical research which is primarily based on central government records stored in the Public Record Office and British Museum still goes on apace, but the regional and local records available in many record offices and reference libraries throughout the country are attracting increasing attention. They now constitute an important growth point in historical studies. Already they have considerably enlarged and modified our understanding of our national past, and they offer good prospects for fresh discoveries to all who continue to work on them with patience and discernment. For this reason they have been given a prominent place in this book.

I wish to thank Professor J. H. Plumb for carefully reading my manuscript and for helping me to improve it.

University of Liverpool
New Year 1970

J.J.B.

Everyone who wishes to read English manuscripts written during the eventful century which separated the execution of Thomas Cromwell from the gruesome disinterment of the remains of Oliver must first master Elizabethan court and secretary hands. In these two styles of writing the very form of the letters is intimidating enough, but abbreviations, contractions, and endless minims, which make no distinction between n, u, and v or between m and w, give the manuscripts an even more fearsome look. Yet two or three hours of perseverance usually dispel the student's worst terrors, and a few weeks of study and practice – particularly practice – bestow on him an ability to read both hands reasonably quickly and surely.

And there are compensations. From Henry VIII's reign onwards, vigorous and expressive English replaced stereotyped medieval Latin in a markedly increasing number of non-legal documents, and several new types of sources, as well as a much bigger volume of records, become available to the student. Rarely does the researcher in any period of English history after 1540 suffer the medievalist's mortification of finding no, or hardly any, evidence on the subject of his quest. At times he may not have all he would like to have – and the most desirable document often perversely appears to be that which has not survived – but he is just as likely to find himself with too much as with too little primary material. A surfeit of evidence poses a new problem for the historian. In selecting appropriate and reliable contemporary descriptions and opinions, he must try to prevent his own predilections and preferences from dictating his choice. Equally, he must revere the sacredness of facts – once he is satisfied that they are indeed facts. Theories and interpretations of the past, however hallowed or long-standing, always remain mortal and expendable. Facts stand unmovable, for truth, the holy grail of all scholars, can only be sought by way of them.

I. QUARTER SESSIONS AND PARISH RECORDS

In pre-industrial days, Britain was far less of a 'tight little island' than it became in the nineteenth century. Measured by travelling time, towns and villages stood much farther apart from each other, and most inhabitants lived entirely within the limits of the local community. The central government at Westminster took responsibility for safeguarding the country from the king's enemies and for punishing major offenders against the king's law, but it looked to the counties, not to a centralized civil service, to administer the country in accordance with the instructions of 'the king in parliament assembled'. From Westminster's point of view *the county* meant the county officers – first, the sheriff, royal nominee and theoretical governor of the county, whose responsibilities by the sixteenth century had dwindled to the care of prisoners in the county gaol, the punishment of minor debtors, the impanelling of juries, the supervision of parliamentary elections, and the collection of extraordinary taxation; secondly, the lord lieutenant, who from Edward VI's reign until Gladstone's first ministry took charge of the county militia and formed the strongest link between central and local government, and, thirdly and above all, the justices of the peace, whose burden of executive duties grew steadily heavier as the years passed.

The crown appointed the justices of the peace from the landed gentlemen of each county. Until 1906, the law required a substantial property qualification for holders of the office. In Tudor times it was 'land or tenements worth £20 a year'; but as money depreciated in value further acts increased the minimum figure. In practice the squirearchy monopolized the office, and the justices' authoritative function in county admin-istration helped to strengthen and maintain the respect which lesser mortals paid to the squires for half a millennium. Most justices took their duties seriously, if only to retain the social cachet of their office, and, without any monetary reward beyond inadequate expenses and occasional modest fees, devoted many hours a month to public work. Their office was neither hereditary nor permanent. At varying intervals, and always at the beginning of a reign, the crown issued new commissions of the peace for each county, and justices who had scamped their duties, or had proved too independent for the monarch's, or the lord chancellor's, liking, often found their name quietly dropped from the list. Westminster might seem safely remote from many parts of Tudor and Stuart England, but the crown had eyes and ears in the assize judges, who, by an act of 1542, were expressly charged with the supervision of the justices, and in the clerks of the peace, one of whose duties was to send to Westminster a list of indictments and convictions made in the justices' courts. Justices of the peace were expected to mediate between aggrieved parties and to see that, in their county, crimes were investigated and criminals arrested. Every justice, single-handed, had authority to acquit or remand in custody or on bail any accused persons whom the parish con-stable brought before him. Two justices working together possessed summary powers over petty offenders, but the full bench of justices, sitting with a jury in quarter sessions, could hear all cases short of treason even though in practice they reserved most serious felonies for the coming of the assize judges. Furthermore, in their executive capacity, the justices in quarter sessions endeavoured to see that county administration worked smoothly, and that parish office-holders did not neglect their duties.

The quorum system was the Tudors' method of ensuring that local justice and county administration would always be legally sound. From each commission the crown picked out a handful of men with legal training or long experience on the bench, and stipulated that one or more of them should always be present whenever two or more justices acted together. The commission document was in Latin – '*assignavimus etiam vos, et quoslibet duo vel plures vestrum (quorum aliquem vestrum A, B, C, etc. unum esse volumus) Justiciarios nostros* . . .': 'furthermore we appoint you, or any two or more of you (of whom we wish A, B, or C etc. to be one) our justices . . .' The word *quorum* (of whom) became transformed into an English noun, so that to be appointed to a quorum was to enjoy an eminence beyond that of a simple justice of the peace. As the seventeenth century progressed, the justices of the quorum tended to be the more experienced squires rather than the professional lawyers favoured by the Tudors, and by the eighteenth and nineteenth centuries, when professional legal advice was more readily available to quarter sessions, very few members of a commission found themselves excluded from the quorum.

Quarter sessions met every three months, theoretically only in the county town, but in most counties, for convenience's sake, in a time-honoured sequence of three, four, or more centres. When need arose, the justices held extra or 'discretionary' sessions, and, of course, every justice, sitting with one or more of his neighbouring colleagues, held frequent petty sessions in his own area of the county to dispatch the trivial cases. At quarter sessions, the justices had the secretarial help and legal advice of the clerk of the peace. He, a trained attorney, presented the business before the bench, guided the court proceedings along correct legal lines, notified all interested parties of judgements and decisions, and, most important for historians, filed the numerous miscellaneous documents known collectively as quarter sessions records. Today, these rolls, books, and single papers are the backbone of every county record office's collection. They illuminate almost all aspects of community life from the sixteenth to the end of the nineteenth century, when the Local Government Act of 1888 transferred the bulk of quarter sessions' non-judicial work to the newly created, elected county councils.

To appreciate the width and variety of the work of the quarter sessions, one cannot do better than study the petitions presented to the court. In Tudor times there were petitions concerning such diverse matters as the building and repair of bridges and roads, militia accounts, vagabonds, and absence from church. As the central government progressively called on the justices to undertake additional tasks, and as economic and social changes gradually made government more complex, such new matters as apprenticeship, industrial discontent, parish settlement, and the organization of schools or the repair of churches became common topics for petitions. Such petitions were presented by private individuals, some by parish officers, some by groups of neighbours, and some by vestries (the ruling bodies of civil parishes) or by manor courts. To all of them the bench listened and gave answer. The short decisions the clerk wrote at the foot of the petition – 'The overseer of the poor to pay the petitioner 9d. a week', or 'To be sent to the house of correction if he does not remove himself within ten days', or, quite simply, 'Yes' or 'No'. The more complicated answers required setting out in separate documents, and these the clerk usually filed under the heading *Orders*.

The general work of quarter sessions the clerk minuted in the Sessions Rolls. Unfortunately, not all the counties have extant records as early as Tudor times, but almost all have substantial records from the mid seventeenth century onwards. Many details of the judicial work done at quarter sessions will usually be found in additional files – Recognizances, Indictments, and Fines. Other bulky bundles of quarter sessions' papers concern administration. The subsections of these administrative papers are not identical in each county, but every clerk of the peace is bound to have kept files upon such common matters as bridges and highways, houses of correction, and, during the nineteenth century, lunatic asylums and police organization. At the same time the law required him to maintain, among other records, registers of alehousekeepers, gamekeepers, dissenters' chapels, savings banks, land tax assessments, and enclosures of land. The nominal custodian of these comprehensive county records was *custos rotulorum*. His office, certainly from Anne's reign if not earlier, was combined with the lord lieutenancy, but, as we have seen, the people who had the day-to-day job of handling the files and registers and keeping them up-to-date were the clerk of the peace and his clerical assistants. For the work of these men in their several generations, all historians, but especially local, economic, and social historians, must be eternally grateful. Without the rich resources of the quarter sessions' records to explore, the primary material upon which the study of history is based would be considerably bereft.

During the Middle Ages the administrative subdivision of the county had been the hundred, and the most usual unit of local government the manor. But the Tudors found the civil parish more practical for their purposes. It was free from the tradition of aristocratic control, but could easily be supervised and inspected by the justices and, when appropriate, by the bishop. In the south and east, the more densely populated areas of sixteenth-century England, the ecclesiastical parish furnished the civil parish with ready-made boundaries, but in the north and west large ecclesiastical parishes had to be divided into two or more civil parishes, each centred not on a parish church but on a chapel of ease. The hundred courts ceased to function, and such manor courts as survived found themselves compelled to fall in line with the vestries, and each year appoint a series of office-holders to carry out traditional and statutory duties. The Highways Acts of 1555 and 1563 required the appointment of *surveyors* or *supervisors* of the parish highways: '... the constables and churchwardens of every parish within this realm shall yearly, upon the Tuesday or Wednesday in Easter week, call together a number of the parochians and shall then elect and choose two honest persons of the parish to be surveyors and orderers for one year of the works for amendment of the highways in their parish leading to any market town ...' The Poor Law Act of 1572 created another new officer, the overseer of the poor, and the comprehensive Poor Law Acts of 1598 and 1601 confirmed him in office and defined the separate functions of himself, the churchwarden and the constable in the administration of the Elizabethan Poor Law. Traditional office-holders, such as the pinder, the hayward and the moss reeve, who had functioned in the medieval manors and vills continued to do much the same work in the new administrative parishes, but some of the officers who had been taken over from the manor – the constable especially – found their responsibilities considerably increased.

At least four officers in each parish – churchwarden, constable, overseer of the poor, and surveyor of the highway – had to collect and dispense public money. Consequently, they had to keep accounts, and, usually each Eastertide, submit them to the justices before either beginning another year of duty, or, more often, handing over their office to a successor. A single sheet of any of these accounts will probably strike the reader as a quaint survival, an oddity of antiquarian rather than of historical interest, but a sequence of accounts for any one parish, or better still for a group of neighbouring parishes, is a detailed record of community activity. Traditions, problems, opinions, personalities, and the pattern of parochial life shine through the humdrum, repetitive entries, made not to enlighten subsequent generations but to satisfy the immediate demand of the justices for an account of a humble and often irksome stewardship.

Just before the Second World War, a volume of church-wardens' accounts of Prescot, Lancashire, turned up unexpectedly. They were exceptionally early accounts; they covered the years 1523 to 1607, a period of dramatic changes in English ecclesiastical law and of stirring and tragic events in Roman Catholic Lancashire. Not surprisingly, a distinguished local historian, F. A. Bailey, gave this battered, partly decayed, and incomplete book his immediate attention, and in two wartime articles and a post-war Lancashire and Cheshire Record Society volume, made the text available to everyone. From these petty, financial accounts can be extracted the story of how this northern parish reacted to the changing laws issued from Westminster. In 1546–7, the wardens were still making the traditional entry, 'Paid for bread and wine to say Mass withal', but three years later, they changed it to 'Paid for bread and wine to celebrate with'. Throughout the second half of the 1540s and the early 1550s, the unusually few and short entries reflect the obvious unease in the parish: for the last two years of Edward's reign the wardens were content to report 'Nothing received nor paid nothing'. But Mary's accession was greeted by the resumption of generous parish giving, the rapid restoration of the Mass, and the return of all the traditional ceremony at the different annual festivals.

Item, in expenses in the parish business by the space of xxii days at Candlemas Term for the obtaining of an indenture and obligation that the church and chapel goods should be restored to that use which they were first given unto   **xxxi s.**

This single item from the accounts of 1553–4 is enough to show with what determination and at what expense the Prescot wardens carried out their part in the Marian restoration, but several other supporting items refer to such matters as the repair of the sanctus bell, the setting up of the paschal candle, and 'the throwing [making] of the Saint Mary candle'. Moreover, the 1555–6 accounts demonstrate the intense interest the parish showed in making good the fabric, especially the windows, of the church after recent years of damage and neglect.

Item, for xii stone of lead	xiiii s.
Item, for xiii pound and a di. [dimidium = half] of old pewter to make solder of	vii s. xd.
Item, paid to the glasser Richard Russell for xxx foot and quarter of new glass, at ixd. the foot	xxiii s. vd.
Item, for setting of ix score foot and one foot and di. of old glass ... at iiiid. every foot	xlv s. iiiid. ob [½d.]
Item, to the same glasser for mending broken holes in the windows	xviid.
Item, for casting off earth from the church walls	iiiid.
Item, for the expenses of one of the church reeves [wardens] for overseeing the glassers and to see them do their duty by the space of vi weeks	xii s.
Item, paid for helping the mason up with stones and for nails to make his tronnges [scaffolding?] with	iiiid.
Item, paid for an eshin [bucket] to carry water and sieve to sieve lime and sand with	vd.
Item, paid to John Tarbock for xxxviii pounds of iron to make hooks of to the steeple	iii s. xid.

These are only some of the items in a long repair bill, but they are sufficient to illustrate the unusual activity of that particular year and to convey across the years a sense of satisfaction and achievement.

Not every parish so openly disliked the Edwardian innovations as Prescot did. The churchwardens' accounts at Yatton, Somerset, for example, are far calmer. Significant entries begin, as expected, in 1547–8.

Paid for the Homilies and Injunctions	ii s.
Paid in expenses for fetching the said books	iiii d.

These two books the crown commended in July 1547. They

upheld that the Epistle, Gospel, and Litany should be read in English, and condemned the superstitious worship of relics and images. Prescot, apparently, ignored this instruction altogether: later it was to delay for a year or more the buying of copies of the First Prayer Book of Edward VI, which was enforced by act of parliament in 1549. But Yatton not only purchased *Homilies* and *Injunctions* in good time, but also acted upon them. For a few lines later in the accounts occur:

Paid in expenses at the taking down of the said
images and the iron in the church   vd.
Paid to W. Sensam and J. Streting for taking down
the same said iron and images   xiid.

and in the following year, 1548–9,

Paid for taking down our Lady in the chancel   iiiid.
Paid for a book called paraphtasus and Erasmus
[Erasmus's *Paraphrase* which the Injunctions of 1547
required every 'parson, vicar, curate, chantry
priest, and stipendiary, being under the degree of
Bachelor of Divinity' to 'provide and have of his
own']   xi s. iiiid.
Paid for a bible of the largest volume [also required
by the Injunctions]   xi s.

In this same year the wardens recorded the sale of the now-unwanted, silver processional cross, and the using of the unexpected cash to repair an important sluice to prevent flooding; the employment of a painter to paint out proscribed Popish pictures and substitute texts on the church walls, and the payment of 8d. to the Reverend Nicholas Poore for translating the Mass into English.

The necessary reversion of this policy after 1553 is entered into the accounts just as calmly. In accordance with law the stone altar had been replaced by a wooden table during Edward's reign. After 1553 it had to be rebuilt at the parish's expense:

THE BUILDING OF THE ALTAR

Item to the masons	viii s.	
Item to the other ii workmen	ii s.	
Item for lime		xiid.
Item to Thomas Clarke		vid.
Item to expenses		xd.

Summa   xii s.   iiiid.

The church at Yatton needed re-equipping in other ways too. The wardens paid 2s. 6d. for a processional (a book containing prayers and hymns used in processions), 16s. 0d. for a missal, 6s. 8d. for a manual, and a further 8d. for expenses 'in seeking' these necessary service books. They bought a new censer, pax and corporal, a net cloth to cover the pyx, and even new tassels for the pyx itself. Next they set about refurnishing and decorating the rood screen and loft, and reimbursed four parishioners who had each advanced 20s. 0d. in order either to buy back the old processional cross or purchase a new one. By the middle of 1557 it would appear that Yatton church had retransformed itself, as had probably most other parish churches, into a traditional Roman Catholic Church after its brief encounter with Calvinistic Protestantism.

But, of course, the restoration of the traditional furnishings of the parish church was as short-lived as the first attempt to change them. Elizabeth's accession in November 1558 was followed, in May 1559, by new Acts of Supremacy and Uniformity, both enforceable by severe penalties against clerical and lay offenders. Even so unwilling a parish as Prescot had to obey before long, and, apparently about Lent or Easter 1560, the first changes took place.

Item, paid to Ewan Garnett for pulling down the high altar viiid.

Item, spent by Robert Prescot, Richard Bower, Hugh Green and Edward Cooper when we took down the other three altars [chantry altars] xiiiid.

The Yatton wardens were no quicker in removing their new stone altar. Probably wardens everywhere were wearying of this expensive game of all change, but every parish had soon to readjust itself to the new services. Considerably less wax was wanted for candle-making, but communion in both kinds required far more wine – the Prescot wardens were soon ordering ten bottles a time – and usually a bigger cup than the customary chalice. In Catholic Lancashire especially, the church authorities had a difficult task putting the law into full operation. As late as 1586, Thomas Meade, the recently appointed vicar of Prescot, considered that the children of the parish were his only hope: '. . . superstition is so grounded in the aged, that without the rare mercy of God death must part it . . .' His predecessor had bought twenty copies of a *Little Catechism* to sell to parishioners. In 1584–5 Meade ordered sixty more, but despite his efforts to get householders to buy it and study the new Anglican doctrines, the wardens noted that they had thirty-eight copies left on their hands at the end of their year of office. Furthermore, the Prescot accounts record not a single instance of collecting a fine for absence from the church on Sundays. The Act of Uniformity of 1559 is straightforward enough on this point: '. . . every person and persons inhabiting within this realm . . . shall diligently and faithfully . . . endeavour themselves to resort to their parish church or chapel accustomed . . . upon pain that every person so offending shall forfeit for every such offence 12d., to be levied by the churchwardens of the parish where such offence shall be done . . .' It is unthinkable that Prescot had no absentees – the recusant rolls in quarter sessions records demonstrate the local strength of the opposition to the Anglican church – and one can only assume that in this parish successive wardens decided that to attempt to enforce this part of the statute would be too difficult and distasteful to be practical. Archdeacons and justices too must have been sympathetic or complacent to allow the wardens to have turned so blind an eye. In many such ways do local records blur, complicate, and make more truthful the neat picture of change which, when used alone, the central government records appear to paint with such well-defined, confident strokes of the brush.

Even in the quiet and more routine years, the office of churchwarden was no sinecure. Church law held him responsible for maintaining the nave, belfry, and churchyard, for providing all books, vestments, and 'furniture' for his church, for collecting, safeguarding, and spending the church rates, and for reporting to the archdeacon's court any moral delinquencies of the rector or parishioners and any variation of the services laid down in the Prayer Book. Repairs to the church fabric were often his most pressing concern. The following extracts from the accounts of Rainham, Kent, for the year 1565–6 have their counterparts in the accounts of every parish at frequent intervals:

Paid to a Carpenter for hanging of the bells	2s. 8d.
Paid for a load of lime and fetching of it	11s. 0d.
Paid for a beam for the Church and fetching of it	10s. 4d.
Paid to Thomas Hicks for Repairing of the Church	33s. 4d.
Spent when the Church was Repaired	9d.
For 1,000 of tile	10s. 0d.
For 150 of Corner tile	6s. 0d.
For fetching of a load of sand	6d.
Paid to Chapman a tiler for 3 days for him and his man and find themselves	6s. 0d.
Paid to James Anderson for iron work divers times	26s. 8d.
Paid to Amye the plumber for old debt mending of the Gutters	7s. 0d.

Two years later there was more tiling to be done:

Paid to Birch a tiler for pointing of the north isle of the Church and for mending of certain decayed places in the Church for 7 days finding himself at 12d. the day	7s. 0d.

As if these were not enough responsibilities for an ordinary, unpaid householder to have to add to his family duties, the state began to pile on civil obligations. The Beggars Act of 1536 required each churchwarden 'to gather and procure' voluntary alms for the relief of the poor. A little later the crown ordered him to assess and receive rates for the relief of maimed soldiers and of prisoners in the county gaol, and to collect money for church briefs, which were documents authorizing charitable collections for the relief of the victims of personal or public disasters. In 1566 Elizabeth's government made churchwardens destroyers of vermin: it held them responsible for collecting yet another rate, and for using the money to reward parishioners who brought along the beaks or eggs of 'noyful fowls', such as crows and hawks, or heads of animals locally classed as vermin – 'all which said heads and eggs shall be . . . in the presence of the said churchwardens . . . burned, consumed, or cut in sunder.' As we have seen, the Highways Act instructed him to convene the annual parish meeting for the elections of surveyors of the highway, and successive poor law acts so increased his responsibilities that at the beginning of the seventeenth century he found himself, aided by the overseers, collecting and administering the parish poor rate and binding the children of vagrants to be apprentices.

On paper, and often in practice, the parish constable too was a busy man, but, if we accept the comments of Shakespeare and other contemporaries, he often failed to match the requirements of his office. His duties included the arrest of vagrants, the pursuit of criminals, the relief of licensed travellers, the maintenance of law and order, the care of stocks and cucking stool, and, when necessary, the raising of the militia. These were far too exacting for one part-time and untrained parishioner to carry out fully and successfully, and therefore he became a stock target for popular fun. 'You are thought to be the most senseless and fit man for the constable of the watch,' says

Dogberry to George Seacoal in *Much Ado about Nothing*, and then when Seacoal vacantly asks what he must do if the 'vagrom man' he has challenged fails to halt, offers the cynical but practical advice, 'Why then, take no note of him, but let him go; and presently call the rest of the watch together, and thank God you are rid of a knave.' Most parish constables had no watch to call out. They could rely only upon the prestige of their ancient office and the strength of their own right arm. Consequently the percentage of undetected crime remained high. Simply because constables had neither time nor inducement to solve any other parish's problems, the effectiveness of a hue and cry could not help but diminish rapidly as it passed to parishes outside the vicinity of the crime. The constable made a perfunctory search for the criminal – the cost of the search was usually less than 6d. – and then thankfully passed on the details to his colleague in the next parish.

During the Middle Ages and the sixteenth century, the official expenditure of most parish constables came out of the county rate which they collected, or out of funds held by the churchwardens. But successive poor law acts increased their duties and their spending, so that an act of 1603 authorized them to levy a rate of their own. Consequently, in the years before the Civil Wars, many parish constables began keeping detailed accounts of their expenditure and submitting them to the annual scrutiny of the court leet – the local court of record – or later, of the justices. These accounts, which became more plentiful as time went on, reveal both the exacting repetition of the constable's duties and the harsh conditions which the law imposed upon unfortunate and destitute citizens. Manchester's constables' accounts have survived from 1612. George Clarke and Rowland Mosley held office from October 1624 to October 1625. During that relatively quiet year they received £70 9s. 0½d. in rates levied on the little town itself and on the 'hamlets thereto belonging', such as Ardwick, Blackley,

Droylesden, and Harpurhey. The following items taken from the beginning of their 'disbursement' accounts show typical ways in which they spent the money entrusted to them:

	s.	d.
October 16 Paid for bringing of John Flood of Carnarthen [*sic*] to the Constables of Stretford		2
Paid for the bringing of Anne Eastwood to the Constables of Newton		3
Paid for the bringing of William Talbot and the whipping of him and his pass and diet all night		11
October 19 Paid for Katherine Horrocks a cripple borne upon a barrow for her whipping pass and diet all night		11
November 3 Received a hue and cry from the constables of Cholerton Row and made a search for one George Cooke that was broke out of Chester Castle and delivering the hue and cry to the Constable of Salford		4
November 5 Robert Cowborne being a blind man and a Fidler and his wife being taken begging she being very great with child and being put in the Dungeon whilst the pass was making being not past half an hour was delivered of a child which was christened and they were both kept of the town's charges till she was churched, which was xiiii days and for their pass and keeping and bringing to Cholerton Row	4	11
For making clean the Dungeon		1
For making precepts to the Constables of the hamlets and delivering them for a subsidy	2	0
Paid for a ladder and ii plate locks for the Dungeon and Cuckstool and for a great round crab lock for the stocks	4	0
November 7 Paid the same day to Ralph Mills and Richard Hunt for walking up and down the Town upon Salford Fair Day for taking of cutpurses and other suspected persons	1	6
November 22 Paid to Luke Knott of Ousdenn [*sic*] in the County of Lancaster a soldier who had His Excellency's [i.e. his commander's] pass and came from Holland		6
December 4 Paid Edmund Buckley of Salford for tending Robert Costerdine who was put in the old stocks for being drunk		2

	s.	d.
December 10 Paid to Ralph Mills and Richard Hunt for carrying Margery Hamilton a cripple who had a pass to the Constables of Cheetham	1	0
Paid the same day for a pass for John Stanger a poor traveller who went towards Lichfield in Staffordshire		2
December 11 Paid to Ralph Mills for bringing John Worrall by the appointment of Mr Prestwich and Mr Mosley to the House of Correction	5	4
December 14 Received a hue and cry from the Constables of Stretford for a robbery committed at Simon Robinson's house at Cowlton [*Colton* (?), North Lancashire or Staffordshire] who had clothes gone and making search and delivering to the Constables of Cheetham to go northwards		6
December 15 Paid Thurstan Knowles for a tree for a pair of stocks	10	0
Paid the same day to John Kay and Richard Lowe for workmanship and for 'ratchemonts' for the new stocks and for making irons	7	0

The full accounts demonstrate how heavy an extra burden the Elizabethan Poor Law thrust on the constable's back. In their first ten weeks of duty, Clarke and Mosley had to superintend a dozen public whippings of vagrants arrested in Manchester, and receive and escort to the next parish at least another score of convicted vagrants or cripples, who, under a justice's order or licence, were travelling back to the parish legally responsible for them. Nevertheless, once the 1601 Act began to work smoothly, most of the poor law responsibilities in the parish were not borne by the constable, but by the overseer of the poor. He exacted regular instalments of poor rate from the parishioners, and paid out tiny weekly sums of money to the chronic sick poor and the temporary disabled. It was his duty to see that no one in the parish starved to death, and that the helpless – infant, crippled, and aged paupers – had somewhere to sleep. But his fellow parishioners, as well as the law, usually insisted that he measured the necessity very narrowly indeed. The following items, taken from the earliest accounts of the overseers of Elmstead in Essex, are typical overseers' expenses:

For a pair of shoes for William Harnis the 1 of July	10d.
Paid for the same William Harnis, for canvas and his apparel making the same day	2s. 8d.
Paid to William Moody the 9 of July	12d.
To John Payne the same day [3 September] for Richard Smith	5s. 0d.
More laid out for a shirt and pair of shoes for Richard Smith	2s. 9d.
For the same Richard Smith for a pair of stockings 21 October	13d.
Laid out for carrying William Harnis to his master [i.e. the overseers were apprenticing him to a trade]	6d.
More to William Moody the 21 December	12d.
More to William Moody the 8 of January	12d.
To the Widow Harnis the same day	6d.
Laid out for a smock for Camplyn's girl the 2 February	16d.
Paid to Ann Harnis the 10 of February	4d.

Even from these few lines there emerges the outline of the story of Widow Harnis and her son. We can imagine the destitution of Smith and Moody, and sense the careful reluctance with which the overseers dispensed the rate money. Such accounts, together with the relevant petitions to quarter sessions, show how the poor law worked out at parish level. For more than two centuries they are the main source for this aspect of social history. They only cease to be available soon after 1834 when, in accordance with the Poor Law Amendment Act, boards of guardians took over local responsibility.

The fourth parish officer regularly to administer public money was the surveyor, or supervisor, of the highways. He came into existence when the Highways Act of 1555 arranged that henceforward the main roads of every parish, 'being now both very noisome and tedious to travel in', should be maintained by the unpaid labour of 'every householder and also every cottager and labourer of that parish able to labour and being no hired servant' for four, and after 1563, six days a year. Very rarely in the sixteenth and seventeenth centuries did parish surveyors present annual accounts, though from their beginning such duties as 'viewing' the roads and ensuring that land-occupiers hedged and ditched along the road side, and that 'statute labourers' had sufficient stones and gravel for their work could not have been done without spending money. But after the Highways Act of 1691, which tightened the grip of the justices on parish road repairs and authorized the levying of a regular highway rate, surveyors' accounts become far more plentiful. As a primary source, they are principally used by economic and social historians studying transport or industrial development in the eighteenth and early nineteenth centuries.

The care of bridges was as tiresome a problem for Tudor and Stuart governments as the repair of the roads. England's growing prosperity depended upon the carting of increasing quantities of goods to and from ports and markets, and no government interested in commerce – if only as a source of revenue – could let this be jeopardized by broken bridges, for which no one would acknowledge responsibility. As early as 1531 the Statute of Bridges alerted the justices: '. . . in every shire of this realm, franchise, city, or borough, four of them at least, whereof one to be of the Quorum, shall have power and authority to enquire, hear, and determine in the King's general Sessions of Peace of all manner of anoysances of bridges broken in the highways to the damage of the King's liege people . . .' The responsibility for the maintenance of many bridges, as for example London Bridge or the Town Bridge at Nantwich, lay with the particular city or borough in which the bridge was situated: sometimes, as at Abingdon and Stratford on Avon, a gild undertook as a pious duty the task of keeping a bridge in repair, and by Tudor times almost all important bridges had succeeded in attracting endowments from local benefactors. The borough of Kingston-upon-Thames had charge of the Great Bridge, a narrow, high-arched, timber structure, which in the sixteenth century offered the next crossing of the Thames above London Bridge. To keep it in repair and administer the bridge funds, the borough annually appointed two freemen to be bridgewardens, and Surrey Record Society has published the accounts which these officials kept during the years 1526–67. These are the earliest accounts extant, but there are later accounts in comparative plenty in the borough archives. Each year, the bridgewardens collected the rents from lands given to the borough for the upkeep of the bridge. Until 1565 when the bridge was made free, they also received an agreed sum – £1 14s. 8d. from 1527 to 1539 and £1 6s. 8d. from 1542 to 1545 – from the speculator who farmed – that is, contracted for collecting – the tolls. In 1542, a normal year in this respect, receipts amounted in all to £20 5s. 10d. – £11 8s. 4d. from rents and farmed tolls; £8 11s. 4d. carried over from the previous year; and 6s. 2d. from the sale of the old timber discarded by the repairers. Out of this money had to come a few rents, the cost of repairs of property administered by the bridgewardens, and payment for occasional requiems for the souls of departed benefactors. But the bulk of the funds was spent on the bridge itself. In the 1542 'discharge' appear thirty-five such items as:

Paid to John Periar for his 3 men for working at the bridge for to set up the rails that the carter fell down   8d.

Paid to John Dowsett for 2 alder poles for to make 'a legges' for the bridge   4d.

Paid to Matthew Price for an iron for the leg at the high pier   4d.

Paid to Edward Buckland and 2 wherrymen for taking up 2 pieces of timber of the bridge's   2d.

Paid to William Wood for 2 days working at the bridge   14d.

Paid for nails   1d.

Paid to John Dowsett for 36½ feet of timber for the
bridge   4s. 10d.

This particular year, the total expenditure, £3 8s. 7d., was low.
The average annual cost for the last twenty years of Henry
VIII's reign was about £8 0s. 0d., but two years when major
repairs were necessary, 1530–31 and 1544–5, cost £22 0s. 8½d.
and £25 9s. 1d. respectively. Unfortunately for the borough of
Kingston, benefactors had endowed the bridge with fixed
sums of money, adequate in their day but rapidly becoming
ineffective as inflation increased the price of labour and raw
materials. Long before the end of the century, the bridgewardens were finding it difficult to keep the bridge accounts
balanced.

'And where in many parts of this realm,' stated the Statute
of Bridges, 'it cannot be known and proved what hundred,
riding, wapentake, city, borough, town, or parish . . . ought
of right to make maintain such bridges decayed . . . then . . .
the said bridges, if they be without city or town corporate,
shall be made by the inhabitants of the shire or riding within
the which the said bridge decayed shall happen to be.' Need-
less to say, the justices had to take responsibility for these
county, and occasionally hundred, bridges. When they required repairing, the justices appointed a surveyor for the job,
advanced him money out of the county rates, and finally, on
the receipt of his account, took back the surplus or paid out
what was still owing. In 1627, quarter sessions estimated
£50 2s. 5d. (of all odd sums) for repairing Garstang Bridge
across the River Wyre. The stone came from Ellel, some seven
miles to the north, and 141 loads of it were quarried and carried
to the bridge at a total cost of £30 16s. 6d. Lime cost £2 15s. 6d.,
paving and walling stones 9s. 0d., timber scaffolding £3 4s. 7d.,
and iron work and wedges 5s. 2d. Almost all the other expenses
were for labour:

To labourers for making mortar	7s. 11d.
To Ellis Davie for paving the bridge	8s. 2d.
To William Gervis, Robert Parkinson and divers other labourers for carrying earth and other labours about the work according to their days	£3 10s. 0d.
For board wages for the workmen	£5 10s. 0d.
Bernard Wood his own wages, 12d. a day. 60 days	£3 0s. 0d.
John Stubbs his wages, 60 days, 12d. the day, the said Bernard and John being chief workmen	£3 0s. 0d.

The total account came to £61 12s. 4d., so that the surveyor appointed for the job had to be given a further £11 9s. 11d. out of the county rate.

The various financial accounts, churchwardens', constables', overseers' or surveyors', have more than one use for the historian. Very few parishes can produce long runs of them all, but the many collections that still exist are obviously reliable guides to the cost of goods, rates of wages, progress of inflation, and methods of employment. Taken altogether from one parish, or if possible two or more nearby parishes, they reveal an intimate cross-section of ordinary life in a particular district at a particular time: taken from several groups of parishes in different parts of England and Wales, or from the same parish or wider area in three or four different generations, they can form the basis of useful comparative studies. As he examines the spending of these petty sums of money, the political historian can see acts of parliament in action, with necessity or local convenience modifying what the legislators decreed. The social and economic historian can find in them information about such matters as food, clothing, furniture, and treatment of the sick, as well as evidence of periods of prosperity or years of plague, bad harvests, or other disasters. And, especially from eighteenth- and nineteenth-century accounts, the industrial historian can study the local effects of a turnpike road, a new canal, or a developing industry. The few short extracts quoted above demonstrate how these accounts are full of people's names. Occasionally they give us sufficient evidence to sketch the character of an outstanding parishioner or a persistent troublemaker. But however brief they may be, the genealogist must always look upon parish accounts as a supplementary source to the parish register, in which the parson regularly recorded baptisms, marriages, and burials.

Parish registers date from 1538. Before that year the odd priest here and there had kept private records, but in 1538 Thomas Cromwell, in his capacity as vicar general, ordered the incumbent and wardens of each parish to record baptisms, marriages, and burials as they occurred. Some parishes were slow to begin, and many incumbents obeyed indifferently by keeping scrappy records in inadequate books. But despite a widespread belief that registers were a fad of Henry's government, registration had come to stay. Edward, Mary, and Elizabeth all confirmed Cromwell's order: the tenth *injunction* of Elizabeth in 1559 reads 'the parson, vicar or curate, and parishioners of every parish within this realm shall in their churches and chapels keep one book of register, wherein they shall write the day and year of every wedding, christening, and burial made within their parish ... and also therein shall write every person's name that shall be so wedded, christened, and buried ...' In 1598, towards the end of her reign, Elizabeth's government ordered parish registers to be kept on parchment. It instructed incumbents to copy into the new parchment books all past records 'but especially since the first year of her Majesty's reign'. Not surprisingly, many incumbents appear to have considered that they had better things to do than copy out sixty years of registers. Others accepted the easier alternative and began their parchment books with the entries for 1558–9, but a few hundred were thorough enough to begin at the beginning. None could have been more meticulous than William Sherlock, the new curate-in-charge at Farnworth, now part of Widnes. His predecessor, who died conveniently in October 1598, had kept the register in abbreviated English:

Mr Henry Greene s. of Mr Edward G. bap.   19 Sept.
John s. to Ric. Davison of Farnworth bur.   24 Sept.
Jane d. to John Smith of Cuerdley bur. in ch.   6 Oct.

– and Sherlock, who obviously considered Latin the proper language for registers, was nevertheless honest enough to copy the old records exactly as he had found them. Below the last entry, 'Edward Baguley Curat of Farnworth bur. 16 Oct.' Sherlock affirmed – in Latin of course – that he had made a faithful copy of all the previous registers from November 1538. He then left space for witnesses to corroborate this claim. But no witness ever signed, presumably because Sherlock could find no one in the parish who had patience or interest enough to check the copy against the original. The next entries are Sherlock's own – in abbreviated Latin:

Thomas f [iliu]s Joh[ann]is Roughsich bap[tizatus] per
predictam Gulielmum Sherlock   18 Oct.
Richardus Barrowe sep[ultus]   19 Oct.
Jenetta uxor Will[el]mi Fletcher sep[ultus] in ecc[lesia]   22 Oct.

Christenings, marriages, and burials follow as they occur, for, as in many other early registers, no attempt was made to record them in separate lists. On the other hand, Leeds and East Grinstead are two examples of parishes which separated entries for baptisms, marriages, and burials from the beginning, which for Leeds was 1572 if the earliest extant register was the first to be kept, and for East Grinstead 1558, since the incumbent in 1598 was one of the many who decided to re-enter in his parchment register all items 'since the beginning of the Reign of our most gracious Sovereign Lady Queen Elizabeth'.

What was entered in a parish register depended partly upon

the intention and whim of the parson, and partly on the conscientiousness of the wardens. Most early registers are brief and staccato. The Edgbaston register, for example, begins in 1636 thus:

Mar.	14 Richard Edwards	bur.
May	15 Joyce, d. of Richd. Griffis	bap.
June	20 Ann, d. of Roger Wilkins	bur.
July	8 Elizabeth, d. of Roger Wilkins	bur.
July	18 Raphel Taylor and Margaret Harwood	mar.

Shorter still were many of the Tudor entries at East Grinstead, where in the baptism and burial sections the parson merely wrote the name and the date without the slightest indication of parents or age. Yet, in the same register, later incumbents were more expansive and gave useful identification details: in the marriages of 1654, for example,

May 1 The Agreement of marriage Between Thomas Baucomb of East Grinstead, Yeoman, and Elizabeth Ke[rest indecipherable] of the said parish, widow, was published the [blank] day of April and the next two Lord's days following And married 1 May.

May 18 The Agreement etc. Between James Linfild [?] of Lingfield in Surrey, Mercer, and Sarah Freeman of East Grinstead, single woman . . .

or in the burials of 1657,

April 25 Elizabeth wife of Thomas Paine of the Town
May 14 Robert Barham, a young man
July 4 Ann Overy, widow of the parish of Godstone in Surrey
August 11 Thomas Lintott of the College
August 12 William Shane, blacksmith

At first sight these details of place, age, and trade might seem too slight to be useful, but anyone who has occasion to use registers to construct genealogical tables finds out quickly how helpful they can be in sorting out people of the same name. Before the improved transport of the nineteenth and twentieth centuries began moving people about more freely, almost all parishes had five or six dominant family names. To seek a particular William Butterworth in Rochdale parish or a Jane Launchbury in Oxford parish is to be spoiled for choice, and demarcation details however tiny are welcome. The economic historian sifts from the registers all mention of trades, although, particularly in the sixteenth and seventeenth centuries when most men, villagers and townsmen alike, retained some direct interest in farming, the distribution pattern of such interesting trades as weaving, nail-making, and coalmining is apt to be masked by part-time weavers, nail-makers, or colliers appearing in the registers as *yeoman*, *husbandman*, or *labourer*. The mention of particular tools or stocks of raw materials in these workmen's wills and inventories often removes part of the mask (see the following section), but the historian can never be sure that he has found more than a fraction of the statistics he has set out to seek.

Parish registers can occasionally be dramatic. The graphs of births and deaths in a particular parish are rarely steady for long. A few ripples even when they are strong can safely be attributed to the vagaries of fortune or weather, but the historian must seek other explanations when figures suddenly bound to unusual heights or fall surprisingly low. For example, there was an extraordinary ripple in the East Grinstead burial figures in 1597. About 1,000 people were living in the parish, and in 1596 the burial figures jumped from an average of 35 during the previous ten years to an unprecedented 63. The following year the number was still high, 45, but by 1599 it had fallen to 30, and it remained quite average in the early years of the new century. On this evidence alone the local historian must *suspect* either an epidemic or, since the heaviest mortality was between February and June, an exceptionally severe spell of winter and spring weather in Sussex in 1597. Signs of epidemic are clearer in the Leeds register in 1587–8. Monthly totals of burials rose from the usual score or so to 37 in September

1587, maintained that high figure in October and November, and then moved further to 63, 61, and 56 in December, January, and February. By June 1588 they were normal again, and in the depth of the following winter tended to be below average. In the registers of the London parishes the plague of 1563 is startlingly plain: in that year St Mary Aldermary recorded 128 burials instead of its usual dozen, St Peter's, Cornhill, 169 instead of a score, and St James's, Clerkenwell, 176 instead of about 30. The worst months in those three parishes were August, September, and October. None of these three registers mentions the word *plague*, but the entries record a number of family disasters. At St Peter's, Gregory Yong, a man of some social standing since he is referred to as *Mr*, buried his wife on 10 September and his daughter two days later. The parson, Mr Gough, buried a daughter in July and a son in September. Yet both these families bore light afflictions compared with that of Peter Docket, a physician living in St Mary Aldermary parish. Between 29 October and 13 December he lost three sons and three daughters. Thirty years later, 1593, plague hit the City of London again: 83 were buried at St Peter's, 66 at St Mary's, and 377 at St James's. This time two of the clerks were more explicit:

[St Peter's] *May 8 Tuesday*. John Ashly, skinner, of the plague, pit [vault] in the cross aisle by the belfry 48 [years].

July 20 Friday. Robert Salisbury, upholsterer, an upright and just man, of the plague, by the vestry 50 [years].

July 20 Daniel Salisbury, his son, buried in the same grave, he died of the plague 10 [years]

[St Mary's] *July 24* Elizabeth and Mary Ward, sisters, servants to Edward Breth, of the plague.

July 25 Elizabeth Moyer, out of Price's house, of the plague

August 1 Isabel Rise, servant to William Hethe, of the plague

August 2 Sara Hering, which died in the street of the plague.

The clerk at St James's continued to do no more than list the names of the victims and the dates of their death, but at the end of his burial entries for 1593, the clerk at St Peter's volunteered figures for the whole of London:

There died in London in all, 25,886
Of them of the plague in all, 15,003

Then in the margin he inserted what we hope was not a boast but a prayer of thankfulness:

In a thousand five hundred ninety and three
The Lord preserved my house and me
When of pestilence there died
Full many a thousand else beside.

The story of another local pestilence is just as clear in the Preston burial register of 1630–31. Trouble there began slowly with a warning 15 burials in December 1630, built up with 29, 39, 54, 62, and 58 in the first five months of 1631, and then reached a grim climax with 92, 328, 279, and 80 burials from June to September. At the end of that year the register states baldly 'the plague ceased': it leaves its reader to imagine what human suffering and loss its bare figures imply, for the 1,063 burials which it records between the beginning of December 1630 and the end of November 1631 represents at least a quarter of the population of the parish. How many deaths it left unrecorded in the confused terror of those summer months it is impossible to tell.

Many statistical studies have been based on parish registers. Pairs of baptism and burial registers can yield valuable evidence on the incidence of infant mortality and the expectation of life: pairs of baptism and marriage registers can show the average age of bridegrooms and brides and the movement of population from one parish to another. In turn these exercises can lead to rough calculations of population figures in pre-census days: 'the dark ages of population history ended in 1538', declares E. A. Wrigley. Parish registers are now being used for more complicated studies such as the triangular relationship between years of scarcity, plague, and the average age of marriage, or possible connexions between developing industrialization, vagrancy, and bastardy. This type of historical study is not idle curiosity. Nor are its tables and graphs barren statistics. On the contrary, as E. A. Wrigley, Peter Laslett, and other members of the Cambridge Group for the History of Population and Social Structure are showing in their books and broadcast lectures, they constitute a sound foundation for social history and often provide a salutary corrective for older, established ideas derived chiefly from contemporary literature.

But, as we can only expect, during four hundred years and more, parish registers have suffered grave damage from their many enemies – careless incumbents, damp walls, hungry rodents, vestry fires, zealots clearing 'rubbish' from rectory cupboards and parish chests, and nineteenth-century genealogists using gall for 'bringing up' faded writing – and, later, for turning the parchment shiny black. Theoretically, the royal injunction of 1598, which required churchwardens to send annual copies of their registers to the diocesan registry, should have provided an ideal defence against all these predators, but it did not do so in practice. Researchers soon find that bishops' transcripts, as the copies are called, are often just as faulty as the registers themselves, if not more so. Had the diocese paid a small fee for regular returns, the transcripts would probably have been much more complete than they are, but, as it is, they are very patchy. A researcher may be lucky enough to find copies of the entries on torn or missing register pages, or of substantial parts of a register which he cannot cajole out of the vestry safe of an uncooperative rector or vicar, but he is just as likely to find that the transcript he is seeking is missing. It was probably never made.

The middle years of the seventeenth century are difficult for register searchers. The general disturbance of civil war, the abolition of bishoprics in 1645, and especially the civil registration of births and deaths in 1653 and the institution of civil marriage in the following year, all upset traditional practice. The Restoration however, abolished all the innovations of the interregnum. The crown and the parish register, were restored together. The register remained unchallenged as the most likely record of most Englishmen's existence until the present system of civil registration was established in 1837.

2. WILLS AND INVENTORIES

To supplement the parish register the genealogist turns naturally to wills. Formerly, these were to be found only in ecclesiastical archives, but now substantial collections of them have been transferred to county record offices. Until 1858 proving wills was the concern not of the state but of the church. The law, revised in 1529, required every executor to place before 'the court of the ordinary' – usually the bishop's consistory court, but occasionally the archdeacon's court – the will, properly signed and witnessed, together with a 'true and perfect inventory of all the goods, chattels, wares, merchandises as well movable as not movable'. Once the court was satisfied that will and inventory were genuine and truthful, it filed copies of both, and gave the executor authority to divide and dispose of the property according to the wishes of the deceased. The Statute of Wills in 1540 made legal the willing of real property, and consequently from that date wills had more significance than they had had in earlier years, when land devolved automatically by the traditional law of primogeniture, and wills were solely concerned with movable property.

Wills were not the prerogative of the better off. Most heads of households made them. 'Infra' wills of £40 and under were proved in the rural-dean's court, but the consistory court dealt with the wills of husbandmen and labourers as frequently as it did those of squires and lawyers. Men who owned property in more than one diocese, however, had to have their wills proved at provincial level, in the prerogative court of either Canterbury or York. Indeed, the prerogative court of Canterbury claimed and practised the right to prove wills and grant administrations for estates, big and small, in any part of England and Wales. During Tudor and Stuart times social convention strongly approved of householders making wills, but if anyone failed to leave instructions about the disposal of his property – and death-bed wishes expressed before witnesses could constitute a legal nuncupative will – his widow or his eldest son had to take out letters of administration (as today) and obtain probate from the same ecclesiastical court. It was usual in these times for a testator to divide his estate into three fairly equal parts. The first he left to his widow, the second he divided among his children, and the third he disposed of as he wished – to charity, to friends, to relations, or in the form of extra bequests to his widow and children.

The will's use to the genealogist is obvious. It gives him the approximate date of the testator's death – for it must lie between the dates of signing and proving – and in addition to establishing the full number of the family, including in-laws, at the time of signing, it often indicates likes and dislikes within the family, the occupations of different members, and the whereabouts of any who have left home. It occasionally sends the researcher scurrying back to the parish register to look for a son or a daughter he never knew existed, or to another parish altogether to trace the descent of a daughter who had married a 'foreigner' or, more rarely before the Restoration, of a son who had set up house in other parts. But a good will does not only help to supplement the parish register and fill gaps in the family tree: it also throws light on the character, interests, and well-being of the testator. It cannot disguise the concern of a loving husband for his wife's future welfare, or the disapproval of an aggrieved father for an erring son, or the generosity of a charitably minded citizen.

... And that I John Whittaker of Durham, [1595] must needs confess that by the virtuous care, and painful and dutiful regard of Anne, my wife, I have received many blessings, and that for her consideration, and good ordering my house and goods under her charge, God hath given good increase and blessed endeavours the better ... And for that, by my death, the best part of her maintenance is taken away, I think the rest that I shall leave, will be little enough to support her estate, therefore, first, I give unto my said wife the house, wherein I now dwell ... together with my whole interest which I have in the orchard ... and the other houses to my said dwelling house adjoining ... as also all my interest of that house called the Geald hall, with two other little houses ... etc.

... And for that my eldest son Anthony Chaytor is not natural unto his brethren and sisters, nor obedient to me, and made me not privy to his last marriage to Margery Thornton of Yorkshire, nor of the assurance of his lands made to his wife (God forgive him, and I pray God to bless him) therefore I do give all those my houses, land, meadows etc., of Fathill and Crossfield within the county of York, unto my son Hugh and his heirs ...

And albeit my son William Sankey hath heretofore as well to my great loss and hindrance, prodigally spent and wastefully consumed a great part of my goods and stock within my shop, has also followed and frequented most wicked, idle and lewd company, to his own shame, discredit and overthrow and my greatest grief, yet, notwithstanding the same, out of my fatherly care and love towards him, hoping of his reformation and amendment of life, I do give and bequeath unto him the other moiety of the said last third part of my said goods ...

... I, William Charlton, clerk, parson of Bangor-is y Coed, Flintshire ... give and bequeath to the poor of the parishes of Bangor, Overton, and Worthenbury £6 13s. 4d., *videlicet* to Bangor £3 6s. 8d., to Overton 40s. 0d. to Worthenbury 26s. 8d. to be divided by the churchwardens of the said parishes amongst the poor thereof. Item, I give towards the reparations of the body of the church of Bangor 20s. 0d. . . .

The 1581 will of Alexander Houghton of Lea Hall, Preston, which has raised extravagant hopes because it nominated William Shakeshafte (Shakespeare?) as a young beneficiary, displays Alexander's keen interest in players and acting:

It is my mind and will that Thomas Houghton of Brinscall my brother shall have all my Instruments belonging to musics and all manner of play clothes if he be minded to keep or do keep players. And if he will not keep and maintain players then it is my will that Sir Thomas Hesketh knight shall have the same Instruments and play clothes. And I most heartily require the said Sir Thomas to be friendly unto Foke Gyllome and William Shakeshafte now dwelling with me . . .

Another Prestonian of a later generation, Thomas Sandes, had similar tastes, for in his will in 1638 he made a special bequest of his 'show called the *Chaos*, the wagon, the stage, and all the joiners' tools and other implements and appurtenances to the said show belonging'. Likewise detailed lists of books betray the bibliophiles, the careful allocation of tools, the dedicated craftsmen, and the scrupulous disposal of expensive articles of clothing the dandies, for where a testator's treasure is there, we can assume, his heart will be also.

The constant enumeration of individual articles of furniture and clothing is a reminder of the expensiveness of such things in Tudor and Stuart times. Shakespeare's notorious 'second best bed' which he willed to his wife was nothing unusual. He, like so many testators of his day, was probably making sure that his wife would have a favourite piece of furniture as well as her share of the whole estate. In some families a 'great table', an 'ark', chest or coffer, or a carved bedstead can be traced through the wills of three or four generations, and second-hand gowns, fur hats, kirtles, and embroidered petticoats were bequeathed – and presumably received – with love and affection.

I, Thomas Wade, of Bildeston, in the county of Suffolk and diocese of Norwich, [1569] . . . give and bequeath to my brother John Wade my frieze gown, my best cloak, my Spanish-leather jerkin, my leather doublet, my black hose, my russet hose, my best hat, my cap, my dagger and my girdle . . . I give Samuel Cole my black coat, and my russet coat . . .

I, Matthew Wood, clerk and vicar of Wybunbury in the county of Chester [1572] . . . do give to my cousin Matthew Wood . . . one featherbed, one bolster, one pillow, one of my best covering, one coverlet, one pair of blankets of cloth, two pairs of sheets one pair of flaxen another pair of canvas. Also the hangings in my parlour with the bed tester and curtains . . . to my niece Alice Wood . . . my best black cow, my best gelding or mare, one featherbed that she lieth in, my best covering, two pairs of blankets one of fustian and another cloth, two coverlets, one mattress, two bolsters, and one pillow with a pillow case, six pairs of sheets three flaxen and three of canvas, and the best standing bed with cords with the tester over the same, my best brass pan etc. . . . Also I do give to Elizabeth Wood one wool bed, one bolster, one pair of canvas sheets, with a coverlet and a twill sheet and four pieces of pewter. Item, I do give unto Margery Wood . . . my fourth featherbed, one coverlet, one bolster, one pair of sheets of canvas, one silver spoon. Item, I bequeath to William Wood, my bastard brother, my black frieze gown . . . and to Ralph Shore one pair of cast hose . . .

The inventories which accompany the wills are only of marginal use to the genealogist, but they are one of the richest sources for social and economic historians. Particularly during the reigns of Elizabeth and of the first three Stuart kings, the authorities insisted upon executors compiling very detailed lists of the deceased's possessions. This was partly to protect the executors from beneficiaries who tried to make claims which the estate could not bear, partly to protect the beneficiaries from being cheated by the executors, and partly to give the court a basis for assessing its fees. All items in the inventory had to be valued. It is difficult to check on the reality of the prices quoted. Most of the goods had been used – many of them exceedingly well used – and descriptions of items are quite general. But in so far as a 'twig chair', or '4 yards of black silk stuff', or 'a flaxen tablecloth' can possibly be compared with similar items bought new from the market, it does appear that executors usually quoted reasonable figures in these inventories.

Historians can use inventories in many different ways. Studied throughout a region, these lists of goods can provide sound facts for distribution patterns of wealth, of social classes, of dialects, of arable or pastoral farming, or of industries; studied over several generations in a particular area they can illustrate in detail such matters as change – or lack of change – in farming tools, house construction and furnishing, methods of earning a living, or the value of money. To examine a series of inventories from a particular social group, trade, or profession is to find out the range of material wealth and living standards among its members. Often the range is surprisingly wide. Four *merchants* – so described by their executors, not by themselves – who lived in the little port of Liverpool in Elizabeth's reign, turned out to have had estates of £44, £188, £238, and considerably more than £400. Two parsons of the same generation, vicars of neighbouring parishes outside Liverpool, had nothing like the same standard of living – one left goods valued at £75, the other at £707 – and of two schoolmasters of James I's reign, Richard Holt, *master* of Rochdale Grammar School, had his estate appraised at £15, but George Swarland, *usher* of Manchester Grammar School, had goods worth £120 and credits, in the form of debts owing to him, of more than £300. It was not just that one of these men was thrifty and the other a spendthrift. The difference in their estates reflected the difference in their incomes.

F. G. Emmison, the archivist who has made Essex Record Office so outstanding a centre for local historical studies, found the same varieties of wealth when, in 1938, he published a series of Bedfordshire inventories of the years 1617–19. There were three clergymen's inventories in the collection. Both the rector of Halcott and the vicar of Riseley had quite well furnished homes: the rector had a comfortable parlour and a fair collection of books in his study, the vicar a well-stocked living room and a thriving farm. But their colleague, the vicar of Flitwick, lived in a poor way. He had not a decent bed in the house, and no more furniture in his living room than three coffers, two boxes, a little table, four stools, a cupboard, and a chair. The whole of his estate amounted to no more than £6 18s. 10d. Tradesmen's estates showed similar differences. John Hall of Potton, a baker but, judged from his inventory, a successful farmer as well, left estate to the value of £225 4s. 0d. But Edward Crash, a baker in Bedford, was worth only a fifth of that, £46 2s. 8d. Thomas Burger of Cardington, a carpenter, died a very poor man: the whole of his possessions amounted to just less than £4 0s. 0d. On the other hand, John King, a carpenter in Ravensden, was comfortably off. William Ardon, a mason from Pavenham, left estate worth £20 2s. 0d., but a fellow mason, William Harberde of Eaton Bray, left almost six times that wealth, £112 2s. 4d. The inventories make it abundantly clear that King and Harberde derived most of their money not from their trade but from farming. King had eight and a half acres under the plough and kept nine beasts and six bullocks: Harberde grew corn, reared sheep as well as cattle, and made extra money out of weaving hemp and woollen cloth.

But the widest categories were the less specific *gentleman*, *yeoman*, *husbandman*, and *labourer*. None of these titles gave any real indication of the person's wealth. Jeffrey Palmer of Ampthill had the kind of household which one would generally associate with the title *gentleman* in early Stuart times. His house had four or five family bedrooms, each furnished with a curtained, four-poster bed. He boasted silver plate worth £21, adequate stocks of linen, brass and pewter, wine and beer. He employed ten or a dozen servants who made cheese and butter in the milkhouse, brewed beer in the brewhouse, ploughed his fields, gathered honey from his five hives, tended his 'seven kine, two nags, a mare and a colt', and fattened his 'three porklings, two barrow[castrated]hogs, three sows, and six pigs'. The appraisers valued his whole estate at £520 6s. 8d. Jeffrey Palmer was not a rich man as gentlemen went, but he must have seemed so to George Button of Maulden. His executors gave him the title *gentleman*, but his inventory reveals that he lived in a one-room hovel. His only possessions seem to have been what he had managed to salvage from palmier days – a standing or four-poster bed, books worth 10s. 0d., clothes worth £3 0s. 0d., and, a little surprisingly, a stonebow. One wonders what personal disaster lies behind this inventory.

Yeomen, husbandmen, and even labourers varied in estate just as much as gentlemen. From the evidence of these inventories it was not necessarily true that a yeoman was better off than a husbandman, although one has to look deeper than the total value of the inventory to discover the real standard of a person's living. Richard Allcocke of Bolnhurst, husbandman, died slightly better off than Robert Scott of Eaton Socon, yeoman. The one was worth £577 8s. 8d., the other £570 15s. 2d. But the inventory details show that Scott, the yeoman, lived considerably more comfortably and graciously than did Allcocke, the husbandman. Scott's house was bigger and better appointed than Allcocke's. The contents of Scott's hall (i.e. his living room) were almost twice as valuable as Allcocke's, and those of his kitchen, discounting his six flitches of bacon hanging from the rafters, almost seven times as valuable. Scott had three good-sized bedrooms, with furniture valued at £15 10s. 0d., £12 10s. 0d., and £8 0s. 0d. Allcocke's best bed was worth £5 and the rest of his bedroom furniture

£2 10s. 8d., but his other two bedrooms the inventory calls 'lodging chambers' and values their contents at a mere £4 10s. 0d. and 10s. 8d. Above all, Allcocke had nothing to match Scott's comfortable parlour with its eight joined stools, two chairs, ten cushions, livery cupboard, and pair of virginals. The same differences could be seen too in the outhouses. Scott had a stable, cowshed, barn, garner, and proper accommodation for his carts, ploughs, and ladders. Allcocke had only a stable, two barns, and a 'backhouse'. He stored his four carts in one 'hovel', and his 'plough timber and other utensils' in another. He tied his beasts in a third 'hovel', and used 'a small shed', worth no more than 3s. 4d., for his calves. He made money during his life, and had over £300 loaned out at interest. But he did not enjoy life's comforts as fully as Robert Scott and his family managed to do.

The hundreds of inventories filed in a single consistory court in a single generation contain sufficient detailed facts to intimidate the most ardent researcher. To set out to explore the possibilities of inventories as a historical source, therefore, calls for a sound plan and self-discipline, the first because the student must know what facts he is seeking, and the second because he must not allow other facts, however attractive and interesting, to distract his attention. Almost every inventory, certainly every sequence of inventories, can be useful in half a dozen different investigations. For example, Alderman John Farbeck of Durham, a mercer who died in 1597, had his estate valued at £373 8s. 10d. His assets were chiefly goods in his shop. The list begins with rolls of cloth:

	£	s.	d.
13¾ yards of Valencia 'grogerine' [?grogram: a course-textured cloth usually made of silk and wool]	1	6	0
17 yards of Lyons grogerine	1	14	4
16 yards of purple Lyons grogerine	1	12	0

	£	s.	d.
10 yards of coarse Lyons grogerine	1	0	0
13 yards of changeable buffine [a new material: woollen mixture]	1	0	6
6 yards of green buffine		9	0
One piece of black rash [an inferior silk or silk mixture cloth]	1	18	0
11½ yards of silk rash	1	12	0
11½ yards of black serge	1	5	0
8¼ yards of French coloured velvet	5	7	0
3 yards of jeans [Genoa] velvet	2	14	0
3½ ells of coloured taffeta	2	2	0
13½ ells of coloured sarsenet	3	15	0
2¼ ells of lockram [coarse linen]		2	8
7¾ yards of buckram		5	4

Other lengths of cloth are in the list – tuft sackcloth, fustian, hollands, flannel, bays, and damask. Then follows a considerable stock of haberdashery:

	£	s.	d.
2 pair of hose		1	8
10 lbs. of twisted fringe, black	2	0	0
2 lbs. 2 oz. of skein crewel		7	0
1 dozen fringed girdles		12	0
3 velvet girdles		3	6
78 yards of velvet lace	1	9	0
1 lb. of stitching silk	1	10	0
9 oz. of Spanish silk		15	0
3 oz. of satin silk		6	0
5 girdles, 3 pairs of garters		14	0
6 pairs of French garters, silk and crewel		4	0
10 pairs of worsted stockings	2	10	0
5 pairs of women's stockings		16	0
2 gross of wood combs		8	0
5½ oz. of bone combs		2	9
32 yards of silver and gold thread		1	6
13½ dozen of women's thimbles		1	9

	£	s.	d.
11 dozen of wrought silk points		19	0
4 dozen shoe buttons		2	8
30 white gloves		8	0

But as the haberdashery list lengthens, unexpected miscellaneous items begin to appear:

	s.	d.
13 oz. of virginal wire	9	0
27 pairs of spectacles	4	9
½ lb. of fine starch	4	0
3 oz. of saffron	7	6
7 Grammars, 4 Terences, 4 Psalters	12	6
30 A B Cies	8	0
2 Venus glasses	2	6
8,000 broad nails	13	6
3 gross 4 doz. copper buttons	5	0
6 oz. of Turkey pepper	1	0
14 quires of large paper and 24 quires of small paper	7	0
4¼ lbs. of turpentine	1	6
1 lb. of arsenic	1	6
42 skins of the best parchment	1 0	0
5 pints of aqua-vitae	3	6

Then, right at the end, the inventory, like a Roman candle, startles us with a bang:

	£	s.	d.
22 dozen hats, lined and not lined	33	17	5
hat bands	2	12	0

Endowed with a shop inventory like this – about one third of the whole has been quoted above – a historian can put the stock back on the shelves and get a fair idea of how the shop looked and smelled. Or from it, and from other inventories of the same kind, he can find out how ordinary townspeople dressed and ate at the end of the sixteenth century. Or, alternatively, he can simply take out of the document valuable information about prices and the relative costs of particular items. He would find it still more instructive to compare this document with other mercers' inventories both in the same area and in other parts of the country, and an examination of shopkeepers' inventories in later generations would almost certainly reveal how and when shops began to specialize in their wares, and at what stage in the seventeenth century Durham shoppers would begin to look upon such crowded 'village stores' as Farbeck's as hopelessly old-fashioned. No literary description is as reliable as a full matter-of-fact inventory, and few are as eloquent.

Visiting the family houses of the gentry has become a fashionable, holiday pastime. As the visitors stand in the entrance hall or the long gallery, the guide sometimes attempts to describe what the house and gardens looked like before Robert Adam and Capability Brown got to work on them in George III's reign. A good inventory does that part of the guide's job far better than he can hope to do it. The appraisers who prepared the inventory usually began in the hall and then passed on to the parlours, dining room, bedrooms or chambers, kitchen, buttery, larder, and cellar in the most convenient order. They listed and priced everything they found:

In my Lord's Chamber

	£	s.	d.
One standing bed with curtain rods, the tester of branched damask green and yellow, with a deep silk fringe of the same colour	10	0	0
One mattress		6	0
One feather bed, 133 lbs., 8d. a lb.	4	8	8
One down bed, 44 lbs., 12d. a lb.	2	4	0
One bolster, 26 lbs., 8d. a lb.		17	4
Two pillows, 10 lbs., 9d. a lb.		7	6
Four blankets whereof 3 are Spanish blankets	1	6	0

	£	s.	d.
One green silk quilt covering	6	13	4
One pair of taffeta curtains green and yellow	10	0	0
A chair covered with green and yellow branched damask	1	0	0
Two stools suitable to the chair		10	0
Two long cushions for the windows [window seats], the one of cloth of gold, and the other cloth of silver		5	0	0
One cupboard with a green carpet fringed with green and yellow silk	1	10	0
Nine bedstaves			3
Two chamber pots		1	8
One pair of fire tongs			4
One iron grate		2	6
Four curtains for the windows red and white	1	0	0
One fire shovel			8
One screen		1	0
Summa	45	9	3

This green and yellow room, dominated by the fourposter bed, belonged to Sir William Norris of Speke Hall. It was the most important of his thirty-seven bedrooms, each of which the inventory, made in 1624, describes in similar detail. Other members of the family and the upper servants possessed, or more often shared, rooms made bright and attractive with such luxuries as 'an orange tawny caddowe [quilt]', 'curtains of blue and yellow taffeta', and 'a chair covered with green velvet, and fringe blue and yellow'. The ordinary run of servants had the necessities without the luxuries:

In the Chamber where the servants lie next the barns, which is on the left side of the stairs.

	£	s.	d.
One pair of bedstocks		1	6
One chaff bed		1	8

	£	s.	d.
One bolster		5	0
Two blankets		5	0
Two coverlets		8	0
One old tapestry covering		2	6
Summa	1	3	8

In the same Chamber

	£	s.	d.
One pair of bedstocks		1	6
One flock bed		3	0
One bolster		5	0
Two coverlets		5	0
Two blankets		4	0
Three forms and two shovels		1	6
Summa	1	0	0

This was by no means the only bedroom for servants – the others included 'the corner chamber at the stair head', the 'porter's chamber', 'the brewer's chamber', 'the chamber next the new bridge where the gardeners lie', 'the chamber next to the brewhouse', 'the chamber where the chimney is' and 'the dove house chamber'. Some fifty beds were scattered over the house; a score of them four-posters, usually fitted for curtains, another score plain bedsteads, and the rest either truckle beds or mattresses laid on the floor boards. The most voluptuous were equipped with heavy feather beds on top of down beds; the most Spartan were straw or chaff palliasses. Despite the size of Speke Hall and the common practice of two or three, gentry and servants alike, sharing beds, there was still, apparently, a shortage of sleeping space. The 'withdrawing chamber' was turned into a comfortable, red and green, family bedroom, and at least four servants slept among the spinning wheels, tubs and casks in the 'workhouse' and another couple in the false roof where the armour was stored 'for my master's use'.

Inventories are just as descriptive about the furnishings of living rooms, or the equipment of kitchens, brewhouses, milkhouses, and butteries, or the stock in the stables, cowsheds, and pigsties. The appraisers opened chests and drawers and enumerated the contents, then poked their noses into the mistress's cupboards to count the sheets, tablecloths, napkins, and yards of gold lace. They examined the master's books to find out what bills he had not settled and who owed him money, and went through his wardrobe to value not only striking, expensive articles such as his 'velvet coat' or his 'gown furred', but also well-worn, humble items such as his 'old pair of breeches', his 'four old caps', or his cravats, 'five that were old ones and the other linen'. Later they walked into the garden, smallholding, or fields to assess the value of crops still growing. Nothing was too private or too petty to escape their recording. For their exacting work faithfully performed social and economic historians cannot help but be eternally grateful.

3. LIEUTENANCY PAPERS

The lieutenancy was a Tudor creation, the latest stage in the development of the defence system of England and Wales. The Assizes of Arms of Henry II and Henry III together with the Statute of Winchester in 1285 had turned the shire levy into a less clumsy, more easily assembled muster of men summoned by commissioners of array: from the middle of Henry VIII's reign the Tudors began to use commissions of lieutenancy in place of commissions of array. The method of summoning was new, but the result – a nondescript force of men, scarcely trained and indifferently equipped – remained much the same. Commissions of array had been addressed to groups of noblemen and gentlemen, whom the king held collectively responsible for carrying out the orders. In 1402 parliament had reviewed commissioners' duties: '. . . to muster

and train all and singular men-at-arms, armed men, and archers
... and to be caused to be armed all those who are of able
body and accustomed to arms ... to distrain on all able in lands
and goods, but weak and impotent of body, that they may
provide ... armour for men-at-arms, also armed men, and
bows and arrows.' The Tudor commissions of lieutenancy
gave similar instructions, but the monarch addressed each
commission not to a group of commissioners, but to a particular nobleman, whom he had created his deputy, or lieutenant,
in a single shire or group of shires. Because the lieutenant was
almost always a nobleman, he became commonly known as
the lord lieutenant.

At first the Tudors used commissions of lieutenancy as their
predecessors had used commissions of array, for specified and
temporary occasions and purposes. Threat of invasion, civil
disorder, or national war would call for a batch of commissions,
informing lieutenants of the threatened danger and ordering
them to prepare to meet it. But once the danger was over, the
lieutenants relaxed their efforts, and waited for the next royal
commission.

> Over each of these shires *in time of necessity* is a several lieutenant
> chosen under the prince, who, being a noble man of calling, hath
> almost regal authority over the same *for the time being* ...

So wrote William Harrison in the second book of his *Description of England*.

Temporary lieutenancies, arbitrarily and variably distributed among the counties, suited the crown's purpose. Deliberately Elizabeth occasionally ignored the lieutenant, and sent
her commission concerning shire levies to the sheriff or to the
justices of peace. During her reign there were always counties
without lieutenants. Nevertheless, the lieutenancy gradually
made itself more permanent and secure. Renewals of temporary
commissions eventually led to more permanent commissions,

appointing certain noblemen lieutenants of specified counties until notice to the contrary. Before the Civil Wars the lieutenancy of several counties was already assuming a hereditary aspect. Lancashire and Cheshire, for example, seemed almost as of right to belong to the Earl of Derby, Somerset and Wiltshire to the Earl of Pembroke, and, until 1694, the President of the Council of the Marches in Wales was ex-officio lord lieutenant of all the Welsh counties. At length the Militia Act of 1662 fully and formally recognized the changes that had gradually taken place in the previous hundred years. Parliament accepted a permanent lieutenancy.

Be it therefore ... enacted ... that the King's most excellent Majesty ... shall and may ... issue forth several commissions of lieutenancy ... to be his Majesty's lieutenants for the several and respective counties ... which lieutenants shall have full power and authority to call together all such persons at such times, and to arm and array them ...

That the said lieutenants ... have hereby full power and authority to charge any person with horse, horseman, and arms, or with foot-soldier and arms, in the same county district ... where his, her or their estates lie ...

Every county was to have its lord lieutenant as naturally as it had long had its sheriff and its quarter sessions.

The lieutenancy was no sinecure. It entailed military and civil duties, but the military duties were the more extensive. The lieutenant had to muster the county levies, soon to be known as the militia. Every fit male from 16 to 60 years old was liable to be mustered, but only a small part of the muster was kept back for training. How many men were retained depended upon the immediate need. 'A sufficient number of the most able' was usually the central government's advice to the lieutenants. Those selected were 'to be sorted into bands, trained and exercised in such sort as may reasonably be borne at the common charge of the whole county'. All soldiers, even these part-time trained bands, cost money. Therefore, lieutenants had always to weigh the threat of danger against the expense of providing a force to meet it: they must not train more men than necessary, or charge the landholders and other inhabitants of their county with more rates than they could easily bear. No lieutenant could shrug off the financial implications of his decision to muster and train, for the crown held him responsible for fixing the quota of the county levy on each hundred, for dividing the hundred's quota among its parishes and townships, and for seeing that each gentleman below the rank of baron contributed his due share of money, horses, arms, and armour. He always needed a good purse of money, for costs were high. His officers required expenses and the men required wages. Private soldiers were usually fed, clothed, and even armed at the public expense: '... always ... there hath been and still are, a certain number of soldiers furnished with armour and weapons, found at the common charge of every township or parish', declared a lieutenancy commission of 1573. In addition the lieutenant carried responsibility for keeping the county beacons in good order and ready for emergency use.

Of course, the lieutenant could not see to all these duties personally. Elizabethan commissions usually authorized him to appoint two, three, or more deputies, and he had the services of his muster master and, after 1589, his provost marshal. He also relied upon the close cooperation of the sheriff, the justices of the peace, and the constables. Each parish had at least one constable, annually chosen, and completely untrained, as we have already explained in Section 1. Supervision of these parish or petty constables was the duty of the high constable, invariably a gentleman and commonly responsible for all the parishes in a particular hundred. These subordinates helped the lieutenant to fulfil his military duties. When he required a muster, he informed the high constable. He in turn informed the parish constables, who each saw to it that at the Sunday service their parish priest announced the date and place of muster. In similar fashion, this same group of officials decided how many men and which particular men should be retained for training. The lieutenant gave each high constable his quota. This the high constable divided among his parishes, and each petty constable then chose his handful of conscripts from his neighbours. Volunteers, who would ease his task, were usually not sufficient, and he often had to make invidious choices. Captain Barnaby Rich, a veteran soldier, said as much in a pamphlet written in 1574.

The petty Constable . . . is loath that any honest man, through his procurement, should hazard himself amongst so many dangers of war; wherefore if within his area of office there hap to remain any idle fellow, some drunkard, or seditious quarreller, a privy picker, or such a one as hath some skill in stealing a goose, these shall be presented to the service of the Prince; and what service is to be looked for among such fellows, I think may easily be deemed.

Lieutenants used their deputies in various ways. Sometimes they gave each of them a specific area to command. Sometimes they employed them all on special duties throughout the whole area of the lieutenancy. In 1587 Lord Burghley attempted to combine both systems:

Though I have limited Lindsey to be under the peculiar charge of you, the Earl of Willoughby and Sir Edward Dymock, and the other parts of Kesteven and Holland to be under the charge of Sir Thomas Cecil and Sir Anthony Thorold, yet my meaning is not but that you all jointly and severally should have care and regard to the whole body of the Shire . . .

When a lord lieutenant was absent on duty, one or all of his deputies took command. It sometimes happened that a county had a deputy lieutenant when the crown had not appointed a lieutenant for him to be deputy to. But however a deputy lieutenant's authority was defined, his duty was clear enough. It was to hold local musters in convenient centres, to keep up-to-date records of men, arms, armour, and stores of powder and shot in their area, to see that their captains held quarterly reviews of men and weapons, and that their sergeants inspected muskets, pikes, and bows every six weeks. 'They shall duly view and peruse, whether the same be cleanly and orderly kept,' instructed a commission of lieutenancy in 1589. Horses and their military equipment – their *furniture* – were probably the most difficult arms to organize. Lords lieutenant had to ensure that the landed gentlemen in their counties were breeding enough horses suitable for war. An act of 1535 laid it down that owners of parklands one mile in compass must keep at least two mares of thirteen hands for this purpose. Owners of big estates must supply the militia not only with the horses, but with their furniture, and with lance, staff, and pistols for the militiamen who rode them. Each sergeant was held responsible for the good state of the furniture for all horses in his squadron, but the horses themselves were stabled 'either by some of the substantialest inhabitants of that division, or else in such other place as shall seem meet and convenient for the same'. The deputy lieutenant arranged the stabling, and saw to it that the levy for maintaining the militia was in his area fairly distributed according to each householder's ability to pay.

Social rank went a long way to determine military rank. Just as the lord lieutenant was almost always an earl or a baron, so the deputies tended to be knights or substantial esquires, and the captains esquires or gentlemen. In a general commission of array in 1573, Elizabeth detailed what she expected her lieutenants to do:

... to choose meetest persons for captains and petty captains, not forbearing any under the degree of a lord of parliament, to the charge of certain numbers, according to their qualities; those of most worship, credit and value to have the charge of more or less according to their degrees, *i.e.* some of the best worship, of two hundred or three hundred; others of meaner degrees and values in living, to take charge under them of each hundred apart; and also with consent of the captains a charge to be made of skilful and expert persons to be lieutenants of every hundred, and necessary officers to govern and lead the said bands. No persons suspected to be unwilling to serve the Queen to have any charge or leading of men committed to them.

In practice, the captains of 'each hundred apart' were the officers who paid the wages of the trained bands. They paid well: in the middle years of Elizabeth's reign, when skilled tradesmen were earning between 4d. and 6d. a day, militia men in training or on service could claim 8d., together with 1d. for every mile they had to carry their armour and weapons between their home, or the storage depot, and the place of training. Unfortunately, regularity of payment depended on public funds being sufficient, and, under the Stuarts especially, arrears of pay became all too common.

Another of the captain's tasks was 'to sort his men's armour and weapons according to the stature of their bodies'. There had to be a balance of arms: Elizabeth laid it down that in every hundred footmen there must be forty harquebusiers and twenty archers. These were the skilled and more useful infantry: the remainder, the pikemen and billmen, were only useful at close quarters – 'at push of pike'. Consequently, infantrymen who could kill the enemy at a distance had to be encouraged and diligently trained. Harquebusiers were licensed to practise at home, and the strong of arm, who were invariably chosen to be archers, were bidden to set a good example and encourage archery as a sport. Throughout Elizabeth's reign, the government had a strong belief in the efficacy of the longbow. Many schools insisted that archery was the only permissible sport for their scholars, and occasional sermons praised the virtue of bows made from English yew, and used by English archers. In truth, the weapon was already obsolete, but national pride, nurtured by stories of Crécy and Agincourt, blinded English eyes to this unpleasant fact.

Since the monarch appointed the lieutenants and the privy council supervised their activities, many official papers concerning the lieutenancy have been preserved among such official collections as the Patent Rolls, the State Papers, and the Acts of the Privy Council. But since, until the reign of Charles II, some correspondence between council and lieutenant and, even more, between a lieutenant and his subordinates, was personal rather than official, the historian has now to seek these letters in family archives. There are many routine letters:

Privy Council to Earl of Suffolk: Whitehall, 15 June 1635.

Give speedy and effectual order to your deputy lieutenants to keep a watchful eye upon all the ports and places apt for landing within those counties, and especially the Cinque Ports; and that upon the first notice of the appearing or approach of any foreign fleet upon those coasts, they cause all the trained bands of those counties, or so many of them as you shall find needful, to be immediately drawn down thither, to repulse the landing of any enemy. Landmen are to be impressed for the supply of His Majesty's fleet.

This letter, preserved in the family papers of E. R. Wodehouse and printed by the Historical Manuscripts Commission in 1892, is typical of many directives sent out when Charles I seemed set on provoking Dutch and French hostility in the North Sea. Luckily, on that occasion no invasion occurred. The Armada threat had been far more serious. Tension had mounted throughout the 1580s. Constant instructions had gone out to lieutenants about quotas of soldiers, training of sufficient men, inspection of arms, and the arrest of those recusants whom the government feared might encourage a fifth column. Urgent preparations were made to repel the expected invasion in 1587. When no Spanish fleet arrived that year, it seemed more certain still that it would come in 1588. On 18 June 1588, a month before enemy ships were sighted approaching the Channel, Elizabeth sent the following letter from 'our manor of Greenwich' to the Earl of Derby and his son, Lord Strange.

Right trusty and well-beloved cousin and counsellor we greet you well.

Whereas heretofore upon the Advertisements from time to time and from sundry places of the great preparations of foreign forces with a full Intention to invade this our Realm and other dominions, we gave our directions unto you for the preparing of our Subjects within your Lieutenancy to be in readiness and defence against any attempt that might be made against us and our Realm; which our directions we find so well performed ... For as much as we find the same Intention not only of invading but of making a conquest also of this our Realme ... Although we doubt not but by God's goodness the same shall prove frustrate, we have therefore thought meet to will and require you forthwith with as much convenient speed as you may to call together at some convenient place or places the best sort of gentlemen under your Lieutenancy, and to declare unto them that considering these great preparations and threatenings now burst out in action upon the seas ... we do look that the most part of them should have upon this instant extraordinary occasion a larger proportion of furniture both for horsemen and footmen, but especially horsemen, than hath been certified. Thereby to be in their best strength against any Attempt whatsoever, and to be employed both about our own person and otherwise, as they shall have knowledge given them. The number of which larger portion as soon as you shall know, we require you to signify to our privy council ...

Elizabeth sent similar letters to other lords lieutenant. The response was fairly satisfactory. The queen's bodyguard at Tilbury probably exceeded 10,000 men, and a further 100,000 or so, scattered through the counties, eventually stood ready under arms to repel the invaders. But it was always difficult to gauge the effectiveness of a militia force. Officers and men were all amateurs. They might have enthusiasm and determination, but these virtues were easily nullified by disastrous staff work, poor supplies, or sheer incompetence of command.

June, July, and August 1588 were busy months for the lords lieutenant. They were holding musters, inspecting defences, arranging for beacons to be ready day and night, and then generally keeping their subordinates alive to the national danger. Lord Derby was on the queen's business in the Netherlands. Therefore Lord Strange was the acting lieutenant for Cheshire and Lancashire. In the middle of June, he sent general instructions to his justices of peace:

... cause to be made ready all such Beacons as are next adjoining unto you, and the Watch to be kept at every one of them. Also, to order the Constables to take all idle and vagrant persons within their Townships and Hamlets; and to take and examine all News and Tale-Carriers, and other insolent Persons that should raise any Rumours among the common people ...

The cost of these preparations and precautions the lord lieutenant arranged to be carefully divided among the parishes and townships of each hundred. This was the kind of apportioning that had to be done in each area:

A Taxation of Money in Manchester Division towards watching of the Beacon of Rivington Pike, and Carrying of Armour from Cross Hall near Lord Derby's home at Lathom

	s.	d.	
Manchester	11	8	
Salford	4	6	
Withington	15	8	
Stretford	4	6	Manchester parish 42s. 4d.
Reddish	4	6	
Chorlton		6	
Cheetham	12		

	s.	d.	
Worsley	4	2	
Barton	6	8	
Pendleton	2	6	Eccles parish 15s. 6d.
Clifton		14	
Pendlebury		12	

Flixton		Prestwich	3s. 3d.	
Urmston	3s. 4d.	Pilkington	4s. 6d.	8s. 0d. [sic]

Summa totalis of the Manchester Division, as the same is here above rated, cometh unto £3 9s. 2d.

Rivington Beacon was a necessary link in the chain of 'red glares' which 'sped the message' of invasion until it 'roused the burghers of Carlisle', but it was not the only charge on Manchester parish. There had to be equipped and maintained the parish's contribution to the nation's defence force – 38 harquebusiers, 38 archers, and 144 infantry armed with pike or bills – and all gentlemen and freeholders had to appear before Lord Strange at Warrington on 16 July, no doubt, in accordance with Elizabeth's letter, to be asked to contribute 'a larger proportion . . . than hath been certified'. Fortunately for the ratepayers the crisis was not long drawn out. On the night of 30 July the English sky was red with beacon fires, and less than a week later most anti-invasion precautions could be safely relaxed. On 24 September, the Earl of Derby, now back from the Netherlands, bade his deputy lieutenants arrange a day of thanksgiving to 'our God'.

Whereas I am credibly Informed that it hath pleased God to continue His goodness towards our prince, church, and country . . . I have thought it expedient in respect of Christian duty we should fall to some godly exercise of thanksgiving . . . Willing you so to commend the business to the clergy of your hundred in their several charges, as our God by mutual consent may be praised therefor. And this is not to be omitted nor delayed in any wise, but to be put in Execution at or before the next Sabbath 29 September . . .

The lieutenancy proved itself during the Spanish Armada crisis. Under the leadership of the lords lieutenant the nation showed magnificent loyalty and determination. However much Elizabeth might fear that the lieutenants might begin to take their local authority for granted, she was bound to retain them in office until the country slowly returned to normal.

The Tudors always assumed that they had the right to order lieutenants to recruit and equip men of their county for service overseas. No more than a month after the Armada thanksgiving, for example, Lord Derby was gathering together a hundred men to sail to Ireland. His deputy lieutenant, Sir John Byron, had to find from Salford hundred 'fourteen tall and sufficient servicemen ... presently furnished with armour, weapon and apparel, with conduct money'. The original estimate of cost for fitting out the fourteen troops was £48 19s. 1d. This the justices collected, but before the troops embarked, the military authorities found many 'defaults of armour, weapons, and other things'. Consequently on 19 November, Sir John Byron was demanding a further £6 19s. 10d. from the hundred 'upon Monday next by ten of the clock in the forenoon of the same day'. By 21 December the men were back home again. Byron wrote again to the justices.

Whereas the Soldiers lately set forth of this Country for her Majesty's service in Ireland, are now thereof discharged and returned home again, every man bringing with him sword, girdle, and dagger. These are therefore to will and require you ... to call before you all the said soldiers now discharged and are returned; And take sword, dagger, and girdle from every of them, and the same safely keep and detain in your own custody for the benefit of the country, and her Majesty's service when occasion shall require ...

There had long been general resentment against equipping and maintaining militiamen for service in distant parts of England or overseas. Popular argument maintained that the militia was a home guard, and that the force was intended for local defence only. But the crown had just as long ignored such a view, and an act of 1557 had assumed that mustered men were liable to serve anywhere the crown decreed. During Elizabeth's reign vexation expressed itself in nothing more dangerous than honest grumbling at the assumed obligation and the expense incurred. But the Stuarts ran into increasing trouble. James I continued to demand soldiers to serve in Ireland, and then, in the last year of his reign, sent militiamen to fight for the Protestant cause in Europe. In the first years of Charles I's reign, lieutenants had orders to raise men for service against the Spaniards and the French. But the crisis was reached in 1638–40, when Charles raised more and more militiamen to fight the Bishops' Wars against the Scottish covenanters. He instructed all his lords lieutenant to raise unprecedented numbers of armed men. He asked for hundreds instead of scores, and thousands instead of hundreds. His orders to the Earl of Suffolk, lord lieutenant of Suffolk and Cambridgeshire, were typical:

... Cause 300 of the 400 in Cambridge shire and 1,200 of the 1,500 in Suffolk to be brought to Yarmouth on 12 April 1639 and to Harwich on 10 April respectively; two parts to be muskets and the third part pikes, and to be transported to such place of the northern parts as shall be appointed by the General of our army ...

Lieutenants had then to relay and interpret these instructions to their deputies, and the deputies to their captains and high constables. This was the circular letter which the deputy lieutenants of Suffolk sent out:

Whereas we have received two several letters from his Majesty under his privy signet together with the commands of the Privy Council importing that under pretence of religion divers disorders and tumults have been raised in Scotland and fomented by factious spirits there ... his Majesty is enforced to arm himself for his own and his loyal subjects' safety ... therefore he hath required us to make several levies both of men and money, whereof 400 men are to be levied, coated, and conducted to Selby upon Ouse, near York, and 1,200 more, to be drawn out of the trained bands, to be conducted, coated, and embarked at Harwich to such place of rendezvous as the Lord General shall appoint; all which charge we have as near as we can, cast up, and find it will amount unto £1,500.

These commands are therefore by virtue of the said letters to require you to bring into Bury St Edmunds, the 8th day of April next, by eight of the clock in the morning, at the Angel, your proportionable part of 1,600 able men, that out of them may be selected such and so many for his Majesty's service, as we are commanded, and also your proportion of £1,500, according to former and usual levies, with your proportion of coats, to be either blue lined with yellow, or grey lined with red, or red lined with white; the price not to exceed the sum of 10 or 11 shillings; all which charge shall be repaid you out of the general levy. You are to pay . . . 8d. a day for every soldier and 6s 8d. a day to every such officer deputed; and to charge so many carts as will suffice to carry their arms. These levies will be repaid out of his Majesty's Exchequer, as in former times.

By the time the Long Parliament met in November 1640, everyone knew what reliance could be placed on 'repaid out of his Majesty's Exchequer'. The control of the militia soon became a major issue. In March 1642 Lords and Commons issued the Militia Ordinance nominating lords lieutenants for all the counties, and placing the control of the levies in their hands. In May Charles condemned the Ordinance: in June Lords and Commons reiterated it. During and after the Civil Wars, the Parliamentarians had their way, but the Militia Act of 1661 acknowledged the king's traditional right to command the armed forces of his realm. In the following year, however, Lords and Commons so arranged the financing of the militia that it became virtually impossible to call it into being for more than a few days without parliamentary consent.

4. STATE PAPERS

The historical sources so far discussed – parish registers and accounts, wills, inventories, and lieutenancy papers – either originated in, or derived fresh significance from, the new government administration which Henry VIII, notably aided by Thomas Cromwell, was creating in the 1530s. This new administration was so different from the medieval as to tempt some historians to describe it as an administrative revolution. Certainly it was fundamental enough to entail a remarkable change in the pattern of national records. The charter rolls, for example, ceased to be necessary. The patent rolls and the lists of inquisitions *post mortem* were among the established records which continued to accumulate new items every day, but their relative importance was steadily eroded by the rapidly growing new categories of official records.

Under Henry VIII and Elizabeth, the privy council developed a most important role in national government and administration. Especially in the last ten years of his reign, Henry not only sought advice from his privy council, but began to entrust it, or particular members of it, with occasional executive powers. Neither Edward's protectors nor Queen Mary checked this development, so that by the 1560s and 1570s the privy council was administering all the routine business of central government. Unlike her father, Elizabeth never attended privy council meetings. She used her secretary – Cecil, Smith, Walsingham, or some other – as the liaison officer, through whom she could convey her orders to the council, and from whom she could receive detailed reports of council business. Nothing was too big or too small for the privy council and its committees to handle. On the one hand, in the name of the queen, it received the ambassadors of foreign kings and negotiated political treaties and trading agreements: on the other, it heard the numerous petitions which attempted to draw royal attention to the grievances, achievements, or alleged transgressions of private citizens. But the bulk of its executive work was the instruction and supervision of the activities of the judges, sheriffs, lieutenants, and bishops, who upheld the queen's authority and carried out her orders in their various spheres of activity. All this business, however big or small, had to be put down on paper. Before long the files were accumulating alarmingly. Storage became a problem; so did the sorting of papers under useful subheadings. There seemed to be too many papers altogether, and the topics and matters they concerned were bewilderingly diverse.

The following items have been taken from the printed *Calendar of State Papers, Domestic* (see below, pp. 70–71); papers received and dispatched by the privy council, or by the council of state. They have been chosen to illustrate the wide variety of council business, but they were not difficult to find. Any couple of pages of any of the volumes of the *Calendar* would yield a selection as varied. Some items record important policy decisions or throw light upon major national events or activities. Most are concerned with the routine, daily business of administration, but a considerable number are either trivial or purely personal without any substantial claim to appear in a collection of state papers.

Dec. 18, 1565 Ric. Longeworth, Master of St John's Coll. [Cambridge] to Cecil. Has prevailed on the members of the College to follow the Queen's injunctions for wearing surplices. Desires to know if common bread may be used in administration of the Sacrament, and whether as often he preaches 'by the hour' in the chapel, to the house only, he may do so without the surplice.

1575 (?) Description of the operation and advantages of a certain newly invented engine of war, whereby twenty-four bullets can be discharged from one piece at a time.

Notes by the inventor touching the engine of war. Expense of making a few at a time. It would require over 100 engines to be employed at once. Desires a yearly pension in consideration of his invention.

April 16, 1580 Bishop Berkeley to the Queen. Certifies the number of
Wells.　　　　 timber trees felled by him since his coming to the Bishoprick of Bath and Wells.

Oct. 24, 1580 The Queen to Edmund Tremayne. To assist Francis Drake in sending up certain bullion brought into the realm by him, but to leave so much of it in Drake's hands as shall amount to the sum of £10,000, the leaving of which sum in his hands is to be kept most secret to himself alone.

July 8 (?), 1602 Warrant to the lieutenants, foresters, and keepers of game in the principality of Wales and border counties to supply game in proportions specified for Lord Zouch, the Lord President and Council there; and also to permit them to hunt in the Queen's forests and to carry away the deer they may kill.

Feb. 5, 1622 Matt. Nicholas to Edw. Nicholas. On his love affair. The lady is very melancholy.

March 3, 1638 Account of Sir William Russell of ship money received and outstanding on writs issued in September 1637. Total received, £35,758 11s.; outstanding £160,655 16s. 8d.

Account of monies levied and remaining in the hands of the sheriffs. Total £12,300, which makes the total collected £48,058.

Oct. 2, 1649 Council of State to the Lord Mayor, Alderman, and Common Council of London. There has been great mischief by the licence and irregularity of the press, and the spreading of foolish, malignant, seditious, and treasonable pamphlets and invectives; great care has been taken to pass an Act that will put an end to that mischief...we desire...that you give special charge to your marshal, etc. to search for all the guilty, and proceed against them without respect of persons.

As we new Elizabethans know only too well, the first Elizabethans' archive problems, big though they seemed to be to them, were tiny when compared with the paper storage problems that lay in the future. Progress tended to follow well behind need, but by the beginning of the seventeenth century the keeper and staff of a newly established State Paper Office in

Whitehall were endeavouring to recover state papers which had strayed into private collections, as well as to conserve and systematize the papers entrusted to their charge. During the seventeenth century, successive keepers made a fair bid to overcome their problems, but eighteenth-century neglect, indifference, and parsimony led to the haphazard destruction of large stacks of filed papers through fire, rodents, and the ravages of damp. The fight back began in 1792 with the appointment of John Bruce as keeper. Slowly and painfully, he initiated reform, and in due course secured better housing and more devoted care for the ever-growing volume of records.

During the seventeenth and eighteenth centuries, there were always a few scholars interested in the state papers as sources for historical research. Most of them used the documents as the basis for their historical narratives, but one or two published the texts of selected documents. In 1704 Thomas Rymer published the first of the twenty volumes of treaties and other political documents which are commonly known as *Rymer's Foedera*, and in 1725 Dumont published a similar collection, including many English documents, under the title *Corps universel diplomatique*. In 1783 both *Domesday Book* and the first records of the medieval parliaments, *Rotuli Parliamentorum*, appeared in print. These pilot schemes aroused considerable interest, and the Record Commissioners, relying upon the labours of scholar-editors, attempted some systematic publication. In 1802 they published the first volume of *Texts and Calendars*, and for the next half century they achieved a creditable average of just over one publication a year. Most of the volumes are large – folio is the usual size – and they contain practically no texts later in date than Henry VII's reign. They are not outstanding examples of good scholarship, but they did stimulate interest in official records, and they drew attention to the possibility of providing students of history with a printed summary of many more of the records in public custody.

By the time Victoria came to the throne, the publication of records had become a favourite academic talking point. Argument went backwards and forwards about documents meritorious enough to be printed in full, about an editor's obligation to annotate as well as transcribe, about the advantages of full texts over summaries and lists, and about the source of the money necessary for publication of any kind. Discussion soon led to action, with the result that the number of historical records and texts published during Victoria's reign is most remarkable. Enthusiasm was not limited to the publication of state papers. Family muniments, letters and diaries of historical interest, ecclesiastical records and accounts, parish and county papers – all found their way to the printers. Print solved the two different problems of availability and preservation. It put the texts into numerous libraries and studies, and, by scattering copies throughout the world, turned the manuscripts from frail and fragile treasures into readily available and robust tools for research. The precious records were free at last from the threat of oblivion by fire, neglect, and old age.

In the late 1840s the Public Record Office began to prepare to publish the State Papers. It decided to begin at 1547, the first year of Edward VI's reign – that is, not at the beginning of the Tudor 'administrative revolution', the date of which would be impossible to determine precisely, but with the first reign after the revolution. Obviously some broad classification of the documents was necessary. The Office decision was to use three major headings, Domestic, Foreign, and Colonial, and to begin with the Domestic papers because they would be 'more interesting to the student, and more available to the advancement of English history'. Sheer bulk and cost put printing each document in full quite out of the question. Yet bare lists of headings would satisfy no one. The accepted compromise was the calendar: the documents were to be listed by date and described as succinctly as possible.

Each separate paper or document is briefly abstracted, the leading facts stated, and the persons and places to which it relates are mentioned sufficiently to indicate to what particular subject it belongs. The student, whether of history, biography, genealogy, or general literature, at however remote a distance he may be placed, can thus ascertain precisely the amount of information existing among the State Papers on whatever may be the subject of his inquiry.

Progress was very slow at first. A good portion of the first volume was in print by 1848, but the volume did not achieve publication for another eight years. But rapidly the work accelerated. By 1872 all the Domestic papers from 1547 to 1625 had been calendared and published. They included a large number of additional papers found after the first volumes had appeared. And in addition, thanks to the ceaseless activities of John Bruce, Mary Anne Everett Green, and other scholars, good progress had already been made on the Domestic papers of Charles I, the Interregnum, and Charles II.

The first volumes of the Foreign and Colonial series both appeared in 1861. They are not so diverse in subject matter as the Domestic series, and the editors have taken more space in order to give fuller summaries of most of the papers. The Foreign series contains both reports to the privy council from ambassadors, consuls, and secret agents working abroad, and the instructions which the council sent back to them. These items must be the groundwork for any study of English foreign policy. But the volumes also include eye-witness or reporter-like descriptions of events abroad, such as the two anonymous accounts of the Massacre of St Bartholomew's Day in 1572, and the following Spanish report on the 'singeing of King of Spain's beard' in 1587.

On the 29th of last month [April], Francis Drake came into the Bay of Cadiz with 27 ships of war; bombarded the city, burned some of the ships in the bay, and put out again on the first of this month, sailing towards the south-west which is the way to the Indies. According to what some English declare that were taken from the fleet, he is going in quest of the fleets and to do all the damage he may in the Indies . . .

The formality of some of the Foreign papers does not obscure the personalities and human problems behind them. In the middle of the sixteenth century, most English representatives abroad had insufficient money to pay their way. Time and again they complained to the treasury about allowances not meeting the high prices they were having to pay, but all in vain. Sir Richard Morison, ambassador to the court of the Emperor, Charles V, opened his heart to Cecil in February 1551. He wrote from Augsburg that he was

wonderfully cumbered for lack of money. At home he had not many that ever he durst open his lips to borrow of them any money; and here he would fain be taken for no beggar, not that he passes so much to be one, as that, being so counted, he shall be less able to do good service. The rest of his calling be able to lash and lay on, and he, poor soul, must oft lose his night's rest for that he cannot day it as others do . . .

The early volumes of the Colonial papers must be the most romantic state papers in existence. A good proportion of their entries are concerned with the voyages of discovery, and the attempts of the Elizabethans to find their way through the north-west and the north-east passages to Cathay. Old expectations and fears and the excitement caused by unexpected achievements bubble through the summaries in the calendars. There is, for example, Michael Lock's description of Frobisher's first voyage to waters north of Labrador. The venture set out from Gravesend on 12 June 1576 and returned to London via the Orkneys on 9 October. The account is sheer adventure-story material, with the romantic touch of the captured Esquimo, who 'was such a wonder unto the whole city [London] and to the rest of the realm that heard of it, as seemed never to have happened the like great matter to any man's knowledge'. It is typical of this collection of papers that the next item should be a preposterous petition from Frobisher asking for letters patent appointing him

... High Admiral of those seas already or hereafter to be discovered by him, with government by land of all people in those discovered parts, also five per cent. upon the clear gain of everything brought from such lands, and one per cent. to his heirs for ever ... and to receive one ton freight of every hundred tons brought thence ...

With such wild expectations, coupled with the lure of further adventure and the assurance he had struck gold, Frobisher prepared his estimates of the requirements and costs of the next voyage, and submitted them to the privy council along with his petition. Fifty years later, this pioneering spirit had given place to more commonplace matters about trading ventures, 'factories' abroad, and established trade routes. Romance is still there in the colonial papers of the Stuart period, but it is more controlled than in Elizabeth's day. In the seventeenth century, there was a little less unknown to explore, and far more known to exploit.

By the end of the nineteenth century the Public Record Office had managed to begin several new series of calendars, including treasury books, acts of the privy council, state papers relating to Ireland, and letters and papers relating to England preserved in French, Spanish, Venetian, Milanese, and Vatican archives, to say nothing of the colossal task of calendaring charter, patent, close and chancery rolls, and other collections of medieval documents. The Victorians did not quite finish what they set out to achieve: 'aiming at a million' they missed 'an unit'. Their successors are still finishing the job, but at a far more leisurely pace. The results of these Herculean labours are lined up on the shelves of all research libraries. Twentieth-century scholars tend to take them for granted, and find it hard to imagine how they would manage without their help.

Calendaring, like all compromises, is not wholly satisfactory. Ideally, every scholar should work from the documents which are the basis of his study. And, of course, historical research which 'advances the frontiers of knowledge' is done in this way. But even the most erudite scholar needs to know what documents are available. The calendar enables him to take a book from the shelf above his head, and find out what documents will be worth consulting for his current research when next he visits the Public Record Office. For him on occasions, and for lesser scholars for most or all the time, the calendar can be enough. Official documents in particular tend to follow set forms, frequently verbose, and many students often require nothing more than the details the calendar gives. After all no student will be relying solely on state papers. Alongside the official documents, a researcher must have more personal sources if he is to be able to study his subject in the round or tell his story in full. A history based on state papers alone would not only be dull. It would also be false and misleading, because it would be so incomplete. For example, the *Calendar of State Papers, Domestic* has the following entries concerning Sir Thomas Wyatt and the rebellion which he led in the first weeks of 1554:

Jan. 22, 1554. Mary instructs 'Sir Edw. Hastings and Sir Thos. Cornwallys to repair to Wiat, and to declare to him the motives of her marriage with Prince Philip. Offers to appoint persons to confer with him hereon'.

Jan. 29. GRAVESEND Norfolk to the Council. Being furnished with 700 or 800 men intends to march towards Rochester. Wiat has fortified Rochester bridge. Recommends that Abergavenny and others should fall on the rear of Wiat's forces.

Incloses Cobham to Norfolk. Informs him of Wiat's intentions to fight it out. Advises the Duke not to advance too far. Cowling Castle, Jan. 29.

Jan. 29. Lord Cobham to the Queen. Consultations as to the best mode of proceeding against the rebels. Norfolk's retreat. *Inclose* Cobham to Norfolk (Copy of above).

Wiat to Cobham. Invited him to join with him and proceed to London. Begs Cobham to make means to arrest Norfolk. Rochester, Jan. 29.

Jan. 30. Cobham to the Queen. Describes Wiat's attack on Cowling Castle. Cobham obliged at last to surrender.

Jan. 31. MEREWORTH Henry Lord Abergavenny to the Council. Called upon the Lord Warden for his aid to fall upon the rear of Wiat's forces. Has marched from Maidstone towards Rochester, but on hearing the Duke of Norfolk's band had deserted, many of his own men had gone off. Blames Norfolk for his rash attack on the rebels.

Feb. 1. SHEERLANDS Sir Tho. Cheyne to the Council. Thinks his letters have been intercepted by the rebels; doubts the loyalty of his own people; the treason of those with the Duke of Norfolk having much discouraged all parties, serving men and others. Advises that Lord Pembroke should not be too hasty to advance against Wiat.

Feb. 2. MEREWORTH Lord Abergavenny and others to the Council. The Lord Warden will join them to oppose Wiat. Mr Moyle and other gentlemen of East Kent are coming with him. *Inclosing,* Cheyne to Abergavenny. Is determined to join him, and to spend his heart's blood in the quarrel. Will be at Rochester on Sunday. Sheerlands, Feb. 1.

Feb. 7. ROCHESTER Sir Tho. Cheyne to the Council. Intention of Wiat to cross the Thames at Kingston. Has appointed to meet Sir Thos. Moyle, Lord Abergavenny, and Sir R. Southwell at Dartford.

Feb. 10. ALLINGTON CASTLE Sir Robt. Southwell (Sheriff of Kent) to the Council. Arrest and committal of various traitors, some to Allington Castle, others to Maidstone Gaol. Specifies to whom he has given the custody of rebels' houses in Kent. Proposes to occupy Allington Castle (Wiat's residence) himself. *Incloses.* Deposition by Sir Anth. Norton of Trocheley, relative to a conversation he had with Wiat at Allington Castle. Feb. 10.

Feb. 24. MEREWORTH Sir Robt. Southwell to the Council. Proceedings of the rebels. Proclamation issued at Tunbridge by Sir Henry Isley, Anthony Knevet, and another gentleman, servant to the Lady

Elizabeth. Arrival of Tho. Culpepper from London, and report that all England was in insurrection to oppose the coming of the Spaniards. Execution of some of the rebel prisoners; desires directions as to disposal of others.

Feb. 25. THE TOWER Sir John Bourne and others to the L. Chancellor and Sec. Petre. Have laboured to make Sir Thomas Wiat confess concerning the Lady Elizabeth and her servant, Sir Wm. St Loo. Wiat declares that Sir James Croft knows more of the matter.

Feb. (?) Note of the armour issued to divers persons out of the armoury of the Tower during Wiat's rebellion; with the value of the same.

March 16. Princess Elizabeth to the Queen, on being commanded to go to the Tower. Protests her innocence, and demands to answer any charge against her. Disavows holding any correspondence with the traitor Wiat, and energetically denies that she ever sent any letter or message to the French King.

March 24. AT THE COURT The Council to Lord Cobham. The Queen is pleased, at the intercession of Count D'Egmont, to order his release from the Tower, and also to extend her clemency to his eldest son (William Brooke) at the intercession of his wife.

Dec. 1558. Account of arms, armour, and weapons issued from the Tower and Westminster, and the Office of Ordnance, at the time of Sir Thomas Wiat's rebellion; specifying the names of all parties receiving the same, the several pieces delivered to each, and the quantities lost or embezzled at the time of the battle, Feb. 1554.

June 7, 1559. Sir Robt. Southwell to Cecil. Further detail of the state of the Offices of the Ordnance and Armoury. Proposes a sale of corslets to gentlemen who are suitors for the same. Answer of the gentlemen who had armour and weapons delivered to them in Wyatt's rebellion.

All these entries are germane to the story. A serious student of the rebellion would be eager to examine most of the originals. He would go to the Public Record Office knowing exactly what he wanted. He would expect no surprises. The calendar would have given him the gist of each document, but from the full texts he might extract a few more useful details. It could well be that from the phrasing and choice of words he could judge the mood and guess the inmost thoughts of the writer. In view of Cobham's arrest and later release, it would be instructive to know if, when he wrote to Norfolk on 29 January, he was chiefly anxious for Norfolk's safety, or was endeavouring to gain time and make things easier for Wyatt. Sir Anthony Norton's evidence about his conversation with Wyatt at Allington Castle might easily contain pertinent information about Wyatt's hopes and fears, and it would be helpful to find out in what tones, bold and confident or shamefaced and cringing, Princess Elizabeth protested against being sent to the Tower on 16 March. Some of these questions the full text will go a long way to answering. His study of Elizabeth's letter, for example, might convince the student that spirited indignation struggled with fear of the immediate future for the mastery of the princess's pen.

If any ever did try this old saying 'that a king's word was more than another man's oath', I most humbly beseech Your Majesty to verify it to me, and to remember your last promise and my last demand that I be not condemned without answer and due proof, which it seems that I now am; for without cause proved, I am by your Council from you commanded to go into the Tower, a place more wanted for a false traitor than a true subject . . . I protest before God (Who shall judge my truth whatsoever malice shall devise), that I never practised, counselled nor consented to anything that might be prejudicial to your person anyway, or dangerous to the state by any means. And therefore I humbly beseech Your Majesty to let me answer afore yourself, and not suffer me to trust to your Councillors, yea, and that before I go to the Tower, if it be possible, if not, before I be further condemned . . . Let conscience move your Highness to pardon this my boldness, which innocency procures me to do, together with hope of your natural kindness, which I trust will not see me cast away without desert . . . I have heard of many in my time cast away for want of coming to the presence of their Prince; and in late days I heard my Lord of Somerset say that if his brother had been suffered to speak with him he had never suffered . . .

Though these persons are not to be compared to your Majesty, yet I pray God the like evil persuasions persuade not one sister against the other ... And as for the traitor Wyatt, he might peradventure write me a letter, but on my faith I never received any from him ...

Your Highness's most faithful subject, that hath been from the beginning, and will be to my end,

Elizabeth.

I humbly crave but only one word of answer from yourself.

But even when the student has extracted all he can from the *Calendar* and the texts of the Domestic series of papers, he will still be far from having a complete story. These Wyatt extracts leave many loose ends. Did Hastings and Cornwallis, for example, actually meet Wyatt as they were instructed to do on 22 January? What is the significance of Culpepper's arrival at Mereworth on 24 February, and why, on 25 February, should Wyatt implicate Croft in the inquiries about Elizabeth's loyalty? In addition to several such unanswered questions, there are wide gaps in the narrative. The *Calendar* tells us precious little about the course of the rebellion. After the attack on Cowling Castle at the end of January, the next we hear of Wyatt is his intention to cross the Thames at Kingston on 7 February. On 25 February Bourne reported that Wyatt was undergoing interrogation in the Tower, but the Domestic papers are silent about what Wyatt did on those eighteen fateful days in between. They are silent too about Wyatt's plans for nation-wide revolt, his character and purpose, the support he received from the people, and his chances of success.

For enlightenment on such important aspects of this subject, the student would have to go to other sources. At least two chronicles contain full contemporary accounts of Wyatt's rebellion: Henry Machyn devoted about eight pages of his *Diary* to it, and the 'resident in the Tower of London' who wrote the *Chronicle of Queen Jane* gave it special attention. Two or three other chronicles make shorter references, and useful information can be culled from contemporary letters and some county and parish records. But the entries from the Domestic series by no means exhaust all the help the state papers can give. Unfortunately, the Acts of the Privy Council, always worth consulting, are disappointingly uninformative about Wyatt. They say no more than that in February the privy council instructed Sir Robert Southwell to take Wyatt's house into his keeping, and in June returned some boats that had been wrongfully confiscated in Kent at the time of the uprising. The Patent Rolls give us a list of all 'the lordships and manors' which 'have come into the queen's hands by the attainder of Thomas Wyatt, knight', and record that Mary granted Wyatt's widow an annuity of 200 marks. But there are several references in the Venetian papers, and, as we might expect since Wyatt was protesting against Mary's proposed marriage to Philip of Spain, there is considerable information in the Spanish papers.

Using these foreign papers calls for caution. They consist largely of confidential dispatches from and to the ambassadors and other foreign representatives resident in England. Few of these papers can be considered as objective accounts. The ambassador usually wants to give the more pleasing, optimistic news. Perhaps he only sees and hears what he wants to see and hear. Perhaps his agents and contacts conspire to keep the worst tidings from him, and, in turn, he conveys to his government more of what he knows will please than what he knows will displease. If possible he himself must cut an influential figure in the story he is telling, in order to show his master he is doing his job properly. Occasionally, he is hoodwinked into sending news which has been deliberately fed to him for political purposes.

Simon Renard, the Imperial ambassador in England, sent several long reports to the Emperor concerning the Wyatt rebellion. He viewed it as a serious threat to Anglo-Imperial relations, and as a potential victory for French diplomacy. On 29 January, when the issue was still much in doubt, Renard and his colleagues made one of their reports. They did not discount the danger that Mary was in – 'it is feared lest certain members of the Council aid and abet the enterprise because of the lack of unison among them, their neglect of public affairs and the Queen's personal safety, and the fact that the decisions they come to are not carried out.' They stated that the French king had offered the rebels help, and even suggested that Charles V should either order them to pack up the embassy because of 'our dangerous position', or send armed help to Queen Mary. Nevertheless, the dispatch laid considerable emphasis on the hopeful signs – that the Council had put Portsmouth and the Isle of Wight in a state of defence against a possible French landing, that 'certain councillors believed' that the conspirators would not accept French help, that Lord Cobham had declared his loyalty, that Norfolk was 'on his way to stop Wyatt', that the rainy weather was 'very unfavourable to the rebels, who cannot camp out', that loyal proclamations had been sent all over the country, that Wyatt was losing support, that 'the Lady Elizabeth' had been summoned to court, and that an attempt at rebellion in the south-west had failed. They ended the dispatch on a hopeful note:

It is believed that Wyatt will be the Queen's prisoner sometime tomorrow, and that the Kentish disorders will altogether cease. I [presumably Renard, although the document is signed by five ambassadors] have advised the Queen to send after Elizabeth and have her arrested at once, for I fear she may escape. Your Majesty will realize that as the French harbour such hostile intentions against the Queen she will not be able to avoid declaring war on them; and I humbly beg you to come to a speedy decision and issue such orders as may seem wise so that relief may be sent to her from Spain.

It is instructive to compare this letter with the one sent by the French ambassador to the King of France on 26 January. The facts are similar, but the outlook and emphasis are quite different. It is rather like comparing leaders which appear in the *Daily Express* and the *Morning Star* on the same day.

... as my Lord Courtenay [Earl of Devonshire] has discovered [i.e. disclosed] the enterprise planned in his favour [i.e. to marry Mary], the authors have been forced to take up arms six weeks or two months earlier than they had intended. I may assure you, Sire, that Mr Thomas Wyatt has not failed his friends, but has kept his promise and taken the field yesterday with forces that are hourly increasing. The Queen and Council are greatly amazed at this, and mean to send the Duke of Norfolk, the Earl of Huntingdon and all the troops they can muster against the insurgents before their numbers swell; but I think the Queen will find it difficult to do this, especially as the very men of whom she now feels sure will soon declare for Wyatt.

The Lady Elizabeth has gone to another house of hers, thirty miles further away, where she is said to have gathered together a number of people, though the Queen frequently sends letters to her because of her mistrust ...

Count d'Egmont and the other Imperialists are here in a state of alarm, and have shut themselves up in two or three houses that open one into the other. On Monday the Queen is to withdraw to the Tower, where there is said to be very little powder ... Others say that she is going to Windsor, for that castle is strong enough to hold out some time against the insurgents ...

The crowned heads and ministers who received these dispatches had to try and calculate the bias in order to get as near to the truth as possible. Historians have to do the same.

Bibliography of Documents 1540–1660

English Historical Documents Vol. V, by C. H. Williams, covers the years 1485–1558. Unfortunately, Vols. VI and VII, which will continue the series to 1660, are not yet available. Miscellaneous extracts from parish and county documents will be found in such books as *The Parish Chest*, by W. E. Tate (1951, revised edition) and *Village Records*, by John West (1962), as well as in the quarterly issues of *The Amateur Historian* and *The Local Historian*, and the vast number of volumes published by local record and historical societies. A most useful guide to society publications is *Texts and Calendars: An Analytical Guide to Serial Publications*, by E. C. L. Mullins (1958). *County Records*, the Historical Association Pamphlet written by F. G. Emmison and Irvine Gray (1948: revised 1961), describes the various categories of records to be found in county record offices.

For the churchwardens' accounts of Prescot, see *The Churchwardens' Accounts of Prescot, Lancashire, 1523–1607*, ed. by F. A. Bailey, Lancashire and Cheshire Record Society publications, Vol. 104 (1953), and articles by F. A. Bailey in Vols. 92 and 95, *Transactions of the Historic Society of Lancashire and Cheshire* (1940 and 1943). *The Churchwardens' Accounts of Yatton*, ed. by E. Hobhouse, are in Somerset Record Society publications, Vol. 4 (1890); those of Rainham in *Archaeologia Cantiana*, Vol. 15 (1883).

The Constables' Accounts of the Manor of Manchester were edited by J. P. Earwaker (2 vols., 1891). Part of the overseers' accounts of Elmstead is photographed in *Elizabethan Essex*, by A. C. Edwards (1961). N. J. Williams edited *Kingston-upon-Thames Bridgewardens' Accounts, 1526–1567*, Surrey Record Society publications, Vol. 22 (1955). The Garstang bridge account is in the Lancashire Record Office.

Reference has been made to the following parish registers:

Edgbaston, 1636–1812, Dugdale Society (1928).

Leeds, Thoresby Society (1891).

East Grinstead, 1558–1661, Sussex Record Society (1917).

Preston, 1611–35 and *Farnworth, 1538–1612*, Lancashire Parish Register Society, Vols. 48 and 80.

St Peter's, Cornhill, St Mary Aldermary, and *St James's, Clerkenwell*, Harleian Society Registers, Vols. 1, 5, and 17.

On the use of registers see *An Introduction to English Historical Demography*, by E. A. Wrigley (1966), and *The World We Have Lost*, by P. Laslett (1965).

County record societies have published many collections of wills and inventories. They include *Wills and Inventories from the Registry at Durham*, Surtees Society, Vols. 2, 38, 112 and 142 (quotations above from Vol. 38); *Jacobean Household Inventories*, Bedfordshire Historical Record Society, Vol. 20; and *Nottinghamshire Household Inventories, 1512–62*, Thoroton Society, Record Series, Vol. 22. Quotations have been taken from these last two books, and also from *Household and Farm Inventories in Oxfordshire, 1550–1590* (1965) and *Wills and Inventories from Bury St Edmunds*, Camden Society Old Series, Vol. 49 (1850). The Historic Society of Lancashire and Cheshire has published the Speke Hall inventory (Vol. 97), and useful articles based on inventories in Vols. 110, 113, and 115. The quotations from the wills of William Charlton and Matthew Wood are from *Lancashire and Cheshire Wills*, Chetham Society N.S., Vol. 3 (1884), and the wills of Alexander Houghton, Thomas Sandes, Richard Holt, and George Swarland can be consulted in the Lancashire Record Office.

For the duties of lords lieutenant see *Lords Lieutenant in the Sixteenth Century*, by Gladys S. Thomson (1923). Quotations have been taken from *Historical Manuscript Commission*, Report XIII, App. IV, and *The Lancashire Lieutenancy*, Chetham Society O.S., Vols. 49 and 50 (1859).

For a complete list of calendars of state papers published before 1957 see *Texts and Calendars* quoted above. Elizabeth's letter will be found in *The Letters of Queen Elizabeth*, ed. by G. B. Harrison (1935). The Camden Society published *The Diary of Henry Machyn*, Old Series, Vol. 42 (1848), and *The Chronicle of Queen Jane*, Vol. 48 (1850).

I. DIARIES, AUTOBIOGRAPHIES, AND CONTEM-PORARY HISTORIES

Samuel Pepys and John Evelyn are far better known today than ever they were in the seventeenth century. Both men enjoyed a wide range of friends and acquaintances; both were known at court, both were members of the recently founded Royal Society, and both were interested ring-side spectators rather than participants in the political fights of their day. But neither man was a pace-setter among his fellows. They both lived long lives, and died within three years of each other – Pepys, the younger of the two, in 1703, and Evelyn, eighty-six years old, in 1706. Gradually, as the people they had known diminished in number, they were progressively forgotten: by the middle of the eighteenth century they had become hardly more than names on a tombstone. But on the publication of their diaries – Evelyn's in 1818 and Pepys's seven years later – they bounded back from obscurity into the spotlight of fame. They have remained there ever since.

This is a pattern of fortune common to diarists, for diaries, like most wines and vintage cars, derive value from their age. A diary of last year, however well kept, has little interest for anyone but the person who wrote it. But if the diarist puts it in a safe place, he can confidently assume that, long after he is dead, it will be of interest to his descendants and probably to the general public of some future age. Unpublishable today, it could be highly publishable in a hundred or two hundred years time. It need have no particular literary merit. What is required is faithful recording of what the diarist saw, heard, said, thought, or did from day to day. If he moves among interesting, influential people and enjoys the good fortune to witness momentous events, as Evelyn and Pepys did, all to the good, but if he lives a more humble and humdrum life, as many seventeenth- and eighteenth-century diarists did, his diary can still be packed with historical interest. For the story he has to tell is often much less valuable than the incidental light, which he cannot help shedding, upon the way of life and the outlook of the times he is living in. If he writes carefully and in some detail, the diarist inevitably puts something more than the narrative on to his paper.

... we lay at Stone that night. We had the next day a comfortable day and journey to Lichfield, and so to Coleshill, where we lay. On March 21st. we had a wet day, and bad way after we parted with the London road, and at Marton an indiscreet maid set us out of the way, and we were entangled in Townfields, dirty and wet and without shelter; and being out of the way did more afflict us than either the way or the weather. It put us late before we reached Southam; but there we found a good house, where they made much care to refresh and dry us; and the day clearing up a little, we adventured the other ten miles that night to Banbury, the way exceeding bad and solitary it being a depopulated country (by reason of the enclosures) in comparison, and we were oft in much doubt of our way ...

So wrote Henry Newcome, an ejected Presbyterian minister, in 1667. The journey itself is of little consequence, but what Newcome has to say is useful comment both upon the slowness and hardship of horseback journeys in Restoration England, and upon the effects of recent agricultural changes.

Or, to take a second example, the short, prosaic, matter-of-fact diary entries of Nicholas Blundell, a Lancashire squire, build up like jig-saw pieces into a detailed picture of country life and agricultural practice in the early eighteenth century.

October 8 [*1711*]. I Breaked 40 Threave of Flax with five Breakers and 24 Swinglers, it was 20 Dizon and eight Stricks of well drest Flax and weighed 90 Pound, they also Breaked about 2 Dizon and a halfe of Richard Newhous his and scutched it once over. The Miller and his son Fidled here after Supper for the Breakers. Whilst William Gray was Shearing in his Burned Ground in Stock Moss I pulled up one Root of Barley which most undoubtedly came from one Grain and had 28 Ears of Corne besides five Strawes which wanted Ears and were I believe snaped of with a Violent Wind . . .

October 16 . . . I payed Thomas Farer the Half years Tax for Windows. William Ainsworth brought home 51 Sheep of John Nicholsons from the Stags Head, I am to have 18d. per Score for keeping them for each Week they stay in my Ground.

October 17. We began to Hatchell [comb] and Spinn this years Flax . . .

October 20. I began to feed my Swine for Fat with Boyled Potatowes. I fetched home 4 Pigs and one Speaning from Ormskirk. I got up the last of my Potatows . . .

Blundell recorded such entries daily from 1702 to 1728 to help him, so he wrote, to defeat his bad memory. They have no pretension to literary style or to reflective thought or to anything beyond a simple record of personal activity. Blundell himself confessed, 'This work of mine may seem to some to be very useless . . . several things that are set down are of no consequence.' But he would have destroyed a valuable social and economic record had he thrown his 'useless' books away, or attempted to cut out the items 'of no consequence'. Contemporaries cannot possibly judge what items future historians will consider of little use, and if Blundell had undertaken to revise his diary he would have been just as likely to destroy the most valuable as the least valuable items. Indeed value is so subjective a matter that entries ignored by one researcher will be treasured by the next. The 'country life' entries, such as have been quoted above, are intermixed in this diary with entries about gathering together goods to be shipped to Virginia, about journeys undertaken both in England and in Flanders, about medical prescriptions and up-to-date cures, about the legal and social handicaps of being a member of the Roman Catholic church, and about the activities, weaknesses, benefactions, and tantrums of Blundell's friends and relations. Half a dozen researchers could use the Diary, and come away with half a dozen completely different sets of notes. It would be meaningless to try and judge which set had the most historical value.

Diary-keeping had become a gentlemanly hobby by the seventeenth century. Few Tudor diaries have come down to us – the diary of William More, the last prior of Worcester, and the journal of Sir Francis Walsingham are among those that have – but from Stuart and later times a host of carefully kept manuscripts have survived. A number, led by Pepys's and Evelyn's, have found commercial publishers and a world-wide market. More still have been published by county record societies; and an unknown number, probably considerably bigger still, are yet in manuscript, prized by those who have inherited them or placed for the use of students in libraries or county record offices. A few of these manuscripts will one day be edited and published, but many, because of their very bulk, or, contrariwise, because of their lack of detail, will never see the light of print. They are doomed to remain unknown to all but a handful of interested people.

What prompts a man to keep a diary? It is an exacting pastime, and very few humans have the temperament to keep diaries for long periods. Many set out on the road, but almost as many soon fall out; the Christmas-gift diary, begun in earnest on New Year's Day, has usually degenerated into an engagement book before the end of January. The resolution to write in it every day has been killed by the pressure of daily life and the precedence given to other interests. It is patent that to be successful the diary has to become a major, if not the most important, interest in the diarist's life. It cannot do this unless it fulfils a satisfying purpose – to be a confidant for the diarist's private ambitions and observations; to be the means of clarifying his thoughts – 'writing maketh an exact man'; to be a record which can have practical uses for him in future years; to be a self-justification or a means of self-expression; to be a substitute for action; or, in some cases, to be a conscious and deliberate attempt to set down a personal history of his own life and times. In one or two families – the Blundells of Lancashire and the Woodfordes of Somerset and Norfolk are examples – diary-making became a family tradition, so that it was almost taken for granted that one member of each generation would keep the family saga going.

To know a diarist's purpose in writing can help the historian judge the worth and bias of his manuscript. But what the historian wants most of all are the entries themselves. John Evelyn was a cautious man. He carried his political cup most steadily through the difficult days of both the Interregnum and the Bloodless Revolution. Just as Philippe de Commines, the supreme chronicler of *his* day, knew the hostile courts of Burgundy and France from the inside, so Evelyn had friends in Cromwell's intimate circle and yet was a personal friend of Charles II. He never intended to publish his diary, for in it he expressed opinions which it would have been impolitic or dangerous to ventilate openly. For this reason the historian can accept what he writes not as diplomatic utterances, but as honest, if highly personal, comment upon events and people. And we are fortunate that in his long life Evelyn met so many outstanding men and women, and that he was actually present on so many interesting occasions. He began writing down his observations in 1631 and did not cease until February 1706, the month in which he died. He lived through the Civil Wars, the Interregnum, the reigns of Charles II, James II, and William III, and part of Anne's reign. He was one of the 'auditors of the greatest malice and the greatest innocency' at the trial of Strafford; he fought in the Royalist army at Turnham Green, or, more correctly and more in character, 'I came in with my horse and Armes just at the retreate' and managed to get back home 'no body knowing of my having been in His Majesty's Army', and he witnessed 'the Magnificent Funeral of that arch-Rebell Ireton'. At a Royal Society meeting in 1662 he watched Robert Boyle produce '2 clear liquors, which being mingled became a hard stone', and at another meeting forty-three years later marvelled at Isaac Newton's new burning-glass, 'which did strange things as to mealting whatever was held to it in a moment'. To his secret disgust he had on occasions to be polite to Nell Gwyn – 'Mrs Nellie as they cal'd an impudent Comedian' – and the Duchess of Cleveland, 'another Lady of Pleasure and curse of our nation'. Less than a week before it was burned down in the Great Fire, he, with Christopher Wren, the bishop, dean, and others, was inspecting Old St Paul's, surveying 'the generall decays of that ancient and venerable Church' and setting down 'what was fit to be don, with the charge thereof'. In 1686 he dined at Judge Jeffreys's table, but disapproved strongly of the lawyers' conversation about 'how long they had detained their clients in tedious processes'. He was present when 'infinite crowds of people on their knees' begged for the blessing of the seven bishops as they were being taken prisoners to the Tower, and present also when William of Orange arrived at St James's. One of his son's tutors was John Milton's nephew 'yet no way tainted by him', and he himself was entertained by Sir Thomas Browne in Norwich and visited by John Dryden at his home at Wotton, Surrey. He deliberately kept out of the way when Charles I was executed, but he was present when Charles II returned to London in May 1660, 'the ways straw'd with flowers, the bells ringing, the streetes hung with Tapissry, fountaines running with wine'. He reported in detail on Charles II's coronation, on the Great Fire, and on the proclamation of the accession of James II. He had an instinct for being in the right place at the right time. Had he been born three hundred years later, he would have been invaluable not as a gossip columnist

– he was too repressed and correct a man for that – but as a special-occasion broadcaster. He and Richard Dimbleby had much in common.

Among his more friendly acquaintances Evelyn numbered Samuel Pepys. He was with him in good times and bad.

4 June 1679. To London: Din'd with Mr Pepys at the Tower, whither he was committed by the house of Commons, for misdemeanors in the Admiralty, where he was Secretary; but I believe unjustly.
30 May 1698. I dined at Mr Pepys's, where I heard that rare Voice, Mr Pate, who was lately come from Italy, reputed the most excellent singer, ever England had: he sang indeede many rare Italian Recitatives, etc., and several compositions of the last Mr Pursal [Henry Purcell], esteemed the best composer of any Englishman hitherto.

Ten years before the first of these two meetings, Pepys had already given up keeping his diary – 'I being not able to do it any longer, having done now as long as to undo my eyes almost every time that I take a pen in my hand'. He was still no more than thirty-six years old, with many active years ahead as clerk of the acts, secretary of the admiralty, and member of parliament. It is possible to trace the rest of his career from the state papers and from his official and semi-official correspondence. But it is doubtful if he would have attracted a single biographer, had he not scribbled away at his short-hand diary between 1 January 1660 and 31 May 1669, and if he had not bequeathed his manuscript to the safe keeping of Magdalene College, Cambridge.

Pepys was a better diarist than Evelyn. He was more meticulous, more impelled to put down the details, and readier to record less obvious facts and impressions. For the historian, Evelyn has the merit of covering an exceptional number of years, but Pepys has the greater merit of using a bigger canvas and, like Bruegel and Lowry, filling it with lots of figures and interesting incidents, out of which the historian can take or throw away what he wants. If Pepys talked in the same way as he wrote, he must have driven his intimates to distraction. Petty, routine happenings abound in his diary.

17 February 1660. In the morning Tom that was my Lord's footboy came to see me and had 10s. of me of the money which I have to keep of his. So that now I have but 35s. more of his. Then came Mr Hills the instrument maker, and I consulted with him about the altering my lute and my viall. After that I went into my study and did up my accounts, and found that I am about £40 beforehand in the world and that is all. So to my office and from thence brought Mr Hawly home with me to dinner, and after dinner wrote a letter to Mr Downing about his business and gave it Hawly, and so went to Mr Gunning's ...

Evelyn would never have made an entry as boring as that: for him nothing worth recording would have happened that day, and consequently he would have taken the common sense view and kept his diary shut. But this conversational vice of piling interminable, tiny, unrelated details one on another is a virtue in a diarist. Unlike the unlucky listener, the reader can always skip the passages that bore him. One can see the value of diary detail by comparing Pepys's description of the Great Fire with Evelyn's account. Pepys, it is true, was the more concerned because his house in Mark Lane was directly threatened, but that is not the sole reason for the difference between the two descriptions. Evelyn is the competent special correspondent preparing an accurate, balanced report for the half column allotted to him: Pepys is the star feature writer and broadcaster, gathering into the story of the disaster as much human interest as he can find and, consciously or unconsciously, taking his reader vicariously through the whole traumatic experience.

... Everybody endeavouring to remove their goods, and flinging into the river or bringing them into lighters that lay off; poor people staying in their houses as long as till the very fire touched them, and then running into boats or clambering from one pair of stairs by the water-side to another. And among other things, the poor pigeons, I perceive, were loth to leave their houses, but hovered about the windows and balconys till they were, some of them burned on their wings and fell down ... Here I saw Mr Isaake Houblon, the handsome man, prettily dressed and dirty, at his door at Dowgate, receiving some of his brothers' things, whose houses were on fire; and, as he says, have been removed twice already; and he doubts (as it soon proved) that they must be in a little time removed from his house also, which was a sad consideration ...

The Fire moved Evelyn to unwonted eloquence, but he did not give us details like these. Perhaps he never noticed them. He was a colder, more reserved man than Pepys. Sympathetic curiosity and instinctive fellow feeling for others helped Pepys to see, as well as to write, in greater detail.

It is always a bonus for the researcher when he can discover two diarists describing the same incident. One account does not only confirm, or clash with, the other, but, taken together, they allow him to view a happening from two different angles. The picture becomes clearer partly because of additional detail, partly because it gains something approaching an extra dimension. At least two diarists recorded their impressions when the Jacobite army marched south through Manchester in 1745. One was a young Presbyterian doctor, Richard Kay, who feared the worst if Prince Charles Edward's supporters were successful:

27 *November* [1745] ... Our Enemies we hear are marching thro' Lancashire and are not far from Manchester on their Journey to London to set a Popish Pretender upon the Throne of England. We all pray and hope that God will not suffer such an unnatural Rebellion to reign long in the Nation. Lord, Suppress the Pride of these Rebells, these rebellious Wretches, in due Times.

28 *November* ... O, How Persons are removing their Families and Effects out of Manchester. We have here [in Bury nine miles from Manchester] a numerous Family. We hear this Evening a Sergeant with one Drummer belonging to the Pretender's Service are come to

Manchester to Day, and have enlisted several into their Service. Lord, Do not laugh at our Calamity, nor mock when our Fear cometh.

The second diarist, Elizabeth Byrom, twenty-three years old and six years younger than Kay, took the whole affair much more light-heartedly. She was thrilled to find herself a witness of such unusual action, and, because she was content to stand aside from the political issue, she could enjoy the experience and its unconscious humour.

27 November. The postmaster is gone to London today, we suppose to secure the money from falling into the hands of the rebels; we expect a party of them here [Manchester] tomorrow. The Prince lay at Lawyer Starkey's at Preston last night; he has marched from Carlisle on foot at the head of his army; he was dressed in a Scotch plaid, a blue silk waistcoat with silver lace, and a Scotch bonnet with J.R. on it. Yesterday the militia were all discharged and sent home, but just in time before the Highlanders came – well contrived.

28 November. About 3 o'clock today came into town two men in Highland dress, and a woman behind one of them with a drum on her knee, and for all the loyal work that our Presbyterians have made, they took possession of the town ... they beat up for volunteers ... 'All gentlemen that have a mind to serve H.R.H. with a willing mind, 5 guineas advance', and nobody offered to meddle with them...

30 November. .... I dressed up in my white gown ... and an officer called on us to go see the Prince, we went to Mr Fletcher's and saw him get a-horseback, and a noble sight it is, I would not have missed it for a great deal of money ... As soon as he was gone the officer and us went to prayers at the old church ... Mr Shrigley read prayers, he prayed for the King and Prince of Wales and named no names ...

Handel's *Firework Music* is still a popular concert piece. It was written for a firework festival in April 1749. One of the spectators was a Miss Greene, aged nineteen and excited to be in London for her second season.

Evening went to Mr Winford's house in Sackville Street to see the

Fireworks in the Green Park by the invitation of Mrs Faz ... The Fireworks continued about an hour; was intended to have been 3 but the Pavilion at one end catching fire they were obliged to put a stop to 'em.

She was disappointed that the show could not last its full time, especially as she had watched the preparations during the previous week, but she put down the comparative failure to ill-luck. But not so sophisticated Horace Walpole. He gave his opinion to his friend Sir Horace Mann:

The Fireworks ... by no means answered the expense, the length of preparation and the expectation that had been raised ... The rockets and whatever was thrown up into the air succeeded mighty well, but the wheels and all that was to compose the principal part were pitiful and ill-conducted, with no changes of coloured fires and shapes: the illumination was mean, and lighted so slowly that scarce anybody had patience to wait the finishing; and then what contributed to the awkwardness of the whole was the right pavilion catching fire, and being burned down in the middle of the show ... Very little mischief was done, and but two persons killed ...

Walpole claimed he had seen *real* fireworks in Paris. Forty people had been killed on that occasion. The French and Italian managers had quarrelled about how things should be done; 'both lighted at once, and blew up the whole'. But Walpole, one suspects, had constantly to be safeguarding his reputation as a wit. When he wrote or talked, his eye was not so much on truth as on the effect his words would produce. He usually wanted to amuse, occasionally to exasperate or shock his readers or hearers out of their complacency. One of his favourite professional tools was exaggeration, but at times he was not above reaching for invention. Therefore, no researcher, without checking, would be wise to accept what he said at its face value. Miss Greene confirms his point about the burning pavilion bringing the show to an end, but it is doubtful if the show was so poor that 'scarce anybody had patience to wait the finishing'.

Theological disputation, so compelling a feature of seventeenth-century England, is strongly reflected in the diaries of the age. Neither Pepys nor Evelyn was a particularly religious man, but both devoted considerable space to the details of texts and sermons. And parsons were quite likely to keep diaries. A fair number have been published. Those of such men as Dr Granville, dean of Durham, Ralph Josselin, vicar of Earls Colne, Essex, and, of course, James Woodforde are Anglican in their point of view, but they tend to be outnumbered by the diaries of Puritan divines. In the Manchester area, where Presbyterians and Independents struggled 'like Jacob and Esau in their mother's womb', there was almost a school of diarists in the Restoration period – Angier of Denton, Jolly of Droylesden, Newcome of Manchester, to say nothing of Oliver Heywood, whose records were not kept in strict diary form, or Adam Martindale, who based his autobiography, the work of his last years, on diary notes kept during his lifetime. Theology did not occupy as much space in these diaries as one might suspect. Out of each one of them can be sieved considerable material useful for the social and economic historian. And, of course, they all show the effects in the parishes of the anti-Dissenter acts of the Clarendon Code, and of the temporary Declarations of Indulgence.

The two outstanding religious testimonies of the seventeenth and eighteenth centuries are the journals of George Fox and John Wesley. They are alike in that each gives us a detailed picture of an extraordinary personality stumping his way through Britain and foreign parts, preaching and teaching his view of God and the salvation of Christ. Both journals are concerned with little else: there is nothing here of small talk or of the routine details of domestic life. Both authors set down successes and failures; sympathetic, hostile, and indifferent receptions; argument and counter-argument. And out of both books come sharp impressions of unshakable conviction, outstanding courage, and endless energy.

As I travelled through markets, fairs, and divers places, I saw death and darkness in all people, where the power of the Lord God had not shaken them. As I was passing on in Leicestershire, I came to Twycross ... There was in that town a great man, that had long lain sick, and was given up by the physicians ... I went up to him in his chamber, and spake the word of life to him, and was moved to pray by him; and the Lord was entreated and restored him to health. But when I was come down the stairs, into a lower room, and was speaking to the servants and to some people that were there, a serving-man of his came raving out of another room, with a naked rapier in his hand, and run at me ere I was aware of it and set it just to my side. I looked at him in his face and said 'Alack for thee, poor creature! what wilt thou do with thy carnal weapon? it is no more to me than a straw'. The standersby were much troubled, and he went away in a rage and full of wrath.

I rode to Nottingham again, and at eight preached at the market-place to an immense multitude of people, on, 'The dead shall hear the voice of the Son of God; and they that hear shall live'. I saw only one or two who behaved lightly, whom I immediately spoke to; and they stood reproved. Yet, soon after, a man behind me began aloud to contradict and blaspheme; but upon my turning to him, he stepped behind a pillar, and in a few minutes disappeared.

One could easily assume that these two typical extracts came from the same journal. But they do not. The first is from Fox's and refers to 1650, the second an entry in Wesley's dated 1741.

The historian cannot dismiss either the Quaker or the Wesleyan movement as being 'just another religious sect'. Both grew out of particular social and ecclesiastical conditions, and both, especially the latter, had a wide and far-reaching influence upon both the way society developed and the new attitude men took towards social problems. The social work inspired by Quakers and Methodists in the last two hundred years compels others besides ecclesiastical historians to study the origin and the aims of both movements.

Fox's *Journal* is not a true diary. It is an autobiography – emotion and events recollected in the tranquillity of prison and put down on paper in 1675 and 1676, when he was regaining his strength at Swarthmoor on the north side of Morecambe Bay. It is obviously based on a clear memory, prompted by note-books, letters, and conversation. It covers the years 1643 to 1675 in considerable detail. Wesley's *Journal* too has been rewritten. He tells us in his Preface that he transcribed 'from time to time, the more material parts of my diary, adding here and there such little reflections as occurred to my mind . . . it is not being my design to relate all those particulars which I wrote for my own use only, and which would answer no valuable end to others, however important they were to me.' Every man has the right to decide what of his writings he wishes others to read, but had Wesley let us have the field notes instead of the edited script, we should probably have found his journal more diverse in subject, and consequently a richer source of historical evidence.

Properly regarded, autobiographies and edited journals such as Wesley's and Fox's are half-way stages between the diary proper and a contemporary history. The diarist is the chronicler: he notes the events as they happen, and the only comment he can possibly make is his own immediate reaction to what has occurred. This is raw material for historians, but not history. For an essential part of the historian's task is to select as well as collect facts; he must evaluate and interpret them, and try to see them in true perspective. The writing of history, therefore, cannot help but lag a reasonable distance behind events. The time gap gives the author a better standpoint from which to view his facts, and, of even more importance, it tends to quieten the emotions and reduce the prejudices which cloud his judgement. To write about issues in which one has been personally involved is inevitably to play the advocate rather than the judge.

Nevertheless, there have been a number of serious and gallant attempts to achieve the well-nigh impossible – to put on paper not merely the story of the writer's own life but a considered appraisal of the times he has lived through. Sir Winston Churchill is the most outstanding contemporary historian of the twentieth century. He seems to have been aware of the weakness as well as the strength of his work. In his preface to *The Second World War*, he pointed out that, since he had been prime minister during the war years, he wrote with exceptional authority, but he also admitted that 'much is constantly coming to light from the disclosure of captured documents or other revelations, which may present a new aspect to the conclusions which I have drawn'. It is true that his next sentence almost discredited in advance any 'new aspects' that did not accord with his own narrative, but it is abundantly clear from past examples that no contemporary history can ever be a long accepted, much less a final, judgement. The author is too near the events and too emotionally involved in the issues to be capable of anything approaching a cool assessment.

Clarendon's *History of the Rebellion* is the seventeenth-century equivalent of *The Second World War*. This work falls into two parts. The first is a reasonably critical account of the Civil War in which the author fought on the King's side, and the second is largely an *apologia* for the part he played in the government of England from 1660 to 1667. The first part, though not infrequently inaccurate in fact, is the better history, because Clarendon viewed the conduct of the war with more detachment than he managed to acquire when assessing his own part in politics. But the whole book is as invaluable a historical source as Churchill's writings obviously are. If involvement makes perspective difficult, it offers the compensation of the author being present on many of the occasions to be described and of personally knowing many of the leading characters.

Gilbert Burnet, created Bishop of Salisbury by William III, wrote *History of My Own Times*. He revised the work continually, and left it to be published after his death. In his day he had a deserved reputation for tolerance, yet he had spoken out so strongly against the Church of Rome that he thought it prudent to exile himself soon after James II came to the throne. After some wandering, he gravitated to Holland, and eventually returned to England with William III's invasion force. He became a confidant of the new king and queen, and as Bishop of Salisbury he exercised considerable influence in church politics until his death in 1715. In his introduction to his *History*, Burnet said that he was writing 'with a design to make both himself and his readers wiser and better', that he wished 'to lay open the good and bad of all sides and parties as clearly and impartially as he himself understood it', and that he intended to tell his story 'without any regard to kindred or friends, to parties or interests'. This was his idealistic aim, but, with the best will in the world, he could not possibly achieve it. Nothing could convince him that all the right was not on the side of the Whigs and of the Anglican church. To him this was self-evident truth. So not surprisingly his 'impartial' history was rejected as fabrication and falsehood by those who, equally one-sided, took a contrary view. Soon after the book had been published, one Jacobite writer condemned it as 'such an uninterrupted series of untruths as will astonish; not mistakes proceeding from negligence or human infirmity, but from a corrupt design to impose on posterity'. This Jacobite saw the mote in Burnet's eye, but was quite unaware of the beam in his own.

Burnet's account of the birth of James Edward in 1688 is a typical example of the way in which his political bias twisted his judgement and, occasionally, pushed aside his common sense. He was not in England at the time of the birth, and, therefore, had to rely upon reports and gossip. He accepted what he wanted to believe, and, probably unconsciously, rejected any evidence to the contrary. The birth of the prince came most opportunely for the Roman Catholic supporters of James II, and shattered the hopes of his opponents that he would soon be succeeded by his Protestant daughter, Mary. Instead of the reign of a Roman Catholic being a short interlude between two Protestant monarchs, it now threatened to become a permanency. To many Roman Catholics this change of prospect appeared to be a miracle. Most Protestants, unable to believe that God would ever serve them in so shabby a way, were ready to believe that the baby was not the child of James and his queen – that in some Gilbertian way it had been smuggled into the bedroom or exchanged for a stillborn child. Yet there was no reason why Mary of Modena needed a miracle to bear James II a son, or why she should resort to trickery. She had had children before, though none of them had lived beyond infancy. This child, born when political tension was at breaking point, was damned from the start.

Burnet never accepted the possibility of the child being a genuine prince. He admitted that the lying-in-room was full of witnesses, but

... No cries were heard from the child; nor was it shewn to those in the room. It was pretended more air was necessary. The under-dresser went out with the child, or something else, in her arms to a dressing room, to which there was a door near the queen's bed; but there was another entry to it from other apartments. The king continued with the lords in the bedchamber for some minutes, which was either a sign of much phlegm upon such an occasion; for it was not known whether the child was alive or dead; or it looked like the giving time for some management.

Not content with this, Burnet went on adding suspicious details – Chamberlain, the usual man-midwife, was not called to the palace; Princess Anne had been denied entrance to the baby's room; and two Papists had been overheard to say, 'The Prince of Wales is dead'. At first, Burnet inferred that no child had been born to Mary; then he suggested that someone else's baby had taken the place of the dead prince.

One, that saw the child two days after, said to me, that he looked strong, and not like a child so newly born ... So healthy a child being so little like any of those the queen had borne, it was given out that he had fits and could not live. But those who saw him every day observed no such thing.

Yet, Burnet went on to record that some weeks later at Richmond the child was indeed suffering from fits. Four doctors thought he was dying, but, 'while the physicians were at dinner', the child recovered.

It was said, that the child was strongly revived of a sudden. Some of the physicians told Lloyd, bishop of St Asaph, that it was not possible for them to think it was the same child. They looked on one another, but durst not speak what they thought.

It would appear from this passage that Burnet intended us to believe that a second masquerader had taken the place of the first.

When, a page or two later, Burnet was telling the story of the 'press conference' at which James II endeavoured to quash evil rumour and convince his privy councillors, judges, and nobles that Mary was the mother of the prince, he threw more unreasonable doubt on the evidence. James had claimed that many people were present at the birth, and that 'they saw the child soon after it was taken from the queen by the midwife'. But, Burnet added,

the midwife was the single witness: for none of the ladies had felt the child in the queen's belly. The countess of Sunderland did indeed depose, that the queen called to her to give her her hand, that she might feel how the child lay; to which she added, 'which I did'; but did not say whether she felt the child or not: and she told the duchess of Hamilton, from whom I had it, that when she put her hand into the bed, the queen held it, and let it go no lower than her breasts. So that she really felt nothing.

Burnet related more of such gossip, and eventually came to the conclusion that James would not have had need to try and convince people had the birth been a genuine one. Just as Tudor historians could not tolerate a good word for Richard III, so Burnet could not believe that James, as a Roman Catholic king, was capable of honesty and honourable intentions. But James Stuart, as a man, was quite a different person for Burnet, After recording his death, he wrote:

He was a prince that seemed made for greater things than will be found in the course of his life, more particularly of his reign: he was esteemed, in the former parts of his life, a man of great courage, as he was quite through it a man of great application to business: he had no vivacity of thought, invention, or expression; but he had a good judgment, where his religion, or his education, gave him not a bias, which it did very often: he was bred with strange notions of the obedience due to princes, and came to take up as strange ones, of the submission due to priests; he was naturally a man of truth, fidelity, and justice; but his religion was so infused in him, and he was so managed in it by his priests, that the principles which nature had laid in him, had little power over him when the concerns of his church stood in the way . . .

Burnet was always doing his best to be fair. He was fully conscious of what a historian should aim to do, and he thought of himself as nothing less than a historian. He would have been insulted if anyone had referred to him as a chronicler, an annalist, a diarist, or a reporter. But he was as human as the rest of us. He made the best use of his eye-witness advantage when he came to describe events he had witnessed, but his partisanship caused him to accept all reports and gossip that were music to his ear, and prevented him from giving proper weight to all unwelcome facts. In short, he was a typical, good contemporary historian.

2. PAMPHLETS AND THE FIRST NEWSPAPERS

In Stuart and early Hanoverian times, the pamphlet was the readiest tool with which to attempt to fashion public opinion. It could be used to publicize fact – to act as a newsletter – but far more often men used it to set out an argument or to popularize a point of view. Every government before 1688 considered pamphleteering dangerous. In 1586 Elizabeth, outraged by the consequences of 'divers contentious and disorderly persons professing the art or mystery of printing or selling of books', required her Council to take strong measures to control the industry. Thereupon the Council ordered the London Company of Stationers to register all existing presses, and gave the archbishop of Canterbury and the bishop of London supervision of the licensing of all new ones. With the exception of one press in each of the two universities, no presses at all could legally exist outside London. But controversy – at this time particularly theological controversy – could not be stifled so easily. The Marprelate press, which published anonymous tracts justifying the Puritan opposition, is the best known of several secret presses which defied the order. In 1622 and again two years later, James I redefined the law, because 'the printing, importing, and dispersing of popish and seditious books and pamphlets and seditious puritanical books and pamphlets . . . is grown so common and practised so licentiously . . .' Henceforward, no pamphlet 'concerning matters of religion, church government or state' could be printed without the licence of an archbishop, the bishop of London, or the vice-chancellor of one of the universities. Although the Court of High Commission already had the duty of searching for 'all heretical, schismatical and seditious books, libels, and writings', this new law had little more effect than the old. A Star Chamber decree of 1637 gave a further twist to the censorship screw, but even the vicious punishments inflicted upon such pamphleteers as Leighton, Prynne, and Lilburne did not silence the government's critics.

The Long Parliament abolished both Star Chamber and Court of High Commission. This produced a spate of writings on all kinds of subjects, religious, constitutional, military, educational, and economic. But the law did not leave the pamphleteer absolutely free: parliament appointed new licensers, the Stationers' Company still claimed the right to register printers, and an author could always be prosecuted for upholding 'popery or prelacy' or endangering civil liberties. In 1643 Parliament made new, stricter regulations, against which Milton protested in *Areopagitica*: 'Give me liberty to know, to utter, and to argue freely according to conscience, above all liberties.' Both the Commonwealth and the Protectorate censored the press, but at the Restoration the Cavalier Parliament turned the clock back almost a century. The Licensing Act of 1662 re-established the stricter censorship of the Tudors and early Stuarts. The Stationers' Company's control was tightened, and every manuscript had to be approved by appropriate authority:

... all books concerning the common laws of this realm, shall be printed by the special allowance of the Lord Chancellor ... the Lords Chief Justices and Lord Chief Baron ... or one or more of their appointments; And all books of history ... or other books concerning any affairs of State, shall be licensed by the principal Secretaries of State ... And all books ... concerning heraldry, titles of honour, and arms, or otherwise concerning the office of Earl Marshal shall be licensed by the Earl Marshal ... And all books to be imprinted or reprinted, whether of divinity, physick, philosophy, or whatsoever other science or art, shall be first licensed and allowed

by the Lord Archbishops of Canterbury, and Lord Bishop of London
... or by either of the Chancellors or Vice-Chancellors of either of the
universities of this realm ...

The last clause of the Licensing Act limited its life to two years,
but this was chiefly to ensure an early review of its effectiveness.
Parliament renewed the law regularly, and it did not lapse
until 1695.

Once rigid censorship had been abolished, the more responsible and moderate critics of government and church
policy managed to make themselves heard. Instead of the
attack on authority and orthodox policies being left to fanatics,
who martyr-like accepted the legal risks they ran, those in
power were henceforward subjected to constant criticism,
some of it extreme and prejudiced still, but much of it reasoned
and helpful. In the political world, the party system began to
grow, because a free opposition could voice objections and
put forward alternative policies. Pamphlet answered pamphlet,
and at White's and St James's coffee-houses, Will's, Button's,
and hundreds of other social and intellectual centres, the arguments were developed or opposed. No man was too elevated
in social rank or too renowned an author to join in. The leading
pamphleteers were among the influential personalities of their
day – Dryden, Defoe, Pope, Addison, Steele, Arbuthnot, and,
probably most effective of all, Swift.

Today the historian goes to the pamphlet when he is seeking
the ideas and opinions of the age he is studying. What men and
women thought, valued, or denounced is as enlightening as
what they did: to understand a particular generation we must
know its ideals and intentions as well as its achievements. The
pamphlet, partial though it is, helps us to gauge what thoughts
were uppermost in people's minds, what new ideas were in
the air, and what were the controversial issues of the day.
Politics and theology were not the only subjects of the pamphleteers. They discussed economic and commercial policies,

indulged in literary dispute and open quarrel, and explored new scientific ideas. Their titles, usually long and involved, varied from half-expected ones beginning *A Review of the Affairs of . . . A true and exact Account of . . .* or *An appeal to Honour and Justice . . .* to more surprising ones such as *A discussion of Apparel or Cloathing, In what manner to remedy Clandestine Marriages,* or *The description of a Plain Instrument: a mathematical treatise.* Some authors disguised their message in allegory (*The Parlement of Byrdes* in mock-medieval spelling) or in satirical humour (*An Elegy on the Death of Trade by a relation of the Deceased*). Others told a straightforward tale, such as *A diary of the Siege and Surrender of Limerick.* Not unexpectedly in the age of the Grand Tour, a number dealt with foreign travel (*A true Description and Direction of what is most worthy to be seen in all Italy*) and a few ventured on such historical studies as *The Vindication of Nicholas Machiavelli* and *The True and Wonderful History of Perkin Warbeck.*

Pamphlets varied as much in length as in subject. They ranged from long, closely reasoned discourses to nothing more than a page or two of prose or verse, either written in haste or heat to be topical, or deliberately planned short to be more effective. Dryden packed argument and invective into terse, quotable stanzas, which, notwithstanding their present status as *literature,* were trenchant pamphlets in their own day. His well-known *Absalom and Achitophel,* published a day or two before Shaftesbury's trial in November 1681, was a vigorous contribution to the Exclusion Bill debate, which was then the only thing London was talking about. Dryden took the side of Charles II and the Court Party: he denounced Shaftesbury and his Green Ribbon Club, and explained Monmouth's 'unworthy' conduct by claiming that he had been misled and ill-advised by the wily Shaftesbury. By putting the story into a quasi Old Testament setting, and by painting the characters not as cardboard heroes and villains but as carefully caricatured individuals, Dryden turned this poetic-pamphlet into an effective weapon against those who wished to exclude James from the succession to the throne. Identifying the characters intrigued and held the attention of the readers, and because, as Dryden said himself, 'there is sweetness in good verse, which tickles even while it hurts', many who did not accept Dryden's politics could not help chuckling at some of his pithy, apt lines. He drew attention, for example, to Shaftesbury's puny frame by paying tribute to his restless energy and 'turbulence of wit':

> A fiery soul, which, working out its way,
> Fretted the pigmy body to decay
> And o'er-informed the tenement of clay.

And he won grudging nods from a good number of his political opponents when he described the mean, inhospitable sheriff of the City of London, Slingsby Bethel, as 'not prodigal of pelf'. He made his point clearer with four lines which Bethel's political friends as well as his enemies must have eagerly committed to memory:

> Chaste were his cellars, and his shrieval board
> The grossness of a city feast abhorr'd:
> His cooks with long disuse their trade forgot;
> Cool was his kitchen, though his brains were hot.

This was far more effective pamphleteering than what he produced when he adopted the commoner practice of his day and cudgelled his detractors with personal satire and invective. In *The Medal*, for example, he lashed out at Shaftesbury more viciously but less memorably with

> Religion thou hast none: thy mercury
> Has passed through every sect, or theirs through thee.
> But what thou givest, that venom still remains,
> And the poxed nation feels thee in their brains.

In defence of Shaftesbury, Thomas Shadwell hit back at Dryden with blinder brute force, and Dryden, recovering his lighter but more deadly style, had little difficulty in demolishing the new champion with mocking contempt. Flecknoe, an Irish priest who mistakenly had considered himself a poet, Dryden imagined to be choosing his heir:

> Shadwell alone my perfect image bears,
> Mature in dullness from his tender years:
> Shadwell alone of all my sons is he
> Who stands confirmed in full stupidity.
> The rest to some faint meaning make pretence,
> But Shadwell never deviates into sense.

Few pamphleteers were as deft or as entertaining as Dryden. But this does not mean that they are less useful to the historian. Some are very helpful indeed. About the turn of the century, for example, an anonymous writer published an eight-page pamphlet arguing the need for annual parliaments. Another in half that space advocated a twice-blessed scheme for increasing exports and putting the poor to work. A third devoted thirty-two pages to advocating compulsory marriage of bachelors in order to increase the population more rapidly – 'England never prospered by the importation of foreigners, nor have we any need of them, when we can raise a breed of our own.' Temptation is strong to dismiss these authors and many others as cranks. Certainly their arguments were often illogical and wrong-headed. But they indicate problems of the day, and tell us something of the solutions that were being advocated. Today the modern counterparts of such seventeenth- and eighteenth-century writers would get themselves interviewed on radio or television, or, in more traditional style, write letters to the newspapers. If their views roused no response, they would disappear as quickly as they appeared; but if they put into words what many other people had been turning over in their mind, or if they propounded a new hypothesis persuasively and logically, they could well initiate an argument which could lead either to legislation and important action or to the replacement of a well-established but worn out policy.

Sir William Petty, a versatile scientist and man of affairs, published several influential, seminal pamphlets during the reigns of Charles II and James II. He was interested in many non-political and non-theological matters as various as land survey, the reform of parliamentary franchise, and the compiling of dictionaries, but probably his most original contribution to the thought of his age was 'political arithmetick', or the application of statistics to economics. This was a new approach, not to begin with a theory, but to 'express myself in Terms of Number, Weight, or Measure' and accept the results. Petty was well aware that his figures were none too accurate. He had no means of improving them, and had to accept them as the best obtainable. But that did not deter him from his calculations and conclusions.

Some have estimated that there are not above 300,000,000 people in the whole world. Whether that be so, or not, is not very material to be known: but I have fair grounds to conjecture, and would be glad to know it more certainly, that there are not above 80,000,000 with whom the English and Dutch have commerce . . . And I further estimate that the value of all commodities yearly exchanged amongst them doth not exceed the value of £45,000,000.

Now the Wealth of every nation consisting chiefly in the share which they have in Foreign Trade . . . we are to consider Whether the subjects of the King of England, head for head, have not a greater share than those of France?

To which purpose it hath been considered that the manufactures of wool yearly exported out of England . . . amount unto £5,000,000.

The value of lead, tin, and coals, to be £500,000.

The value of all clothes, household stuff etc. carried into America £200,000.

The value of silver and gold taken [i.e. bought] from the Spaniards £60,000.

The value of sugar, indigo, tobacco, cotton, and cocoa, brought from the southward parts of America, £600,000.

The value of the fish, pipe staves, masts, beaver, etc. brought from New England and the northern parts of America, £200,000.

The value of the wool, butter, hides, tallow, beef, herrings, pilchards, and salmon exported out of Ireland, £800,000.

The value of coals, salt, linen, yarn, herrings, pilchards, salmon, linen cloth, and yarn brought out of Scotland and Ireland, £500,000.

The value of the saltpetre, pepper, calicoes, diamonds, drugs, and silks brought out of the East Indies, £800,000.

The value of the slaves brought out of Africa, to serve in our America Plantations, £20,000.

Which with the Freight of English shipping trading into foreign parts, being above £1,500,000, makes in all £10,180,000.

Which computation is sufficiently justified by the Customs of the three Kingdoms, whose intrinsic value is thought to be nearly £1,000,000 *per annum* ...

But the value of the French commodities brought into England is not above £1,200,000 *per annum;* and the value of all they export into all the world besides, not above three or four times as much ...

So as France not exporting above Half the value of what England doth ... and having withal more people than England: it follows that the people of England have, head for head, Thrice as much Foreign Trade as the people of France, and about Two parts out of Nine of the Trade of the whole Commercial World; and about Two parts in Seven of all the Shipping ...

Petty's technique and argument will certainly not impress modern economists and statisticians, but in his day this was a revolutionary way of approaching economic and social problems.

Helped by John Graunt, Petty began such studies about 1660. In 1682 he published *An Essay in Political Arithmetick, concerning the people, housing, hospitals, etc of London and Paris,* and followed this with a similar analysis of the growth of London and Rome, and *Five Essays in Political Arithmetick*. In 1690, two years after Petty's death, his son published a comprehensive pamphlet, which would have been published a dozen years earlier had it not threatened to injure Charles II's wooing of Louis XIV. This work had the usual long title, but is commonly known as *Political Arithmetic*. It is a wide-ranging study of why the tiny United Provinces had recently become so prosperous and powerful, and why extensive and potentially rich France was not keeping pace. From the conclusions that arose from his facts and figures, Petty was always on the look-out for lessons that England might profitably learn.

Petty began by establishing that 'France be in People to Holland and Zealand as 13 to 1; and in quantity of good Land as 80 to 1; yet it is not 13 times richer and stronger, much less 80 times: nor much above thrice.' He then set out to discover why this should be so. It would be tedious to list all his reasoned arguments, but in view of the majority opinion in his own day, and of what became respectable thinking many years later, it is worth while examining at least three of his conclusions.

The first is his conviction that wealth from manufacture and trade is considerably greater than wealth from agriculture. Most Englishmen were still doubting that fact in George III's reign, but a century earlier Petty was already arguing that England should be promoting trade and industry at the expense of agriculture.

There is much more to be gained by Manufacture than Husbandry; and by Merchandise than Manufacture ... the Hollanders have rid their hands of the old patriarchal trade of being cow-keepers; and in great measure, of that which concerns the ploughing and sowing of corn: having put that employment upon the Danes and Poles; from whom they have their young cattle and corn.

Now here we may take notice, that as trades and curious Arts increase, so the trade of husbandry will decrease . . . and consequently the rents of lands must fall.

For proof whereof, I dare affirm that, if all the husbandmen of England, who now earn but 8d. a day or thereabouts, could become tradesmen [artisans] and earn 16d. a day (which is no great wages, 2s. 0d. and 2s. 6d. being usually given): that then it would be [to] the advantage of England to throw up their husbandry, and to make no use of their lands, but for grass, horses, milch cows, gardens, and orchards etc. Which, if it be so, and if Trade and Manufacture have increased in England . . . and if the price of corn be no greater now than when husbandmen were more numerous and tradesmen fewer; it follows from that single reason . . . that rents of lands must fall . . .

He did not shrink from his argument's logical conclusion that England would become dependent upon the foreigner for her food. He saw no harm in it. If corn prices began to rise in England, he said, 'corn would be brought in to us, as into Holland, from foreign parts, where the state of husbandry was not changed'. Cobden and Bright were to be no more out-spoken than Petty was upon this issue.

Another of Petty's arguments which must have astonished his contemporaries into thought was that it would pay England to entrust her defence to foreign mercenaries. To him soldiering was a trade 'of greatest turmoil and danger, and yet of least profit'. The Hollanders, he maintained, sensibly hired troops

from England, Scotland, and Germany, to venture their lives for sixpence a day; whilst they themselves safely and quietly follow such trades, whereby the meanest of them gain six times as much. And withal, by this entertainment of such strangers for soldiers, their country becomes more and more peopled: forasmuch as the children of such strangers are Hollanders, and take trades; whilst new strangers are admitted *ad infinitum* . . . And, consequently, by this way of employing of strangers for soldiers, they people the country and save their own persons from danger and misery, without any real expense.

The argument was neither heroic nor particularly moral, but

in Petty's eyes it logically evolved from the statistics he had examined. To him national pride and renown were better centred in economic prosperity than in military valour. At the end of his pamphlet he even proposed selling English land to foreigners in order to increase the national capital available for trade:

Where note, that selling of lands to foreigners for gold and silver, would enlarge the Stock of the Kingdom: whereas doing the same between one another, doth effect nothing. For he that turneth all his land into money, disposes himself for trade: and he that parteth with his money for land, doth the contrary: but to sell land to foreigners increaseth both money and people, and consequently trade.

This might be the purest economic reasoning that Petty could deduce from his statistics, but he could hardly have expected it to be readily accepted by his fellow Englishmen.

A third unusual argument for Petty's day was his justification of religious toleration on economic grounds. Whereas, he reasoned, the principal care of the vast army of clerics – '100 to 1 to what they use or need' – in France and Spain was to ensure that there was uniformity, the Dutch tolerated their dissenters, 'for the most part, thinking, sober, and patient men; and such as believe that labour and industry is their duty to God: how erroneous soever their opinions be'. He went on to demonstrate that 'Trade doth not, as some think, best flourish under popular Governments', but wherever there are dissenters to devote their lives to developing it – Jews and Christians in the Turkish Empire, Jews and 'non-Papist merchant-strangers' in the Italian cities, and Huguenots in France.

From whence it follows, that Trade is not fixed to any species of Religion, as such: but rather, as before hath been said, to the hetero-dox part of the whole: the truth whereof appears also, in all the par-ticular towns of greatest trade in England ... From whence it follows, that for the Advancement of Trade, if that be a sufficient reason, indulgence must be granted in Matters of Opinion: though licentious actings, as even in Holland, be restrained by force.

Petty made a particular point of the economic backwardness of the countries that had maintained their allegiance to Rome: three-quarters of European trade was 'in the hands of such as have separated from that Church'. Little wonder that it was not until William of Orange was on the English throne that the authorities licensed this pamphlet to be published.

Pamphlets and newssheets grew up together. No one would take them for twins, but everyone acknowledges that the family likeness is unmistakable. In Stuart times such newspapers as were published were either bald lists of rumoured happenings – 'It is reported from Holland that ...' or 'Last Thursday His Majesty dined at ...' – or editorial comment upon the events of the day. The Licensing Act made the publication of any kind of news very difficult. The inadequate but licensed *News* and *Intelligencer* appeared weekly for a couple of years in the mid-1660s, but for the next dozen years the *London Gazette*, at that time a non-newspaper if ever there was one, was the only licensed journal in England. The Titus Oates and Exclusion Bill furore made it quite impossible to suppress illegal newssheets circulating round the tables of the coffee and tea houses. For a few years the authorities were content to turn a blind eye to what was going on, but James II brought back censorship in all its severity. Under William relaxation returned. Newspapers flourished as never before. There were plenty of them, but none were distinguished, and all died in infancy or, at best, in childhood. The lapsing of the Licensing Act in 1695 increased their number yet again.

Such copies of these early *Mercuries*, *Posts*, and *Newsletters* as still remain are even less enlightening to historians than they were to their original readers. Their scraps of news and gossip are unreliable, and only when they resort to comment, as some of them do very readily, do they acquire the same kind

of historical value as a pamphlet has. But from the first years of
the eighteenth century – perhaps it is fair to say from the first
journal written by Defoe – newspapers achieved a higher
rating as a historical source. Defoe's newspaper, which tried
several titles before settling on *A Review of the State of the
English Nation*, was published from 1704 to 1713. It carried
serious comment upon the political events of the day, and, in
the section headed 'Advice from the Scandalous Club', satirical
observations upon London life. It had numerous imitators
and competitors: both in Anne's and George I's reign Londoners
seem to have had a choice of between a dozen and a score of
regularly published newspapers and journals. Most were
weeklies or bi-weeklies, but the *Daily Courant*, first issued in
1702, was as good as its name and maintained a daily issue for
several years.

For almost all the newspapers published in Anne's reign, the
progress of the War of the Spanish Succession was the domin-
ating news item. But any student planning to use the newspapers as a source for a study of Marlborough or for a history
of the war should heed Addison's warning in the *Tatler:*

They [the news-writers] have been upon parties and skirmishes
where our armies have lain still, and given the general assault to
many a place when the besiegers were quiet in their trenches. They
have made us masters of several strong towns many weeks before our
generals could do it, and completed victories when our greatest
captains have been content to come off with a drawn battle. Where
Prince Eugene has slain his thousands, Boyer [editor of *The Postboy*
and *The Supplement*] has slain his ten thousands.

The best-remembered newspapers of Anne's reign are the
Tatler and the *Spectator*. Both were the work of Addison and
Steele, and both are remembered not for the quality of the
news they carried, but for the grace and wit they exhibited in
commenting upon life around them. The *Tatler*, which Steele

began in April 1709, set out with the intention of commenting on political affairs, but fairly quickly dropped politics altogether in favour of social and literary topics. It lasted for 271 issues, but after a three months' break Steele and Addison collaborated again on a second journal, the *Spectator*, which ran from March 1711 to December 1712.

In the modern sense of the word, the *Spectator* was not a newspaper at all. Each daily issue consisted of an essay. Addison, Steele, or one of their occasional contributors such as Addison's cousin, Eustace Budgell, or the Dissenter, Henry Grove, would undertake to write the whole of an issue, much in the manner of those journalists who today contract to write a column for a daily paper or a weekly journal, But the writers of the *Spectator* were not plagued by the need to be topical; never was their copy scrapped in order to make way for a more urgent message or a more-up-to-date topic. They wrote leisurely and elegantly, almost as if they were writing for the Third Programme, or composing a talk suitable to be broadcast between the two acts of an opera relayed from Covent Garden. But the limitation of their copy was not that it must last fourteen and a half minutes precisely, but that it should fill, but not exceed, four narrow columns on both sides of a single sheet of foolscap. Addison professed to see advantages in enforced brevity. On 23 July 1711, he devoted the whole paper to explaining that although authors of books could afford dull passages – 'rests and Nodding-places' – 'those of us who publish their Thoughts in distinct Sheets ... must immediately fall into our Subject and treat every part of it in a lively Manner'.

Had the Philosophers and great Men of Antiquity, who took so much Pains in order to instruct Mankind, and leave the World wiser and better than they found it; had they, I say, been possessed of the Art of Printing, there is no Question but they would have made such an Advantage of it, in dealing out their Lectures to the

Publick. Our common Prints would be of great Use were they thus calculated to diffuse good Sense through the Bulk of a People, to clear up their Understandings, animate their Minds with Virtue, dissipate the Sorrows of a heavy Heart, or unbend the Mind from its most severe Employments with innocent Amusements. When Knowledge, instead of being bound up in Books, and kept in Libraries and Retirements, is thus obtruded upon the Publick; when it is canvassed upon every Table; I cannot forbear reflecting upon that Passage in the *Proverbs*, *Wisdom cryeth without, she uttereth her Voice in the Streets*. . .

Unlike most contents of modern newspapers, the *Spectator*'s essays were not intended to be ephemeral. Addison and Steele gathered them into more permanent monthly collections, and eventually published them in book form. This, of course, has given the researcher far easier access to the text.

The *Spectator* was well named. Most of the essays describe some aspect of the daily scene, and straightforwardly, satirically, or by analogy make personal comment on the chosen topic. On 22 August 1711 Budgell wrote on dress and fashion. He strongly upheld the convention that required a man to dress according to his social rank. Those who dressed beneath their 'Quality and Estate' – 'who walked in Masquerade' – deserved all the disrespect which they encountered. Far better for a man 'to appear in his Habit rather above than below his Fortune', for 'I have indeed my self observed, that my Banker ever bows lowest to me when I wear my full-bottom'd Wig; and writes me *Mr* or *Esq.* accordingly as he sees me dress'd'. Two months later, Addison turned the thoughts of the subscribers to that 'loose Tribe of Men' who 'ramble into all the Corners of this great City, in order to seduce such unfortunate Females as fall into their Walks':

Were I to propose a Punishment for this infamous Race of Propagators, it should be to send them, after the second or third Offence, into our *American* Colonies, in order to People those Parts of her

Majesty's Dominions where there is a want of Inhabitants, and in the Phrase of *Diogenes* to *Plant Men*.

On 29 January 1712, Addison discussed with his readers the perpetual problem of balancing the authority of the central government against the freedom of the individual. He had nothing new to add to the old argument, but in the context of the age in which he lived, it is somewhat startling to hear him say of that precious commodity, individual liberty:

But the greatest Security a People can have for their Liberty, is when the Legislative Power is in the Hands of Persons so happily distinguished, that by providing for the particular Interest of their several Ranks, they are providing for the whole Body of the People: or in other Words, when there is no Part of the People that has not a common Interest with at least one Part of the Legislators.

Most nineteenth- and twentieth-century radicals would have applauded such a statement, but, as the rest of that day's *Spectator* shows, Addison would have been appalled to see how they would have interpreted the principle in practice. He was quite content with the composition of the Commons of his day. The evils he was denouncing were not restricted franchise and unequal distribution of seats, but the tyranny which he found so widespread in Europe, and that 'lowest State of Slavery' which he asserted existed in nine-tenths of the world.

Richard Steele wrote as diversely as Joseph Addison. It was he who, in the second issue, introduced the readers to Spectator's friend, Sir Roger de Coverley:

The first of our Society is a Gentleman of *Worcestershire* of antient Descent, a Baronet, his Name SIR ROGER DE COVERLY. His great Grandfather was Inventor of that famous Country-Dance which is call'd after him. All who know that Shire are very well acquainted with the Parts and Merits of SIR ROGER. He is a Gentleman that is very singular in his Behaviour, but his Singularities proceed from his good Sense, and are Contradictions to the Manners of the World, only as he thinks the World is in the wrong.

Sir Roger was fictional but his character and his actions were based on actuality. His creators (for Addison wrote about him as freely as Steele) caricatured him gently, but they did not distort him beyond recognition, nor even make him untypical of eighteenth-century squires. His behaviour in church, for example, illustrates the eccentric but tight hold many squires had on their tenants:

As SIR ROGER is Landlord to the whole Congregation, he keeps them in very good Order, and will suffer no Body to sleep in it besides himself; for if by Chance he has been surprized into a short Nap at Sermon, upon recovering out of it he stands up and looks about him, and if he sees any Body else nodding, either wakes them himself, or sends his Servants to them. Several other of the old Knight's Particularities break out upon these Occasions: Sometimes he will be lengthening out a Verse in the Singing-Psalms, half a Minute after the rest of the Congregation have done with it; sometimes, when he is pleased with the Matter of his Devotion, he pronounces *Amen* three or four times to the same Prayer; and sometimes stands up when every Body else is upon their Knees, to count the Congregation, or see if any of his Tenants are missing.

On the same fictional visit to Worcestershire, Steele reported what Sir Roger had to say about his kinsman, Sir Humphrey, 'the Honour of our House'. It is a list of characteristics and achievements which the eighteenth century found virtuous in a land-owner of honour:

... he was in his Dealings as punctual as a Tradesman, and as generous as a Gentleman. He would have thought himself as much undone by breaking his Word, as if it were to be followed by Bankruptcy. He served his Country as Knight of this Shire to his dying Day; He found it no easie matter to maintain an Integrity in his Words and Actions, even in things that regarded the Offices which were incumbent upon him, in the care of his own Affairs and Relations of Life, and therefore dreaded (tho' he had great Talents) to go into Employments of State, where he must be exposed to the Snares of Ambition. Innocence of Life and great Ability were the distinguishing Parts of his Character; the latter, he had often observed, had led to the Destruction of the former, and used frequently to lament that Great and Good had not the same Signification. He was an Excellent Husbandman, but had resolved not to exceed such a degree of Wealth; all above it he bestowed in secret Bounties many Years after the Sum he aimed at for his own use was attained. Yet he did not slacken his Industry, but to a decent old Age spent the Life and Fortune which was superfluous to himself, in the Service of his Friends and Neighbours.

After the *Spectator* had come to the end of its short but distinguished life, Steele turned to political journalism, upholding the Whig cause as fiercely as Swift wrote on behalf of the Tories. The last months of Anne's reign, the accession of George I, and the frustrated 'Fifteen Rebellion all inflamed party strife. Addison commented that no sooner did children begin to speak than they were mouthing *Whig* and *Tory*. The taunts, outrageous statements, and libellous articles of the newspapers reflected this dominance of party issues. During the reigns of the first two Georges, the London newspapers were more remarkable for their multiplicity – '200 half sheets per month', according to the *Gentleman's Magazine* – than for their serious comment on social or political matters, but several of them began to carry reports of parliamentary debates. By 1722 the Commons were formally objecting to being reported, and from time to time during the next forty years individual members or the House as a whole denounced the practice anew. Yet the volume of reporting increased rather than diminished, and it is to the files of such journals as the *Gentleman's Magazine* and the *London Magazine* that we must go for accounts of parliamentary debates before the reign of George III. They are far from being full accounts. Memorized speeches were extensively touched up, and, to try to avoid libel actions, names of speakers and opponents were frequently reduced to an initial letter. But they were accurate enough to be eagerly read, and to rouse the anger of those members who considered that reporting 'reflected on the dignity of the House'.

The average edition of these early newspapers has to be reckoned in hundreds rather than in thousands of copies, but their influence was not so restricted as these small numbers might suggest. Not only were individual copies shared and passed on, but also, from the first years of the century, an increasing number of provincial printers were selecting items from the London press to put in their weekly local newspapers. *Norwich Post*, *Bristol Post-Boy*, *Exeter Post-Man* and other such papers retailed to their readers as much of the war news, party controversy, and London excitement as they could stuff into their few columns. Apparently their readers were not interested in local happenings; most local news transmitted itself rapidly enough by word of mouth. Their appetite was for British victories against the French, caustic debates in the Commons and Lords, scandals of high society, London market prices, self-styled exclusive 'inside' information, details of the mortality lists from London parishes, and even the latest jokes and riddles. Local printers satisfied this appetite by openly plagiarizing the London press. On market day they offered their customers their weekly digest of news from all the London papers and private newsletters which they had been able to buy during the previous seven days. When news was plentiful and stirring, local newspaper selling, despite the Stamp Acts, was simple enough. Difficulties arose when Britain was at peace, when the Jacobites were not threatening, and when no particular political issue or social scandal was the talk of the town. Such dog-days brought many a local paper to an early grave. C. A. Cranfield, in *The Development of the Provincial*

Newspaper, 1700–1760, calculated that over 130 provincial papers were published between 1701 and 1760, but that only 35 were in existence at the end of that period.

During the reigns of George I and George II, local newspapers attracted an increasing quantity of advertisement. It gradually became standard practice to publish in the back-page columns details of houses and estates to be let or sold, notices of cattle for sale or stallions at stud, and appeals for the apprehension of runaway apprentices or for the return of lost property. Doctors, schoolmasters, and various tradesmen advertised their skills or wares; merchants luxuries such as tea, coffee, and wines; theatre managers their plays; and, increasingly, coach proprietors their timetables and fares. Along with these notices, which had to be local to be effective, came occasional items of local news. Local prices might be quoted alongside London prices, or there might be comment on Methodist activities, or turnpike trouble, or riot and murder in the area. But it is not until George III's reign that provincial publications begin to give local historians such colour and detail as the London newspapers of Queen Anne's reign provide for those interested in life in the capital.

3. HEARTH TAX AND POLL TAX RETURNS

Not until the nineteenth century do historical records begin to yield accurate and regular population statistics. To assess the number of inhabitants living in parishes, towns, and counties before the first census figures of 1801 and the first tables compiled by the statistical societies which were being founded in the 1830s and 1840s, historians are driven to various indirect means. As we have seen, parish registers are a favourite source of the necessary facts. Tax figures are another: medieval poll tax returns are useful in counties in which records have survived, and the lay subsidy rolls, especially for 1524 and 1525, are better still if they are available for the required area. The Anglican church took a census of families in 1563, of communicants and recusants in 1603, and again, but this time only in the province of Canterbury, of communicants, Roman Catholics, and Nonconformists in 1676. And during the eighteenth century, there were a number of 'surveys', 'scrutinies', 'counts', 'censuses', and 'returns' for different towns, counties, and dioceses. The accuracy of these various tables of statistics varies considerably. In the last section we saw that Sir William Petty longed for more exact information upon which to base his political arithmetic. For current population figures in England and Wales, he used the contemporary hearth tax returns. If, in common with the majority of his contemporaries, he thought the tax an insufferable intrusion into personal privacy and an unjustifiable financial burden, he saw no reason why the collectors' lists and figures should not be put to good use. Demographers and economic historians in plenty have followed his lead.

The hearth tax, an idea borrowed from France, was one of the Cavalier Parliament's ways of raising additional taxation. Although it suffered considerable and constant abuse, and although the collection of it provoked several riots, it was based, in the government's opinion, on the equitable principle of the broadest backs bearing the heaviest burdens. The individual sums demanded were roughly proportional to the individual taxpayer's ability to pay. Since richer men lived in bigger houses than poorer men, the argument ran, and since the size of a house could be approximately assessed by the number of fireplaces it possessed, counting hearths was a cheap, quick, and fair way of assessing the new tax. Few people would deny that it was more equitable than the subsidy which it partially replaced. At first the parish constables were made responsible for drawing up the assessment lists for the hearth tax; if they doubted the figure given by the householder, they had the legal right to enter the house and count the hearths themselves. Quarter sessions gathered together the returns from the parishes, and the local collectors and, later, the detested chimney men – the officials specially appointed to collect the tax half-yearly – worked from the list which the clerk of the peace issued in the name of the quarter sessions bench of justices. The act of 1662 required every head of household, unless he was in receipt of poor relief or not inhabiting a house worth at least £1 0s. 0d. a year, to pay 2s. 0d. a year for every hearth or stove in his house. In theory nothing could have been simpler or more straightforward to assess, but several times Charles II's government sold the annual yield to tax farmers rather than face the trouble of collecting it through the normal channels of constables and sheriffs. As soon as William and Mary came to the throne, the tax was repealed.

Those who wish to use hearth tax returns as a historical source are not particularly concerned with the unpopularity of the tax or the difficulties of collection, but they have to decide what trust they can put in the figures. The percentage of error must be considerably greater than in the later census figures. There would always be the problem of constable and householder deciding when a hearth was not a hearth, and, since the tax was so detested throughout its life, the degree of evasion, which vitiates the accuracy of all tax returns, would tend to be higher than usual. On the other hand evasion would be difficult without the cooperation of a sympathetic constable. Hearths are not easy to hide away, especially if the assessor is local enough to know the houses well.

The most complete record of hearth tax returns is in the Public Record Office. County records offices usually have some material, and some record societies have printed lists for particular parishes. From 1664 onwards, the lists were required to show the names of those excused payment as well as those expected to pay. The details are as brief as they could possibly be. The following short extract from the 1672 returns from Bingley in the West Riding is typical:

Tho. Smith	1	James Keighley	2
Mary Smith	1	Mr Bentley	3
Thomas Keighley	2	Michaell Slater	1
William Scott	3	Tho. Scarron	1
Robert Leach	3	Tho. Murgatroide	6

Further south in the West Riding is Saddleworth. In the 1668 return for that township, there were 173 householders altogether. Three paid for four hearths, ten for three hearths, and eleven for two hearths. Eight householders – one less than in Bingley – were exempt because of their poverty, and the rest of them lived in single-hearth cottages. The centrally built fireplace and chimney stack would be designed to warm both rooms on the ground floor and any bedrooms there might be above. It would appear, therefore, if we rely upon an average of five men, women, and children to a household, that in 1668 the population of Saddleworth fell considerably short of 1,000. The houses were mostly small cottages: it would be a fair assumption that practically everyone lived uncomfortably close to the poverty line but very few became dependent on the parish. The constable who collected the tax and handed over the money to 'Mr Toby Humphrey, one of the subfarmers and collectors of the sayd Revenew' paid for one hearth. His name was George Schofield, and the list contains many names which are just as common as Schofield in that Pennine area today – Lees, Shaw, Buckley, Winterbottom, Whitehead, and others.

Hearth tax returns for 1673–4 paint a markedly different picture of social conditions in the Isle of Thanet in the northeast corner of Kent. This is the summary of the information:

	Hearths on which tax was paid	Houses which paid tax	Excused
St John's (Margate)	552	174	100
St Peter's	393	168	42
West Borough (St Laurence)	253	100	107
Ramsgate	234	92	73
Birchington	230	79	27
Minster	211	76	8
St Nicholas	94	34	4
Monkton	90	31	3
Sarre	47	17	—
All Saints Borough	30	7	—
	2134	778	364

The number of householders too poor to pay the tax is surprisingly high, especially in an area where the average number of hearths to a house suggests a moderate prosperity. It could well be that the assessors interpreted the regulations leniently. Even so, in contrast with Saddleworth's housing, which was monotonously uniform, Thanet's offered some strong contrasts as early as the 1670s. It must be remembered that the popularity of sea-bathing which was going to make that coast such a desirable holiday area was still three or four generations away.

If we cannot get exact figures out of hearth tax returns, we can at least find reliable comparisons. In the area north-west of Birmingham, for example, the figures show that in 1665, on the eve of changes that were to lead to remarkable industrial development, Wolverhampton, with 858 householders, bore about the same relationship to Walsall, 645 householders, as it does today. On the other hand, Wednesbury, with 218 householders, was two-thirds the size of West Bromwich, with 311 householders, whereas today it is only one-third the size.

And Darlaston, 145 householders, was substantially bigger than Tipton, 115 householders. Today, the reverse is true. Indeed the study of the growth of a modern industrial town could well begin with the hearth tax returns, for in the pioneer areas of industrial England, such as south Lancashire and Tyneside, they give us the population picture just before bigger-scale industry began to grow. It is hard to believe, for example, that Restoration Liverpool was so small a borough. The hearth tax returns of 1673 give only 252 householders. Exactly a hundred years later, a town 'survey' listed 8,002 families crowded into 5,928 houses. There was then an average of six people living in every house.

Some very interesting work has been based on the hearth tax returns for the city of Oxford. The original work of Thorold Rogers in 1891, amended by H. E. Salter thirty years later, has built up a detailed picture of Oxford at the beginning of Charles II's reign. Rogers came to the conclusion that the 1665 returns, with their 998 householders and 3,653 hearths, gave the city a population of just over 7,000 in full term. But Salter's re-examination of the lists disclosed details which Rogers had missed. The lists, for example, did not include the exempt houses. Therefore, argued Salter, the true figures would be higher than Rogers's – about 1,250 householders and probably 4,000 hearths. Salter also discovered that the houses were listed in sequence along the streets. This enabled him to show that the houses with the largest number of hearths were all inns.

Jane Hallam	xii	The Crown Tavern, Cornmarket
Mathew Loveday	xx	The Blue Boar in St Aldate's
Ralph Flexney	xvii	The Bear Inn, High Street

The colleges were taxed like all other dwellings – Merton 82, Balliol 40, All Souls' 60, Brasenose 65, and Christ Church the vast number of 243.

The baldness of the hearth tax lists limits their use for the genealogist, the social historian, or any researcher who is looking for more than rough estimates of population figures. But if they can be matched against a detailed household inventory, or against a building or row of buildings still standing, or against a later or earlier hearth tax return, or against a reasonably contemporary description of a street or a town, they can provide a sturdy framework on which to hang attractive detail. Where they still exist, poll tax lists also make useful supplementary documents for hearth tax returns. Unless he was receiving parish relief, everyone over sixteen years of age had to pay poll tax, which was levied at irregular intervals from the early years of the Restoration to the end of William III's reign. Office holders and servants paid 1s. 0d. for every £1 0s. 0d. they earned in profits and wages. Lawyers and doctors paid a higher rate still, and in addition the tax demanded 1 per cent of the value of everyone's personal estate. There were graded payments for those who held a recognized rank in society, the church, or one of the professions – a baronet paid £15 0s. 0d., an archdeacon £2 0s. 0d., a doctor of laws £5 0s. 0d., and so on. The result is that poll tax returns give considerably more detail about people than do hearth tax returns.

Salter put the Oxford poll tax returns of 1667 against the hearth tax returns of 1665. Not only did the one confirm the other, but the poll tax returns gave the name and status of many people other than the heads of households. The following, for example, are the hearth tax returns for three houses in High Street, Oxford:

John Johnson	v	[hearths]
Alexander Wright	vi	„
John Lazenby	xvi	„

Of the same houses two years later, the poll tax returns give these details:

	£	s.	d.
John Johnson and Mary his wife		2	0
His wages at St John's and Bayly Colledges		2	6
In monies	1	0	0
Jane Peirce, Mary Peirce, John Johnson, Mathew Eliz. and Anne, children		6	0
Thomas Pusy, apprentice		1	0
Alice Potter, wages 20s.		2	0
Alexander Wright and Kath. his wife		2	0
Alexander and Martine, their children		2	0
Laurance Tayler, apprentice		1	0
Eliz. Warner, 20s. wages		2	0
In moneys £100	1	0	0
John Lazinby [host of the Mitre], wife and 8 children		10	0
Margaret Ashley, no wages		1	9
Isabell Ellis, wages £2		3	0
Aron Nicholes, chamberline		1	0
Robert Lankett		1	0

It was the second document which enabled Salter confidently to revise the population figures which Rogers had hazarded for Oxford after his study of the hearth tax returns. Of the 8,566 people who contributed to the poll tax in Oxford, 6,499 were ordinary citizens and 2,067 were members of the university. In addition an unknown number of citizens were exempt because they were too poor to pay. So, with very good reason, Salter raised Rogers's estimate of ordinary citizens from 'under 4,500' to 'about 7,000', and reduced his estimate of 'nearly 3,000' for the university population to 2,067.

Poll tax returns are not plentiful, but it is worth a local historian's time to look for them. The tax was levied at haphazard intervals. In 1512 Henry VIII's government revived it, but soon afterwards abandoned it for the subsidy. In course of time, the subsidy lost favour – the gap between the fixed assessments of taxable property and economic reality grew so wide that the rich were often paying little more than the poor – and after 1663 Charles II's parliament brought back the poll tax again. The last time it was levied was in 1698.

Although, as we have seen in the evidence from Oxford, poll tax returns are more detailed than hearth tax returns, they are frequently not so reliable a guide to total population. The Chetham Society, for example, has printed the poll tax return for Manchester in 1690. It enumerates 2,535 persons. But, if this return is to be used to assess Manchester's population, there must be added to this figure an unknown number of inhabitants who were exempt from paying the tax – those too poor to pay poor rate, all children of day labourers, agricultural workers under sixteen years of age, and children under sixteen of all parents having more than four children but not worth more than £50 a year. It is impossible to count the number of souls in such categories. They could in theory fall well short of the number of taxpayers, but in view of other evidence it looks likely that they substantially exceeded that figure in Manchester. The hearth tax collectors of 1666 had returned 1,368 hearths liable to tax. If we accept the low estimated average of four people to each hearth and include the hearths not taxed, the total population of the town would work out at about 6,000 in the first decade of Charles II's reign. From other plentiful evidence, it is obvious that during the next half century Manchester's population grew considerably, because cottage spinning and weaving, increasingly organized by Manchester clothiers and mercers, was beginning to feel the effects of a quickening overseas trade based on Liverpool and other Lancashire ports. By 1710 the town authorities estimated that 8,000 people were living within its boundaries. It would seem from this evidence, therefore, that Manchester's population would be about 7,000 in 1690. The poll tax figure of 2,535, standing by itself, could be very misleading.

However, if poll tax returns are not reliable guides to population, they can help us piece together a detailed picture of the distribution of wealth in a town. We cannot accept the returns as the whole truth, for when it comes to fixing assessments most people take a pessimistic view of their assets. But the figures can guide us to some fairly accurate conclusions. There are several items, for example, which indicate that Manchester was nothing like so rich a town as it was to become in the following hundred years. Seven or eight people out of every ten were assessed at the minimum of 1s. 0d., and only 118 people paid tax on estates. This last fact will strain the credulity of the informed reader, especially when it is further revealed that, out of these 118, 109 estates were assessed at £200 or less, and that only one estate, that of John Lever, was assessed at as much as £500. The following is the list of assessments for Ancoats Lane on the edge of the growing town:

	£	s.	d.
John Cartwright and wife a man and maid		4	0
Richard Morte gent.	1	1	0
wife a man and maid		3	0
Oswald Mosley Esq.	5	1	0
wife and 4 children		5	0
4 men and 2 maids		6	0
Mrs Jane Mosley widdow to Nich. Mosley Esq.	1	14	0
two daughters £100 each	1	2	0
a maid servant		1	0
Thomas Tildsley and wife		2	0
Lawrance Holland and wife and daughter		3	0
William Baley and wife and daughter		3	0
Edward Charnock and wife		2	0
John Robinson and wife		2	0
John Baxter and wife		2	0
Robert Robinson and wife and sonne		3	0
John Worthington 2 daughters and man		4	0

As the figures show, moderate wealth and humble living were near neighbours. So it was throughout the town: there was no quarter reserved for the better off. The overall impression is that most of the townspeople were constantly struggling to make ends meet, although one cannot help thinking that such people as Oswald Mosley and Jane, his mother, got off with pretty light assessments. Again, in an age when domestic help was cheap and easy to get, very few Manchester families apparently employed servants. Just over 200 houses recorded servants, and these would include inns and business premises. Altogether 142 men servants and 259 women servants were assessed, and, most surprisingly, a mere 23 apprentices. But, of course, these figures are subject to considerable amendment. The historian's difficulty is deciding how many people in each category succeeded in claiming exemption or in escaping the assessors altogether.

4. COLONIAL RECORDS

Colonies creep into English history early in the seventeenth century. The impetuous Elizabethans had tried to plant colonies earlier than this, but both in Newfoundland and in Virginia they had been too impatient for profits to spend enough time and money making sure their plantations took root. We have to wait until the Stuarts are on the throne before we can record successful plantings, first in James I's reign, in Virginia, Massachusetts, Barbados, and St Kitts, and, later, in Charles I's reign, in Maryland, Connecticut, St Lucia, and a number of other places on the eastern coast of North America and in the West Indies. The Commonwealth and Protectorate governments took colonies seriously, and during the reigns of the later Stuarts, England's prestige as a colonizing power increased considerably. She seized the initiative from the Dutch and Portuguese both across the Atlantic and in India, but soon came into serious conflict with the French. This Anglo-French struggle reached its climax in the middle decades of the eighteenth century. The War of the Austrian Succession and the Seven Years' War – both fought ostensibly to settle the future of Silesia – resulted in Britain defeating the French challenge in India and North America and in her navy taking a firm grip on the sea routes which connected the mother country to her children in distant parts of the world. By 1763 the first British Empire was fully established.

The records which relate this fascinating story are scattered all over the world. Most British historians study the subject from the mother country's point of view. They look west across the Atlantic, south to the African coast, and south-east to India. But it is just as reasonable to take one's stand in a particular colony and, as the colonists did, gaze in the very opposite directions. Indeed, the only way to reveal historical truth more fully is to study subjects from different angles. British colonial legislation usually appeared less intelligent in Boston or Jamestown than it did in Westminster. Plantation owners in the West Indies, to say nothing of the slaves themselves, did not justify slave-trade profits in the way the merchants of Bristol and Liverpool did, and both the Indian princes and those Englishmen who braved the dangers and enjoyed the perquisites of 'factory' life in Surat or Fort St George felt they knew more about the rights and wrongs of the East India Company's monopoly than those British merchants who wanted the charter revoked. One can easily appreciate that there were these different opinions and points of view, but it is far more difficult to take them all fully into account. The very size of the problem destroys the best intentions. Students who set out to master British colonial history find either they have to be content with a general grasp of the whole subject based on the writings of specialist historians, or they have to concentrate upon a particular aspect of the subject if they wish to verify facts and come to conclusions of their own by plunging into primary sources. The basic information is contained in many different types of documents. What the student is seeking determines which category of documents he must consult. In the next few pages, we shall examine the strength and weaknesses of the principal mother-country sources for studying, first, the evolution of British colonial policy up to the reign of George III; secondly, the statistics of colonial trade; and, thirdly, the personal experiences of men involved in colonization and colonial expansion.

During the 180 years which separated Sir Humphrey Gilbert's ill-fated attempt to plant Newfoundland (1583) from the recognition of Britain's colonial supremacy at the Peace of Paris (1763), the attitude of Englishmen towards their colonies changed considerably. Each generation had its own purpose and its own theories: it criticized past policy and opinion and, in turn, was itself criticized by its successor. These different viewpoints can be studied from two main sources. Legislation concerning colonial matters usually makes clear the accepted opinion of the day: individual writings, in the form of books, essays, or pamphlets, can either point the way ahead to future policy, explain current opinion, or express regret that an approved policy or attitude has been abandoned for one which the writer considers less desirable. With some vigour the Elizabethans debated their reasons for attempting to plant colonies. All professed a desire or a duty to 'reduce the natives to civility' and convert them to Christianity – that is, to Anglicanism – and all expressed an urgent wish to annex new lands for the queen. But, when it came to more mundane motives, they found themselves divided. Walsingham was one who saw colonies primarily as naval bases useful in the unending war against Spain. Burghley and Peckham preferred colonies to be further north than Walsingham advocated, so that they could supply England with shipbuilding materials, fish, and furs. Gilbert agreed with them, but also argued that colonies would prove to be the solution to the vagabond problem at home, partly by stimulating demand for exports, and partly by selected emigration:

... we might inhabit part of those countries, and settle there such needy people of our country which now trouble the commonwealth, and through want here at home are forced to commit outrageous offences, whereby they are daily consumed with the gallows ...

Hakluyt put forward the interesting idea of establishing a 'stapling place' – a second Calais – on the other side of the Atlantic, and, with Christopher Carlile, looked forward to the day when English colonies in America would supply all the raw materials which at present England was obliged to buy from foreign countries. Dreams and visions there were in plenty. Peckham's imagination even sketched the delights of country life and of unlimited land-owning and farming which awaited the settler. The writings of these enthusiasts clearly illustrate the optimism of the planners. It was not an armchair enthusiasm, for, if the writers had not crossed the Atlantic to see for themselves, they had usually consulted those who had. Yet such on-the-spot reports as have been gathered together in the Hakluyt Society publication, *The Roanoke Voyages*, show how the dream boats foundered on the rocks of insufficient preparation and unexpected practical difficulties.

One of the Elizabethans' faults was that they tried to succeed too quickly. They saw the advantages of colonization and wanted to enjoy them before earning them. Francis Bacon understood this. In his essay *Of Plantations* he wrote:

Planting of countries is like planting of woods; for you must make account to lose almost twenty years' profit, and expect your recompense in the end; for the principal thing that hath been the destruction of most plantations, hath been the base and hasty drawing of profit in the first years.

Bacon, however, was not ahead of his time. He wrote this particular essay in James I's reign, and by that time, men were recognizing that planting required patience and careful planning. The experience of the successful colonists in Virginia after 1607 was the basis of some of Bacon's other wise thoughts:

It is a shameful and unblessed thing to take the scum of people and wicked condemned men to be the people with whom you plant ... The people wherewith you plant ought to be gardeners, ploughmen, labourers, smiths, carpenters, joiners, fishermen, fowlers, with some few apothecaries, surgeons, cooks, and bakers. In a country of plantation, first look about what kind of victual the country yields of itself to hand ... Then consider what victual or esculent things there are which grow speedily ... Above all, there ought to be brought store of biscuit, oatmeal, flour, meal and the like, in the beginning till bread be made ...

Virginia was founded as a commercial colony. The main purpose of promoters and settlers alike was to develop trade with England. The Pilgrim Fathers, however, went to Plymouth in New England in 1620 primarily to enjoy religious freedom. So did the Dorchester emigrants who founded Salem five years later, and the Roman Catholics who settled in Maryland in the 1630s and 1640s. The servants of the East India Company who undertook to live in India were colonists in quite a different sense: they planned to return to England after their tour of duty. In the West Indies, there were English colonists of both kinds, those who went out to settle, and those who intended to make money and go back home. Naturally, the true colonists soon developed a point of view different from that of chartered companies, from that of the trader and colonial administrator, and from that of the home government. Before long, the big debate was not about the best method of founding colonies, but about the right relationship to establish between colonies and mother country. The easiest way of tracing the development of this important controversy is in the official decrees of successive governments.

The beginning of this aspect of the colonial story lies in the charters granted to the various trading companies and colonial pioneers. Both Tudor and Stuart charters gave trading companies the same basic rights – exclusive control of trade between England and their specified territory; official recognition of the companies' organization and constitution; and the right to manage their own affairs abroad so long as this did not prejudice the rights of the crown. For these valuable privileges, which were to be enjoyed for a limited number of years, each company paid substantial fees. The agreement satisfied both company and crown. The company recovered its fee by charging its customers dear, and the crown had the satisfaction of knowing that in fifteen or twenty years' time the company would only be too willing to pay higher fees for the renewal of its charter. No one but company and crown had to be considered, for the customer did not count, and such 'colonists' as were involved were salaried servants of the company. With colonial pioneers circumstances were rather different: they were Englishmen forming permanent settlements overseas. Particularly at first, the crown recognized that inducements to settle and protection for the colonists were both necessary. The first charters granted to Virginia, for example, were considered to be not ungenerous to the colonists. The charter of 1606 made provision for a resident council, chosen from the settlers, to manage local administration under the direction of the nominated Royal Council of Virginia in London.

... And we do also ordain ... that each of the said colonies [two separate settlements were at first envisaged] shall have a Council, which shall govern and order all matters and causes ... within the same several colonies, according to such laws, ordinances and instructions as shall be in that behalf given and signed with our hand or sign manual, and pass under the privy seal of our realm of England ...

For the first seven years, said the charter, the colonists were to be privileged to 'transport the goods, chattels, armour, munitions and furniture, needful to be used by them ... out of our realms ... without any custom, subsidy or other duty'. But when, two years later, this charter was seen to be too restrictive, James I's government tried again. It transferred the real executive power from the Royal Council to the directors of the Virginia Company, and allowed the colonists to hold their land as freeholders and not as royal tenants. This experiment lasted ten years. In 1619 Virgina held its first representative assembly. Four years later the Virginia Company lapsed, and from 1625 the colony enjoyed a substantial degree of self-government under the supervision of a governor, nominated by and responsible to the king. These changes were all practical experiments. They were not based on predetermined theories: in the jargon of present-day politics they were 'pragmatic'. The texts of these charters, supplemented by other government papers to be found in the *Calendar of State Papers* and the *Acts of the Privy Council*, are sufficient to explain the details of the successive changes and to understand the official reasons for making them.

Virginia prospered steadily. Together with the success of such companies as the East India Company, the satisfactory development of West Indian trade, and, above all, the shining example of Dutch prosperity based on overseas commerce, the growing wealth of Virginia was one of the main reasons why the next generation of Englishmen took such a lively interest in colonies. However divided on other important matters, Interregnum and Restoration governments were united in this – they were both determined to develop England's colonies, chiefly for the greater glory and increased prosperity of the mother country, but at the same time recognizing that this desirable end was closely linked with the prosperity of the colonies themselves. The Navigation Act of 1651, reaffirmed and strengthened by the Navigation Act of 1660, aimed at establishing a large English and colonial merchant fleet. Colonies were to import only from England, and they were to sell their own main exports – sugar, tobacco, ginger, indigo, cotton, etc. – only to England. Moreover, all imports and exports were to be shipped in English or colonial ships manned chiefly by their own nationals. To help maintain colonial prosperity, the Tobacco Act of 1660 left the colonies with the monopoly of tobacco growing, and the Naval Stores Act of 1704 gave them special consideration as suppliers to the navy of tar, pitch, hemp, masts, bowsprits, and other similar commodities. Such colonial privileges cost the mother country very little. It was very different when the manufacture of woollen cloth in the colonies threatened to restrict the sale of English woollen cloth abroad. The Woollen Act of 1699 attempted to stamp out that danger before it became uncontrollable. It prohibited the export of wool from England and Ireland, and made it illegal for the colonies to export woollen cloth. The petition which led to the Act put the issue very clearly:

Upon the whole matter, we cannot but observe, that the woollen manufacture of this kingdom will receive the greatest encouragement by a due consumption of it at home, the largest vent of it abroad, and the hindering, as much as is possible, the growth and increase of it elsewhere: and that therefore, amongst other things, the exportation not only of wool from Ireland, but also of their woollen manufactures, and of the wool, and woollen manufactures, of the respective English plantations in America to other parts than England, ought to be prohibited or discouraged, by the most coercive and proper means ...

When it came to keeping exports high and imports low, and so preserving with individual foreign countries the favourable balance of trade so dear to all mercantilists, there were few things the home government was not prepared to do. In 1699, for example, a mere two votes saved parliament from discussing a preposterous bill to compel all women servants 'in England and the English plantations whose wages exceed not five pounds per annum' to wear 'felt hats of the manufacture of England'. To the promoters, it seemed the only way to stem the decline of the export of felt goods from Chester.

Mercantilist theory, of course, dominated colonial policy as strongly as it did all other economic thinking. Its control was even tighter under the first two Georges than it had been in the reign of Charles II. The seventeenth-century Englishman looked on the English colonist as a junior partner, and planned that they should stand together against the foreigner. The eighteenth-century Englishman still preferred the English colonist to the foreigner, but he was resolved that where the colonies were in the slightest danger of curtailing English profits, the issue should be firmly settled in England's favour. Bacon had professed that he could 'look at the mother and the daughters with an equal and indifferent eye, remembering that a colony is a part and member of her own body'. The promoters of the Navigation Act professed that they were aiming to strengthen colonial as well as English shipping, and later, when the colonists protested that the Act was doing no such thing, Sir Josiah Child, in his *Discourse on Trade*, argued that without the Act the colonies would have lost all their trade to the Dutch. In his *Essay on the East India Trade*, published in 1697, Charles Davenant even questioned the wisdom of tying colonial trade to the mother country: freer trade could well benefit both England and India. But by the time Sir William Keith came to write his *History of the British Plantations in America* (1738), influential Englishmen were giving very little thought to the well-being of the colonists. They were only interested in the wealth of the mother country.

When either by the Deficiency of a sufficient Quantity of our own Product to be exported ... or when by a greater Share of Industry we are outdone by Foreign States ... then the Wisdom of the

State has sometimes thought fit to send such of their People as could be spared, to settle themselves in various Climates, where some new Species of Products might be raised, and sent home to revive Commerce, and to assist the Public by restoring to it again the lost Balance of National Trade.

And this being the original Intention of, and the only justifiable Reason that can be given for the Practice within these last Two Centuries, of making Settlements and planting Colonies on the uninhabited vacant Lands of America, whose People are protected by, but made subservient to, and dependent on their respective Mother States in Europe ...

... the Profits arising to British Subjects in America, from their exchanging Lumber, etc. with the Product of foreign Plantations, either to be used in America or returned to Europe for British Account, must terminate in the Advantage of Great Britain; who thereby reaps a certain Gain from the Labour of Foreigners, as well as from that of her own Subjects, besides engrossing a larger Share of such Commodities as the better enables her to govern the European Market ...

... the most effectual and profitable Way of restraining the Subjects in the Plantations from interfering with Great Britain in her Home Trade and Manufactures, will be to take due Care that the Colonies be always plentifully supplied with British Cloths, and other European Commodities, at a much cheaper Rate than it is possible for them to raise and manufacture such Things within themselves: And Likewise, that the Importation of all such Product and Manufacture from the Colonies, as are fit to supply the Wants of Great Britain, and to assist the Public in the Balance of National Trade with other countries, be properly encouraged ...

Contemporary attitudes towards the slave trade ran on parallel lines. Most British merchants in the middle decades of the eighteenth century deplored the way opportunities were being missed to develop the African trade. One anonymous pamphleteer in 1745 considered that the French were driving the British out of the slave trade. If they succeeded, it would mean the end of British colonies altogether.

But if the whole *Negroe Trade* be thrown into the Hands of our Rivals, and our Colonies are to depend on the Labour of *White Men* to supply their Place, they will either soon be undone, or shake off their Dependency on the Crown of *England*. For *White Men* cannot be obtained so cheap, or the Labour of a sufficient Number be had for the Expence of their Maintenance only, as we have of the *Africans* . . .

Were it possible, however, for *White Men* to answer the End of *Negroes* in Planting, must we not drain our own Country of *Husbandmen, Mechanicks,* and *Manufacturers* too? Might not the latter be the Cause of our Colonies interfering with the Manufactures of these Kingdoms . . . In such Case, indeed, we might have just Reason to dread the Prosperity of our Colonies; but while we can be well supplied with *Negroes,* we can be under no such Apprehensions; their Labour will confine the Plantations to *Planting* only; which will render our *Colonies* more beneficial to these Kingdoms than the *Mines* of *Peru* and *Mexico* are to the *Spaniards.*

Such arguments and outlook dominated British thought on colonies for most of the eighteenth century. They were to be attacked by the pamphlets of Josiah Tucker and the arguments put forward by Adam Smith in his *Wealth of Nations*. But this was not until the reign of George III. And Britain did not reap practical benefits from Tucker's and Smith's free trade theories until the mid nineteenth century.

Changes in economic colonial policy were accompanied and supported by parallel changes in constitutional machinery. Progressively, governments at home endeavoured to tie ever closer the bonds that held the colonies to the mother country. As early as July 1660, less than six weeks after his return to England, Charles II issued an order in council setting up a committee for plantations 'to receive, hear, examine and deliberate upon any petitions, propositions, memorials or other addresses which shall be presented . . . by any person or persons concerning the plantations . . .'. This committee, which met twice a week, was matched by a similar one for trade. Both committees contained representatives of the chartered companies as well as eminent privy councillors and secretaries of state. They advised the privy council, and, through the privy council, the crown took what action was deemed necessary. After five years of useful service, these two committees lapsed. They came to life again towards the end of the sixties, combined together in 1672, and lapsed again in 1675. Nevertheless, until the Revolution of 1688, colonies remained a matter for the privy council. The order in council of 1675, which replaced the lapsed combined committee with a permanent committee of the privy council, gave the councillors power 'to send for all books, papers and other writings concerning any of his Majesty's said plantations, in whatsoever custody they shall be informed the same do remain'. But with the coming of William and Mary, parliament began to claim control of colonial affairs. It did not succeed immediately, but increasingly, from the benches of Lords and Commons, the voice of the City of London complained about such things as colonial violation of the Navigation Laws, the carrying of colonial exports to Ireland and Scotland, and the activities of the Scottish Darien Company in Africa and the Indies. In 1696 the new board of trade, responsible to parliament, took over from the privy council all matters concerned with trade and plantations. Its powers and duties were very wide. In general terms it was charged with promoting 'the trade of this our kingdom and inspecting and improving our plantations in America'. But the order in council which established the board went into significant detail as well:

... to inquire into and examine what trades are or may prove hurtful, or are or may be made beneficial, to our kingdom of England ...
... to consider of some proper methods for setting on work and employing the poor of our said kingdom and making them useful to the public, and thereby easing our subjects of that burden ...
... to take into your care all records, grants and papers ... to inform

yourselves of the present condition of our respective plantations . . .
and to enquire . . . how the same may be rendered most useful and
beneficial to our said kingdom of England.

. . . to inform yourselves what naval stores may be furnished from our
plantations . . . and the best and most proper methods of settling
and improving in our plantations such other staples and manufactures
as our subjects of England are now obliged to fetch and supply themselves withal from other princes and states . . .

. . . to find out proper means of diverting them [the colonies] from
such trades and whatsoever else may turn to the hurt of our kingdom
of England . . .

Little concern is expressed for the welfare of the colonies. The
board is to devote itself primarily to increasing English profits
and safeguarding English interests. Those merchants who were
members of the Lords and Commons strove to keep the board
up to the mark throughout the eighteenth century.

Thanks to countless hours of labour by devoted editors, the
student today can find many of the relevant original documents
in print. Sometimes they are given in full: more often they are
calendared. In addition to the *Acts of the Privy Council* and the
Calendar of State Papers Colonial already mentioned, the Public
Record Office has published the *Journal of the Commissioners for
Trade and Plantations* for the years 1704–82. What is more,
L. F. Stock has gathered together information on parliamentary debates and bills concerning the North American colonies.
This compendium saves the student much trouble, for in these
pre-Hansard days, when for many years it was illegal to report
parliamentary debates, records of parliamentary activities have
to be culled from many sources, some official, such as *Statutes
of the Realm* published by the Record Commissioners, and
others unofficial, such as the appropriate volumes of Cobbett's
Parliamentary History of England or private letters and diaries
preserved in family muniment rooms. Stock has arranged his
material chronologically and has given the source of each

item. Like all calendaring his work has the time-saving advantage of allowing the researcher to survey the collection of material quickly and reasonably comprehensively. But calendaring never does away with the necessity of reading the full text of the key documents.

If the student has difficulty in establishing the chronological details of the colonial story, he will find it harder still to chart the ebb and flow of colonial trade, our second chosen aspect of this subject of Colonial Records. To work with nineteenth- and twentieth-century commercial records is to enjoy the advantage of having plenty of reasonably reliable statistics; but the preliminary to studying the growth of trade in the seventeenth and early eighteenth centuries is to attempt to assess the accuracy of such incomplete figures as are available. Mercantilists had a natural interest in statistics. They had to match exports against imports in order to calculate the all-important balance of trade, and merchants needed figures if they were to persuade the government to protect a particular industry with a higher import duty, or to curtail colonial competition in a particular overseas market. We have already seen that in the later seventeenth century, Sir William Petty, John Graunt, and others were publicizing their new science of 'political arithmetic'. They had many converts. When, in 1701, John Arbuthnot argued in a pamphlet that 'the public accounts of the nation' should be carefully kept and calculated, he was partially preaching to the converted. Already William Culliford had been working for five years as inspector general of imports and exports at the board of trade. His job was

to make and keep a particular, distinct, and true account of the importations and exportations of all commodities into and out of this kingdom, and to enter from what places the same are exported or imported, and out of the said account once in every year . . .

make and present a fair and exact scheme of the balance of trade (as it then stands) between England and any other part of the world ...

In theory, therefore, import and export statistics are available to the historian from 1696 onwards. But these figures are both incomplete and suspect. They consist of quantities and prices of goods which merchants declared to the custom authorities they had either imported or intended to export. Their accuracy depended upon the alertness and integrity of custom officers as well as on the honesty of merchants. Undoubtedly some officers were bribable and some merchants imported quantities of prohibited goods under false labels, just as others avoided the strictures of the Navigation Acts by concealing the country from which they had originally bought their cargo. Alderman Smuggler, a character in George Farquhar's play *The Constant Couple*, complains bitterly that the custom officer insists that the so-called Portuguese wine he is importing is in truth French wine in Spanish casks: 'These tide-waiters [custom officers] and surveyors plague us more with their French wines, than the war did with French privateers.' Likewise, merchants were not above pricing their goods falsely, or exaggerating or diminishing the quantities of goods which they officially declared they were exporting, if they felt either deceit would outwit a rival or bring them extra profits. 'A ship and cargo worth £5,000,' declared Alderman Smuggler, 'why 't is richly worth five hundred perjuries.' Not until 1759 had the inspector general power to check doubtful figures by demanding to see the cockets, the lists of goods actually put on board ship before it sailed. And, of course, none of these official figures include either invisible exports or the quantities or values of smuggled goods. In the eighteenth century, the high rate of excise duties made smuggling so profitable that a substantial, if incalculable, percentage of imports and exports never went through the customs. All these facts and possibilities the researcher must keep in mind when using the statistics compiled each year by the inspector general's office.

Yet, despite their imperfections, these official figures are far from useless. Without any processing, they can offer helpful comparisons: they can indicate, for example, the comparative volume and buoyancy of trade of different colonies, upward and downward trends in the demand for particular goods, and dramatic increases in certain imports, such as the import of raw cotton in the 1780s. It is also possible to check the credibility of many of the given prices by comparing them with prices in contemporary inventories and account books, or, often more conveniently, with the figures given in J. E. Thorold Rogers's *History of Agriculture and Prices in England*. The ledgers of the inspector general are still in manuscript in the Public Record Office and the Custom House, but summaries and extracts have been printed from time to time in specialist histories and local studies.

More readily available in reference libraries are a number of eighteenth-century statistical compilations. Of these, four are probably the most useful for studying colonial trade – Joshua Gee's *Trade and Navigation of Great Britain Considered*, first published in 1729, Malachy Postlethwayt's *Universal Dictionary of Trade and Commerce*, 1751–5, Sir Charles Whitworth's *State of the Trade of Great Britain*, 1776, and David Macpherson's *Annals of Commerce*, 1787. None of them, however, limits itself to trade with the colonies. Despite the title of his book, Whitworth is concerned only with English trade, but he does cover *all* English trade. He gives annual summaries of accounts from 1696 to 1773, chiefly to establish balances of trade with individual countries. From these can be picked required colonial figures – unfavourable balances of trade with Barbados and Bermuda in 1739, for example, turned into substantial favourable balances twenty years later, or exports to Madras and Calcutta climbing from £36,977 12s. 6d. in 1715 to £217,395 6s. 0d. in 1739. The same method can be used with the annual summaries printed in the third and fourth volumes of Macpherson's *Annals*. The following items have been extracted from his tables for 1762:

Countries, Etc.	Imported into						Exported from					
	England			Scotland			England			Scotland		
	£	s.	d.	£	s.	d.	£	s.	d.	£	s.	d.
America in general				326,347	17	11				169,962	9	9
Belle-isle	715	3	0				21,625	7	9			
Hudson's bay	12,119	14	5				4,122	2	9			
Newfoundland	23,436	8	11				35,387	13	1			
Quebec	32,079	9	6				148,478	4	2			
Nova Scotia	1,144	6	5				25,071	2	4			
New-England	41,733	17	6				247,385	18	3			
New-York	58,882	6	5				288,046	16	10			
Pennsylvania	38,091	2	2				206,199	18	8			
Virginia and Maryland	415,709	10	9				417,599	15	6			
Carolina	181,695	10	3				194,170	14	1			
Georgia	6,522	17	7				23,761	18	10			
West Indies				48,761	16	7				68,149	2	8
Antigua	249,367	0	9				125,323	9	0			
Barbados	254,860	17	6				213,177	4	5			
Bermuda	988	15	0				7,786	7	0			
Grenada	26,560	16	9				119	6	1			

But previous to 1760 as well as afterwards when he begins to print annual summaries, Macpherson quotes occasional figures concerning specified trades or single colonies. These shed brighter if more restricted light than the annual tables. The following figures concerning the Hudson's Bay Company's sale of furs in 1743, for example, emerge when Macpherson is examining 'a controversy in the press' between Arthur Dobbes, governor of North Carolina, and Captain Christopher Middleton, a servant of the Company. At the Admiralty's bidding, Middleton had spent 1741 and 1742 trying to find the elusive north-west passage. His failure convinced him that no passage existed. Dobbes continued to assert that the passage must be there: had the Hudson's Bay Company been more active and enterprising, it would have discovered the way into the Pacific long before this. Trade in Hudson Bay, therefore, should be 'laid open' to give others a chance to develop it and explore further. To support this argument, Dobbes quoted these figures:

	£	s.	d.
26,750 beaver skins, sold for	9,780	4	0
12,370 marten's skins	4,242	7	0
2,360 damaged ditto	442	10	0
590 otter's skins	413	0	0
850 cats	765	0	0
260 damaged ditto	52	0	0
320 foxes	200	0	0
600 woolverines	205	0	0
170 damaged ditto	27	12	0
320 black bears	368	0	0
1,580 wolves	1,580	0	0
270 ditto, damaged, and stags	123	15	0
40 woodshock skins	22	6	0
10 mink skins	1	10	0
5 racoon skins		16	0
120 squirrel skins	2	0	0
46,615 of all sorts, sold for	18,226	0	0

He added the following articles, but without their prices:

130 elk skins, 440 deer skins, 3,170 pound weight of bed feathers, and 220 lb. in a tick, 140 castorum [type of beaver], 470 whale fins, 23 casks of whale oil, and 8lb. of wesaguipaka.

And in their March sale 40,125 beaver worth	14,670	0	0
Unvalued goods, about	400	0	0
Total amount of their sales in the year 1743	33,296	0	0

The figures need checking if only because they are provided

by a man with an axe to grind, but the general pattern of the year's business can be accepted. Beaver and marten skins, obviously dominated the market, and apparently no one in George II's reign thought much of mink.

The Calendar of Treasury Books published by the Public Record Office gives details of custom receipts from 1666 to 1745. There is still a gap of a few years in George I's reign in this unfinished series, but the type of figures the series gives supplements the more general figures recorded by the inspector general. On the receipt, or 'charge' side of the custom accounts, figures are given for each type of duty for each port; for example, the following are some of the figures for the year 1705–6:

Out of the New Subsidy which commenced 8
  March 1701–2
  London port: Grand Receipt (including Planta-
    tion Goods and Wines)

	£	s.	d.
	238,032	9	10
Outports			
Barnstaple	970	10	8¼
Beaumaris	13	7	3½
Berwick	132	14	9¼
Boston	141	18	2½
Bridgwater	151	8	5
Bristol	19,929	6	4
Bideford	1,001	13	5
[etc.]			

Duty on Coals which commenced 15 May 1703			
London port	83,059	12	9
Outports			
... Colchester	2,051	18	5
Dartmouth	88	9	2½
Dover	668	19	1¼
Exeter	445	0	0
Feversham	524	9	2¾
[etc.]			

Money due and payable to her Majesty ... for the
said New Impositions on Wines and Vinegar
London port
Sir John Shaw [Receiver for Plantation Goods]   91,110   4   0½
Outports
... Fowey   4   10   0
    Harwich   8   14   11¼
    Hull   2,412   10   3¾
    Ipswich   0   15   4½
    Liverpool   699   2   0¼
               [etc.]

Silks and Linens: General Account
London port   175,308   6   10
Outports
... Lancaster   8   3   9¾
    Liverpool   970   5   6
    Looe   2   13   8
    Lyme   155   15   5¾
    Lynn   1,659   4   10
               [etc.]

New Impositions on Tobacco
London port
Sir John Shaw   81,858   16   8½
Outports
... Milford   533   18   0
    Padstow   3   19   9½
    Penzance   1,262   10   6
    John Williams, succeeding Collector there   18   7¾
    Charles Jones, succeeding him there   31   1   10
    Plymouth   7,613   0   9½
    Portsmouth   0   8   3½
    Whitehaven   22,534   11   7

On the 'discharge' side of these same accounts are given the overpayments made by some of the collectors of customs, and the lists of salaries and fees paid to custom officials both at home and in the colonies:

	£	s.	d.
Thomas Byerley, Collector at New York from 10 November 1702 to Xmas 1704	116	15	0
Thomas Collier, Surveyor at Williamstadt in Maryland	52	10	0
William Carter, Comptroller at New York	55	0	0
Richard Chichester, Collector at Rappahannock River in Virginia	120	0	0
Robert Dacres, Comptroller at Corytuck in North Carolina	75	0	0

Of course, the treasury was not only concerned with customs. Its business was with all income and expenses of the crown. Therefore, the costs of defending the colonies both by land and sea are to be found among a mass of 'declared expenses' for army and navy. In this same year of 1705–6, for example, such items as the following stand out as colonial expenses:

	£	s.	d.
Four Companies of Foot at New York (Visct. Cornbury: Officers and 400 men)	6,052	13	4
Independent Company of Foot at Bermudas (Capt. Benjamin Bennett: Officers and 50 private men)	717	3	11
Company of Foot at Newfoundland (John Thurston, agent: Officers and 80 private soldiers)	759	0	5
Capt. Tho. Lloyd and the executors of Capt. Samuel Powell for provisions and clothing for the Company at Newfoundland and for spies, French prisoners and persons employed to sound the harbour	573	3	1
John How for provisions furnished for 92 Officers and soldiers of Newfoundland for one year from 25 December 1703	739	10	0

But it is not easy to find naval expenses, especially in a war year such as 1705–6 was. The cost of 'services and wages' are listed roughly alphabetically, ship by ship:

	£	s.	d.
Assistance (1 July 1703 – 30 June 1704)	3,822	6	$11\frac{1}{2}$
St Antonio (26 May 1700 – 30 June 1703) Humphry Pudner, master	924	16	4
Anglesea (1 July 1702 – 30 June 1704) Baron Wild, Commander	5,809	15	$1\frac{1}{4}$
Advice (1 July 1703 – 30 June 1704)	3,655	5	$7\frac{1}{2}$

It depends where these ships were serving whether their maintenance can be attributed to colonial costs or not.

To supplement and check these board of trade and treasury statistics, economic historians seek and find additional figures in a number of other archives. Board of trade correspondence files and the reports of occasional parliamentary inquiries into this or that aspect of colonial trade can prove useful sources. So can custom records, especially the Plantation Registers kept at each port to list owners' declarations about ships and cargo in accordance with the Act of 1695, and the Wool Registers to record imports and exports of wool as required by an Act of 1739. Although concerned only with the tonnage and nationality of ships entering British ports, the General Register of Shipping adds its quota to statistical evidence, and even the numbers of sixpences officially deducted each month, from 1726 to 1810, from seamen's pay for the upkeep of Greenwich Hospital have been pressed into the historian's service. To these more general records can be added a number of local sources, such as the accounts of port, as distinct from custom, authorities; the growing number of county and town directories in the eighteenth century; the business records of trading companies; private letters and diaries; newspaper articles and advertisements. None of the statistics derived from any one of these sources is necessarily accurate. As usual, the historian faces the inescapable task of assessing the worth of each source he uses. Yet, taken together, there are usually sufficient reasonably reliable figures for him to piece together a picture which is accurate enough to accept as a working hypothesis, and detailed enough to correct many long-lived, false impressions. Local economic studies, such as M. M. Schofield's *Economic History of Lancaster, 1660–1860*, are surprisingly full of significant statistics. More recently, Robert Craig's statistical study of the port of Chester in the eighteenth century has considerably modified the conventional opinion that Chester's overseas trade was hardly worth talking about in that century. To find the statistics for their wider canvases, such historians as Elizabeth Donnan and A. P. Wadsworth and Julia Mann have searched similar varied central and local sources: Donnan brought together a comprehensive collection of documents on the American slave trade, and the other two scholars produced an enlightening study of the Lancashire cotton trade in the seventeenth and eighteenth centuries. And, of course, for statistics concerning the colonies, all the sources are not British. The former colonies have archives too.

Our third chosen aspect of colonial history – the personal experiences of men involved in colonization, trade, and colonial expansion – is one of wide appeal. Colonial policy and the statistics of colonial trade are subjects that only interest the dedicated few, but stories of exploration and colony-founding fascinate almost everybody. The discovery of the unknown, adventure and travel, danger and hardship spiced with occasional tragedies, triumphs, and unexpected treasure, these are perennial ingredients of exciting story-telling. Novelists, dramatists, and film-makers – especially film-makers – have all exploited colonial narratives. Historians have used them just as freely, but more soberly. For it is no part of their task to invent additional characters, imagine unrecorded incidents, or deliberately heighten the drama of the story. Their aim is not to rouse their readers' emotions or to hold audiences spellbound in their seats, but to try to depict from the evidence available what colonizing really entailed for those who sailed across the seas or pushed further into the interior.

Fortunately, printed colonial narratives are not hard to find. The Hakluyt Society alone has published well over 200 volumes and is still publishing. It is a society founded to print original accounts of voyages of discovery, and other contemporary documents which concern the establishment of overseas trade and the founding of colonies throughout the world. Titles range chronologically from *The voyages of the Venetian brothers Nicolò and Antonio Zeno to the Northern Seas in the fourteenth century* to *The Journal of William Lockerby, sandalwood trader in the Fijian islands, 1809–9;* in subject from *The natural and moral history of the Indies* to *Bombay in the days of Queen Anne*; and in area of the globe from *A true description of three voyages by the north-east towards Cathay and China* to *Reports on the discovery of Peru* or to *The Discovery of the Solomon Islands*.

Of course, other colonial narratives and topographical books were in print long before the Hakluyt Society published its first volume in 1847, for the first Elizabethans and seventeenth- and eighteenth-century Britishers were as eager to read of adventure and new lands as we are. In 1672, for example, Richard Blome published his *Description of the Island of Jamaica with other Isles and Territories in America*. Twelve years later, John Esquemeling published *Bucaniers [sic] of America*, and in 1748 R. Walter edited Anson's account of his *Voyage round the World*. These books sold well. So did the official accounts of James Cook's three voyages, while William Dampier's *Voyages round the World* and *Voyages and Discoveries* were required reading for all well-educated eighteenth-century gentlemen. At least three notable omnibus collections preceded the Hakluyt Society's publications – J. Pinkerton's seventeen volumes of *Voyages and Travels*, published between 1808 and 1814; A. and J. Churchill's eight volumes with the same title, published between 1744 and 1747; and the pioneer of them all, Richard Hakluyt's *Voyages and Discoveries*, the first edition of which appeared as early as 1589. Yet, despite all this printing, the stock of worthwhile manuscripts is still not exhausted. Many narratives, log-books, diaries and collections of 'letters from abroad' are stored away in public and private archives, libraries, and junk rooms all over the world. The Hakluyt Society is in no danger of running out of good raw material for many years to come.

Bibliography of Documents 1660–1760

Three volumes of *English Historical Documents* cover this period: Vol. 8, ed. Andrew Browning (1953); Vol. 9, ed. D. B. Horn and Mary Ransome (1957); and Vol. 13, ed. Merrill Jensen (1955).

Quotations have been taken from the following diaries, letters, and contemporary histories:

The Diary of Samuel Pepys, ed. H. B. Wheatley (1895).

The Diary of John Evelyn, ed. A. Dobson (1906).

The Diary of Rev. Henry Newcome, ed. T. Heywood, Chetham Society O.S., Vol. 18 (1849).

The Great Diurnal of Nicholas Blundell, ed. F. Tyrer, Record Society of Lancashire and Cheshire, Vols. 110 and 112 (1968 and 1970).

The Diary of Richard Kay, 1716–51, ed. W. Brockbank and F. Kenworthy (1968).

The diary of Elizabeth Byrom in *The Private Journal of John Byrom*, Chetham Society O.S., Vol. 44 (1857).

The diary of Ireland Greene in *Isaac Greene, a Lancashire lawyer of the 18th Century*, R. Stewart-Brown (1921).

Letters of Horace Walpole, ed. Mrs P. Toynbee (1903–5).

The Short Journal of George Fox, ed. N. Penney (1925).

Journal of John Wesley, ed. N. Curnock (1906–16).

History of My Own Times, Gilbert Burnet (1833).

The two most important collections of pamphlets are *The Harleian Miscellany*, 8 vols. (1744–6) and *The Somers Tracts*, 16 vols. (1748–52). The text of the *Spectator* was reprinted in the Everyman Series in 4 volumes (1907). For local newspapers see G. A. Cranfield *Hand-List of English Provincial Newspapers and Periodicals, 1700–1760* (1961).

Hearth tax figures have been quoted from the following:

Miscellanea, Thoresby Society Publications, Vol. 2 (1891).

'The Hearth Tax in Saddleworth, 1668' in *Palatine Note-Book* (1883).

Archaeologia Cantiana, Vol. 12 (1878).

History of Wednesbury, J. F. Ede (1962).

Oxford City Documents, J. E. Thorold Rogers, and *Surveys and Tokens*, H. E. Salter, Oxford Historical Society, Vols. 18 (1891) and 75 (1923).

Chetham Miscellanies, O.S. Vol. 57 (1862).

The chief collections of official colonial documents are *Acts of Privy Council of England, Colonial Series*, 6 vols. covering 1613–1783 (1908–12); *Calendar of State Papers, Colonial Series*, 42 vols. covering 1513–1736 (1860 – in progress); *Journal of the Commissioners of Trade and Plantations*, 14 vols. covering 1704–82 (1920–38). The following books are mentioned in Section 4 of this chapter:

Proceedings and Debates of the British Parliaments respecting North America, L. F. Stock, 5 vols. to 1754 (1924–42).

Documents Illustrative of the History of the Slave Trade, Elizabeth Donnan, 3 vols. (1930–32).

The Cotton Trade and Industrial Lancashire, 1600–1780, A. P. Wadsworth and J. de L. Mann (1931).

Guide to English Commercial Statistics, 1696–1782, G. N. Clark (1938) is a most useful book.

ECONOMIC AND TOPOGRAPHICAL
RECORDS

Although in 1760 Britain was in the middle of yet another war with France, many British historians have looked upon that year as 'a turning point'. If it is necessary to have new chapters in our national history – and there is no denying their organizational convenience – 1760 is as good a break as we shall get in the eighteenth century. In October of that year the peace-seeking George III replaced the petulant George II. Within six months Lord Bute had been appointed secretary of state, and Pitt's influence on government policy was decidedly waning: if one chapter had closed with a 'year of victories' and the establishment of British supremacy in Canada, India, and on the seas, the next chapter was opening with a desire for peace with France and a determination to free Britain from inconvenient alliances in Europe.

For less obvious reasons, many economic historians have been prepared to join their political-history colleagues in regarding 1760 as a year of unusual change. About that time the first British Empire achieved its greatest size and wealth: the new colonial chapter was to be concerned not with additions to British overseas power but with military defeat and loss of territory. The significance of that change is easy to appreciate. It is, however, more difficult to accept that 1760 marks the beginning of a new chapter in the Industrial Revolution. The complexities of all social-economic movements make it impossible to cut through the intricate pattern without leaving very ragged edges. There are no clean cuts or tidy ends: a specific invention might begin a new era in a single industry, and an individual Act might bring to an end a particular social evil, but the industrialization of Britain, with all its social and economic effects, was a many-sided transformation. Erratically as it moved forward, it gathered increasing momentum, but it is impossible to determine at what point the initial slow glide developed into a walking pace, or in what year the speed of the movement first threatened to get out of government control. Nevertheless, in the first half of George III's long reign, the Industrial Revolution made faster progress and dislocated society far more severely than it had done in the days of the first two Georges. Better communications and more efficient machinery constantly increased production. More factories meant even bigger concentrations of workers in towns. Britain's wealth was growing beyond expectation, yet the twin scourges of vagrancy and social unrest were increasingly harassing successive governments. No one year can ever be fixed as the beginning of this phase of the industrial movement, but since it is associated with George III's reign, it is convenient to accept the first year of that reign as a conventional beginning.

I. PRIVATE ACTS OF PARLIAMENT

Documentary sources from which the Industrial Revolution can be studied are as manifold as the aspects of the movement itself. Changes in the patterns of employment, the growth of towns, the effect of industrial change on political thought or social conscience, technological development, transport, trade unions, changes in education – all these and many more are facets of the study of the industrialization of Britain. In addition to the ample general sources – newspapers, contemporary publications, letters, diaries, and the like – which have the potential to illuminate all aspects of the Revolution, each facet has its distinctive special sources. The study of the topographical transformation of Britain, for example, cannot help but be substantially based upon private Acts of Parliament. The definition of 'private Act' is not universally agreed. Traditionally, Acts divided naturally into public and private: statutes were *public*; Acts concerning inheritance, divorce, or naturalization were *private*. But as the eighteenth century advanced, an increasing number of Acts authorized such undertakings as new roads, waterways, and enclosures. They were too local to rank as national statutes, and yet too public in their effect to be private Acts in the accepted sense. In 1797 parliament classified them as *public local and personal*. In their passage through the Lords and Commons, they were to follow the procedure laid down for private Acts, but, since many people needed to know their content, 200 copies of each were to be printed.

It is these 'public local and personal' Acts – still properly listed under the general heading of private Acts – that help us to study the way the new Britain was built. Each Act records the addition of another upright, beam, or joist to the growing structure. For although no one required parliamentary permission to build a factory, invent a machine, demand higher wages, or move from a village cottage to a terraced cottage in the town, it was not possible to turnpike a road, 'navigate' a river, dig a canal, re-site a bridge, construct a dock, build a railway, drain a fen, or enclose common land without first seeking and obtaining the authority of parliament.

Unlike a public Bill, which is almost always introduced into the Commons or Lords by a minister of the crown, a private Bill is usually initiated by a person or group of persons outside parliament petitioning Commons or Lords for permission to present it for consideration. If the Bill is concerned with the disposal of estates, parliament, since 1706, has referred it immediately to two judges: if it is a Bill for a public work, such as a new canal, drainage scheme, or street widening project, parliament, since 1792, has required detailed plans to be deposited with the text. Once the sponsors have carried out the necessary preliminaries, the private Bill follows the usual course of first reading, second reading, committee stage, and third reading in both Houses, except that the committee stage is turned into a judicial examination of the proposals. This is the supreme opportunity for opponents of the Bill to state their case. If they can convince the committee of the House that the Bill is not in the public interest, then the only way for the sponsors to raise the matter again is later to petition for permission to introduce a revised Bill. This procedure is well illustrated by the struggle to obtain parliamentary authority to build the first passenger railway, that from Liverpool to Manchester, which was opened eventually in September 1830 by the Duke of Wellington.

The concept of a railway from Liverpool to Manchester was first seriously discussed in 1821. Joseph Sandars, a Liverpool corn merchant, was determined to break the canal companies' monopoly of the carrying trade between the two rapidly developing industrial and commercial centres. He arranged with William James of Manchester and George Stephenson the engineer for a preliminary survey to be made for a possible railway route, and at the same time, as discreetly as possible, canvassed support among the leading business men in south Lancashire. By 1822 the press was discussing the project, but not for another two years did the supporters take positive steps to get the Bill prepared. In May 1824 they floated a company, the Liverpool and Manchester Railroad Company, with £300,000 capital. In October they issued a prospectus which argued their case with facts anyone could understand – 33 miles of rail against over 40 miles of canal; four hours of train travel compared with a day and a half by barge; carrying charges reduced by at least one-third, and new outlets for coal and agricultural produce. Sandars supplemented this document with a vigorous pamphlet, copies of which were sent to members of both Houses and distributed widely among people likely to support the railway. John Gladstone, the father of the future prime minister, thought it wise, as a member of parliament, to withdraw from the Company, but he was a most effective advocate inside the Commons. He spoke in debate, and presented the railway case privately but persuasively to such influential political friends as Canning and Huskisson. In the meantime, other keen supporters of the project endeavoured to lobby as much preliminary parliamentary support as they could.

The Company presented its first petition at the beginning of February 1825. On 11 February parliament gave leave for the Bill to be introduced into the Commons. The second reading took place on 2 March: in the debate both Huskisson and Brougham were distinguished supporters. But the committee stage was not so easy. It began on 21 March and did not cease until 1 June. Counsel appeared for both sides. Stephenson was the principal witness for the Bill. Gladstone and William Brown gave evidence that Lancashire businessmen were in favour. But the opponents of the Bill were stronger still. They were a strange mixture – the canal companies protecting their vested interests; engineers like Francis Giles arguing that Stephenson's proposed method of crossing Chat Moss would fail; landed proprietors resenting possible threats to their estates; Liverpool Corporation opposing the route the railway was taking into the borough; and men like Thomas Creevey and the archbishop of York just hating the thought of 'intersecting the country with railways'. The opponents won the vote in committee, and, of course, killed the Bill.

The Company, however, had the courage to try again. They did what they could to anticipate their opponents' arguments by commissioning John and George Rennie to make a fresh survey, and by amending the route here and there to meet recent criticism in Liverpool and Manchester. They increased both their capital and propaganda, and issued a new and less provocative prospectus. Early in 1826, parliament gave its consent to introduce the second Bill. This time it passed all the stages in the Commons, helped considerably by the preliminary work which had won it new friends, including Liverpool Corporation. It then faced the stiffer hurdle of the Lords. Lord Derby spoke against it, but, thanks to good witnesses and very capable counsel, the promoters won a more resounding victory in the Lords' committee stage than they had done in the Commons. The rest was formality. The royal assent was given in May 1826. The following month, the Company appointed Stephenson as its engineer, and work began. Three amending Acts were necessary before the line was finished four years later. The first, in 1827, gave the Company permission to raise additional capital: the other two, in 1828 and 1829, authorized amendments to the original plan – a bridge over the River Irwell and an extension at the Manchester end of the line. On each of these three occasions the full procedure of petition, plans, and Bill had to be followed, but, fortunately for the success of the project, none of the amending Bills met serious opposition.

All the extant documents concerning this and other private Acts are available to students in the House of Lords' Record Office. In addition to the original petition and the Act itself, there are deposited plans, estimates of cost, lists of subscribers, and transcripts of the evidence given during the committee stage in both Houses. Unless the documents he most requires were among those destroyed by the Commons' fire of 1834, the most exacting scholar can hardly want more information than this. In many cases, however, he can discover what he wants outside Westminster. Largely because, after 1792, promoters were required to deposit duplicate plans with clerks of the peace, every county record office and many another local archive has its collection of local petitions, plans and Bills.

None of these collections is likely to be complete. Early Bills are rarer than later Bills. Railway documents are more numerous than most, partly because they are all comparatively late in date and partly because promoters were required by law to deposit their plans with the clerk of the peace of every county through which they intended the railway to run. Then again, once parliament had passed the Bill, the official printer printed copies for public purchase. Since it was natural that the company, trust, or corporation charged with carrying out the project should be anxious to preserve a copy of its authority, printed texts of Acts are frequently found in minute books of turnpike trusts, of canal and railway companies, and of appropriate committees of borough councils.

Much of the information the researcher requires is also to be found in well-known reference books. The many folio volumes of *The Journal of the House of Commons*, beginning with the year 1547, and of *The Journal of the House of Lords*, beginning in 1509, give considerable detail about the progress of Bills through both Houses. On 17 February 1798, to take a typical example, the Kennet and Avon Canal Company petitioned the Commons for permission to introduce an amending Bill. The *Journal* does not quote the petition in full, but it gives all necessary details about the proposals:

... if the Line of the said Canal was varied in certain Parts, in the county of *Wilts*, from the Course originally intended for it, namely, from, and out of, a Piece of Arable Land in the Parish of *Bishops Cannings*, in the County of *Wilts*, lately belonging to *Thomas Rigge*, Esquire, deceased, to a Piece of Ground, in the said Parish, belonging to *R. E. Drax Grosvenor*, Esquire, and from the Turnpike Gate at the West End of *Devizes*, in the said *County*, to a Close of Meadow Ground belonging to *Henry Penruddocke Wyndham*, Esquire, in the Parish of *Rowde*, in the County, the Line of the said Canal would be considerably shortened and improved ...

The entry goes on to explain the Company's second proposal –

'to carry the canal into the River Avon at or near *Dole Mead* in the Parish of *Lyncomb* and *Widcombe*' instead of at Bath Easton Mill as originally intended. Later entries in the *Journal* record parliamentary progress. The House referred the petition to a committee, on whose advice it gave authority for the Bill to be introduced on 20 February. From 1 March to 19 March the Bill was examined in committee. Several objectors were heard, and minor amendments made. On 28 March the Commons gave the amended Bill a third reading, but in the course of this last debate added a further clause:

... nothing therein contained shall prejudice any Agreement made by the Company of Proprietors with the Tenants of *Sir James Pulteney* and *Lady Bath*.

By the beginning of April, the Bill was in the Lords. That House passed it with yet another amendment on 27 April. Four days later, the Commons accepted the Lords' amendment, and on 7 May the Bill received the royal assent.

The two sets of *Journals* complement each other. To extract all the facts from these records, the student must use both. He is bound to come across repetition, but the Lords' *Journal* adds details which the Commons' *Journal* does not give, and *vice versa*.

For further detail still there is *Mirror of Parliament*, a series of volumes which summarizes parliamentary speeches and business for the years 1828–41. The *Mirror* lists petitions and counter-petitions, and, in summary form, covers much private business which the earlier volumes of *Hansard* omit. But of all these records *Hansard's Parliamentary Debates* give us the fullest treatment of general parliamentary business. The first series covers the years 1813–20, the second the 1820s, and the third 1830 to 1890. These volumes, unlike *Hansard's* later volumes, do not give verbatim reports of speeches, but they record the more important debates in considerable detail. The second series, for example, devotes three pages to the third reading in the Commons of the successful Liverpool Manchester Railway Bill on 6 April 1826. It reports the speeches of the proposer and seconder, General Isaac Gascoyne, member for Liverpool, and William Peel:

... The population on the thirty-one miles which intervened between Liverpool and Manchester was nearer in amount to 1,000,000 than 800,000 persons, and, therefore, it was impossible that some inconvenience must not be suffered. But, assuredly, inconvenience ought not to prevent a general public improvement ...
... The trade of that port [Liverpool] had been calculated to have doubled every twenty years since 1760, and the trade in cotton to have doubled every ten years ... The principal opposition to the Bill arose from the proprietors of canal shares ...

There follow long summaries of the main opposition speech, given by Edward Stanley, member for Preston, and of William Huskisson's reply, in which he reproved 'his gallant friend' for not voicing his objections at the earlier committee stage. A few lines each suffice for three further speeches, and the entry concludes abruptly with the figures of the vote – '88 for, 41 against: majority 47'.

It often happens, however, that the researcher does not need much detail. If he is concerned with the industrialization of a region, or with a national study of such features as canals or railways or the supply of water to growing towns, his needs, or at least his immediate needs, probably require no more than a list of particular acts, with their dates and main provisions. If this is so, he should consult *Statutes at Large*, which lists the *titles* of all private Acts passed between 1509 and 1869. The titles are full enough to indicate clearly the purpose of each Act. The following six Acts, for example, received the royal assent on 11 March 1808:

1. An Act to continue and amend an Act of the Thirty-second Year

of His present Majesty, for repairing the Road from the Town of *Middleton in Teesdale*, to the Gate in the new Inclosures, called *The Edge*, in the Parish of St Andrew's Auckland, and a Branch therefrom to Eggleston Bridge, in the County of *Durham*.

2. An Act for amending and enlarging the Powers of an Act of His present Majesty, for paving, cleansing, lighting, and watching the Streets and Public Passages in the City of *Winchester*, and several Parishes in the Suburbs thereof, and for removing and preventing Nuisances therein.

3. An Act for amending and enlarging the Powers of the several Acts relating to the *Oxford* Canal Navigation.

4. An Act for continuing and amending Two Acts of the Fifth and Twenty-seventh Year of His present Majesty, for repairing the Road from *Hurstgreen* to the Extent of the Parish of *Burwash* in the County of *Sussex*.

5. An Act for enlarging the Term and Powers of Two Acts of His present Majesty, for repairing the Road from *Scole Bridge* to *Bury St Edmunds*, in the County of *Suffolk*.

6. An Act for enclosing Lands in *Chapel Allerton*, in the West Riding of the County of *York*.

The first, fourth, and fifth of these Acts are marked 'b' in the printed list to show that, like most Acts concerned with the creation and extension of turnpike roads, they were limited to a term of twenty-one years. The sixth Act is marked 'q P', the sign for a 'quasi-public' Act. In 1870 the annual volumes of *Statutes at Large* gave way to a new series, *The Public General Statutes*. These new volumes still listed local Acts, but a little more tersely than their predecessors had done. The following are taken from the first few entries for 1870:

An Act to authorise the Chester United Gas Company to raise additional Capital.

An Act for supplying the town and parish of Mansfield in the county of Nottingham with Water.

An Act for extending the power of 'The Leicester Lunatic Asylum and Improvement Act, 1865', and for other purposes.

An Act to confirm Orders made by the Board of Trade under the Sea Fisheries Act, 1868, relating to Boston Deeps and Emsworth.

The last of these items is marked 'P' to indicate that it is a 'public Act of a local character'. In 1884 the series changed its title to *The Public General Acts*, but until 1919 the list of local Acts still appeared under a new heading – 'Table of the Titles of the Local and Private Acts arranged alphabetically'. Since 1962, after a gap of forty-two years, *Public General Acts and Measures* has again listed local acts under yet another title, 'Lists of Personal and Local Acts'.

In the first years of the nineteenth century, George Bramwell, a lawyer, found, as scholars still find, 'that searches for private acts in the tables prefixed to the statute books were attended with great labour, and consumed a most inconvenient portion of time'. Accordingly, he prepared *Analytical Tables of the Private Statutes between 1727 and 1812*, which he published in 1813. Presumably the tables saved him and his colleagues precious time, but they are of restricted use to historians. He defined 'private statute' more narrowly than usual: such Acts as 'those which relate to drainage, roads, navigations, bridges, churches, piers, workhouses, prisons, docks or harbours, or to the improvement of cities or towns' he deemed to be public Acts. Therefore, he listed only Acts concerned with divorce, the disposal of estates, enclosures, changes of surnames, and naturalization of foreigners. Alphabetical lists of Acts for each year he followed first with a list of estate Acts under subject-matter headings – copyholds, deeds, jointures, leases, and the like – and then with two concise alphabetical lists of estate Acts and enclosure Acts. Of much more general time-saving use, however, is the *Index to Local and Personal Acts, 1801 to 1947*, published by H.M. Stationery Office in 1949. This includes Bramwell's 'public Acts'. The first of its fifteen sections is headed 'Bridges, Ferries, Roads, Subways and Tunnels', the second 'Transport, Railways, Road, and

Miscellaneous including Air Transport', and the third 'Canals, Rivers, and Navigations'. The *Index* packs all kinds of details into a most compact form. The following extract from Section IV gives a good idea of its brevity:

Exeter:
  Petty customs and
  quay dues   3 – 4 V.c. lxxiv

Exmouth:
  Construction etc.
  of pier   26 – 7 V.c. 104
  Construction of
  docks, railway, and $\left\{\begin{array}{l} 27 - 8 \text{ V.c. cccxix} \\ 33 - 4 \text{ V.c. cxlii} \end{array}\right.$
  works
  Abandonment of
  certain works: new
  works: expendi- $\left.\right\}$ 16 – 7 G5. c. xcii
  ture of capital by
  S.Ry.Co.

Eyemouth:
  Improvement and $\left.\begin{array}{l} 2 - 3 \text{ V.c. xxxvi} \\ 37 - 8 \text{ V.c. clxxxv} \end{array}\right\{$ Repealed $\left\{\begin{array}{l} 45\text{--}6 \text{ V.} \\ \text{c. lviii} \\ 10\text{--}11 \text{ G5.} \\ \text{c. cxxi} \end{array}\right.$
  maintenance of
  harbour guarantee
  by burgh commrs. $\left\{\right.$
  etc.   45 – 6 V.c. lviii (Repealed in pt 10–11 G5.c. cxxi)
        47 – 8 V.c. ccxvi

  Amendment of
  1882 Order: in-
  crease of rates etc.   10 – 11 G5. c. cxxi

Fairlie:
  Provision as to
  rates chargeable by
  L.M.S. Ry. Co.   23 – 4 G5. c. lv

Unfortunately this useful index does not begin before 1801.

And not all counties are as well blessed as Lancashire, whose archivist has compiled a classified list of local Acts from 1415 to 1800 to serve as a useful forerunner to this national *Index*.

Such Acts with their deposited plans have obvious uses for both national and local historians. No story of the development of canal or turnpike or railway networks can be attempted without them. They are essential for the study of the growth of towns, ports, and social and industrial development – and for the necessary counterpart of this urban change, the re-organization and transformation of the countryside. But the researcher should handle these documents with care. Acts and plans are proof of intention, not of achievement. Several companies went to the trouble and expense of obtaining parliamentary authority only to change radically or even abandon their plans later. The majority of local Acts are amending Acts: these can either augment or restrict the original plan, and they must always be studied along with the original documents. But an abandoned project need leave no positive evidence at all. The sponsors could just let the project lapse. Therefore, the researcher has to check that each Act was fully implemented. In many cases he has no need to check by documents – the dock or the railway, or the waterworks concerned can yet be in use, the canal may be out of commission but is still there, and the characteristic mile-stones alongside A 123 or B 456 still show where the turnpike trustees built their road. Where there is no material evidence left, however, ordnance survey maps and local newspaper files frequently come to the rescue. The map shows the location or route of the public work; different editions of the newspaper often supply details about the opening, the success or failure of the venture, the later additions, and the final abandonment. If map and newspaper do not answer all the student's questions, he must then see if he can find what he wants in the British

Transport Historical Records Offices in London, York, or Edinburgh.

Just as useful a historical source as the Act and plans is the petition which originally begged leave to introduce the Bill. This is the advocate speaking in favour of the new proposal. Like all good pleaders, it gives prominence to facts which promote the project, and slides over, or attempts to explain away, facts which threaten to hinder it. But the petition does give *facts* – lies would be too easily discredited at the subsequent committee stage – and often the facts are historically enlightening. A petition for a turnpike road in 1766, for example, revealed that there was no bridge over the River Tame, east of Lichfield, between Hopwas and Salters' Bridges, a distance of at least six miles as the crow flies. Both these bridges 'are dangerous in flood, because they are too low'. There are, the petition continued,

three separate fords which are oftentimes impassable ... except at one of the said fords near Elford Hall, where passengers are conveyed over in small ferry boats, and in high floods are obliged to walk from the boats over the meadows, through the water.

When, in 1762, Liverpool Corporation decided to build its third dock, its main argument for a Bill was that

the trade and shipping of the town and port of late years is greatly increased, and the ships and vessels are more numerous and of larger dimensions ... That the two wet docks [The Old Dock and Salthouse Dock] and dry pier already constructed are not sufficient for the ships resorting thereto: that vessels, especially His Majesty's Ships of War stationed at the port, are obliged to lie in the open harbour, exposed to the rage of tempestuous weather and of rapid tides and currents, in imminent danger of shipwreck.

In February 1769, the commissioners charged 'with paving, cleansing and lighting the Squares, Streets, Lanes and other places within the City and Liberty of Westminster, and other Parts therein mentioned' petitioned for powers to raise more money. Part of their argument was that parish rates in their area were unequal, and that rates in the parishes of Covent Garden and St Martin's were particularly low. To support this argument, the treasurer of the commissioners quoted the following figures:

		£	s.	d.
Paving rate for Charing Cross	1765 –	346	0	0
	1766 –	270	10	0
„ „ „ Cockspur Street	1765 –	156	7	6
	1766 –	116	14	0
„ „ „ part of Strand	1765 –	757	16	0
	1766 –	573	1	6
„ „ „ Half Moon Street	1765 –	29	14	0
	1766 –	21	18	0

For those four streets alone, the commissioners in 1766 received £308 0s. 0d. less than the sum – itself inadequate – they had received the previous year.

Such topographical details as these might not surprise the local historian. Their main value is that they confirm facts and impressions gained from other sources, and occasionally add an otherwise unknown detail or two. It is much the same with the counter petitions presented to parliament at the committee stage. Most of them are predictable. No change, however beneficial to the public, can help but tread on someone's toes, and when people are about to be hurt, they shout. In the late eighteenth century, turnpike trusts steadfastly opposed canal-building: in the following generation turnpike trusts and canal companies became natural allies against the railways. Landowners usually protested against selling their land for a waterworks or sewage farm, and there were always ratepayers who shrank from the prospect of authorizing improvement commissioners to begin bringing their town up to date. Occasionally, however, there are counter petitions that are more unexpected than these. It is not immediately obvious, for example, why merchants and shipowners employed in the Newcastle-upon-Tyne coal trade should oppose, as they did in May 1810, the proposal to cut a canal from the Thames at Abingdon to the Kennet and Avon canal. Nor would one be expected to guess that, in 1802, the main reason for the land-owners and tenants of several townships round Ilkley and Otley opposing an extension of the turnpike road from Otley to Skipton was because it seemed likely to raise the price of carting lime to their fields. But one can be sure that altruism prompted counter petitions as rarely as it was the motive force of the Bills themselves. Behind every petition for a 'public local and personal' Bill there were vested interests. Most of these Acts served the public well. Collectively they transformed both the economy and the topography of Britain. But prominent among the promoters of each Bill were men whose dominant thought was that, directly or indirectly, it would help to line their pockets. As Adam Smith expressed it, the private profit seekers were 'led by an invisible hand' to promote public good.

2. COUNTY MAPS AND TOWN PLANS

Few people fail to find old maps fascinating. The artistic em-bellishments, the quaintness of the spelling, and the unusual cartographical conventions attract the eye and engage the interest. But old maps are more than fashionable, colourful decorations for the dining-room wall. They can be informative and valuable historical documents. 'Can be' are the key words, for in map publishing plagiarism has been rife. To take ad-vantage of the consistent popularity of maps, many publishers, with little more than a fresh date and a few superficial additions, have printed new maps from copper-plate engravings that were generations out of date. For a historian's purpose, the competence of the survey is paramount. He wants to know what the mapped area looked like at a certain date, and therefore no cartouches, imaginative decorations, ingenious symbols, or gay colours can ever compensate him for a poor or patchy survey.

Certain eminent map-makers stand out from the ruck of British cartographers. The first two are Christopher Saxton and John Norden, both Elizabethans. Their work outshines anything that had been done earlier. Nevertheless, they owed part of their success to a small band of worthy predecessors. Just as dramatists like Kyd and Marlowe earlier essayed the kind of plays that Shakespeare wrote far more successfully, so at least a trio of Tudor cartographers, George Lily, Humphrey Lluyd, and Laurence Nowell, showed the possibilities of a new approach to mapping. Their work led directly to the achievements of both Saxton and Norden.

Saxton, a Yorkshireman, surveyed thirty-four counties for his *Atlas of England*, which was published in 1579. His maps are both attractive and, by the standards of his day, advanced in their technique. But they far from satisfy the rigorous standards of the modern cartographer. The sugar-loaf hills, the conventionally marked woodlands, the paled parklands, and the other semi-pictorial symbols must be interpreted hardly more literally than the serpents which he showed cavorting in the sea. Saxton used a collection of sugar-loaves to show a hilly area, a ring of palings to indicate a gentleman's park: he never intended his patrons to be able to calculate the heights of individual peaks or measure the extent of a particular estate. In much the same general way, Saxton waggled his streams and rivers across a county without strict regard to where the bends in reality occurred. Here and there he misplaced a river – or accidently invented one. And though he marked bridges, he made no attempt to show roads. Norden did put main roads on his maps. He used a simpler scale than Saxton, and by means of marginal numbers invented a quick reference system. But he confined his work to the southern counties.

Yet despite their imperfections, Saxton's and Norden's maps are precious historical documents. They were based on keen, if sometimes hurried, observation and measurement. They paint a good general picture of what the counties looked like in Elizabeth's reign: they show the relative sizes of the towns, the approximate area of woodland, marsh, and waste, and give us the Tudor pronunciation of many place names. At one and the same time, these maps are a demonstration of the Elizabethans' newly discovered, boastful pride in 'this precious stone set in a silver sea', and a by-product of the developing scientific outlook, which had recently produced the Copernican theory and was soon to be responsible for Kepler's *New Astronomy*.

John Speed's *The Theatre of the Empire of Great Britain* was the next important cartographical achievement. It was published in 1611. Speed unblushingly used the surveys of Saxton and other predecessors, and the advanced techniques displayed in his maps emanate more from the skill of his Dutch engraver, Jodocus Hondius, than from his own art. But Speed added one or two valuable town plans to each of the county maps he published. He usually chose the county town, but here and there surveyed a second: his *Kent*, for example, has plans of Canterbury and Rochester, his *Staffordshire* Stafford and Lichfield. Plans, or, more correctly, artistic impressions, of English towns were not new. Norden had inserted town plans on some of his county maps, and G. Braun's and F. Hogenberg's *Civitates Orbis Terrarum* (1572–98) had included pictorial plans of London, Canterbury, Exeter, Cambridge, Oxford, Ely, Norwich, Chester, and York. Speed used these surveys, but drew plans of another sixty-four towns, the streets of most of which he had paced out himself. Speed's plans had a long life. Some eighteenth-century publishers were still passing them off as up-to-date.

Maps lost none of their popularity during the reigns of the Stuarts. As the Tudor antiquary George Owen said of Saxton's maps, they remained 'usual with all noblemen and gentlemen, and were daily perused by them for their better instruction of the estate of this Realm'. Thanks chiefly to Dutch cartographers and engravers – Jansson and Blaeu are the two best known in this country – the technique of map-making improved considerably, but not until John Ogilby and his assistants began tracing and measuring the main roads of Britain with their 'wheel dimensurators' or 'perambulators' did we get anything that was significantly new. Ogilby published his book of road maps in 1675, the year before he died. He mapped the roads on what was considered to be a big scale, one inch to the mile; and he drew them in strips, similar to the strips prepared by motoring organizations today. Six or seven strips occupied each page of his atlas: the reader began at the bottom left-hand corner of the page, passed from the top of the first strip to the bottom of the second, and eventually finished the page in the top right-hand corner. The maps are full of information. They distinguish between open and enclosed fields, show inclines and declines, and record the destinations of all important side roads. Armed with an Ogilby map, the traveller could check his position either by using the compass point which indicated the direction of each strip, or by keeping his eye open for the marked inns, country houses, churches, mills, and occasional gibbet.

Ogilby's road maps were reprinted in several editions, and of course their information was quickly 'borrowed' by other cartographers. Robert Morden's county maps were among the first to superimpose Ogilby's roads on superficially revised old surveys. Nevertheless, Morden's 1695 maps – drawn particularly for a new edition of Camden's *Britannia* – were much more satisfactory than his 1676 maps, which had been published as *The 52 Counties of England and Wales described by a pack of cards*. Not only were they bigger – usually about four miles to the inch – but they marked latitudes and longitudes (based on degrees west of the City of London), traced several minor roads in each county, roughly indicated the changing depths of coastal and river waters, and went some way towards modernizing the spelling of place-names. Morden based some of his maps on Saxton, and some on later surveys. Therefore, the researcher has to use his maps with caution: alongside near-contemporary truth, he is likely to find details that were only true a hundred or more years earlier. And no serious student of Roman Britain will waste time on the Roman names which Morden put on his maps. This is not Morden's fault. He recorded the archaeological information of his day. It is later scholarship that has shown several of his Roman town names to be wrong, and a few of his Celtic tribes to be out of place.

Emanuel Bowen was the most popular cartographer of the first half of the eighteenth century. He was responsible for two major publications – *Britannia Depicta or Ogilby Improved* (1720) and, in collaboration with Thomas Kitchin, *The Large English Atlas* (1750–2). Both were successful ventures: the first went through twelve editions before 1764, and the second ten editions before 1800, despite the fact that in most counties it was superseded by far more accurate maps in the 1770s and 1780s. Bowen's *Atlas* maps, on big scales, sometimes approximately two miles to the inch, were well engraved. They marked main roads, many of which were newly turnpiked, hundred boundaries, latitude and longitude (not always accurately), vicarages and rectories, market towns, charity schools, and parliamentary boroughs. They even told the reader the market days of each market town. But their distinguishing feature was the topographical observations and titbits of historical detail which filled the margins and empty spaces. Unfortunately, these short paragraphs rarely if ever throw new light on the eighteenth century. They often do no more than list the prominent features of a township: occasionally they fail to mention anything of important recent changes. On the map of Cheshire, for example, Bowen wrote the following obvious comments on Malpas:

Malpas or Malopasous (said to be so called from the bad Road leading to it) is situate upon a high Hill, on which there also formerly stood a Castle; now in ruins. The Church is a stately Building, standing in the highest part of the Town and is remarkable for having two Rectors belonging to it. Here is a Grammar School and an Hospital founded by Sir Ranulph Brereton.

This information is correct enough, except that the bad road which gave its name to the place was the Roman road in Norman times, and not the pot-holed road of the eighteenth century which Bowen seems to imply. But the adjacent comment on Northwich was well out-of-date when the map was published:

... the Salt is not so white, nor made with so much ease, the Brine Pit being deep, and the Water drawn up with great toil in Leather Buckets.

Bowen apparently did not know that the discovery of rock salt at the end of the previous century, the navigating of the River Weaver in the 1730s, and the more recent use of mechanical pumps had transformed the salt industry at Northwich. He was better informed, if still imprecisely, on Manchester:

The Fustian Manufacture called Manchester Cottons which for a long time has been considerable in the Town has been of late very much improved by some modern Inventions in Dying [sic] and

Printing, which together with a great variety of other Manufacture as Ticking, Tapes, Filleting etc. distinguished by the Name of Manchester Wares have rendered both the Town and its Neighbourhood both rich and prosperous ...

Bowen dedicated each map to an influential aristocrat in the county, and prominently listed the seats of the county gentry, his chief patrons. But he did not resurvey the counties, and, from a cartographical and historical point of view, that was a task that was long overdue.

In 1759, the Society of Arts offered £100 to anyone who 'shall make an accurate Survey of any County upon the Scale of one Inch to a Mile'. Already there had been several attempts to do this. Gascoyne had produced a new survey of Cornwall as early as 1700, and in the 1720s there had been published new one inch to the mile maps of Denbigh and Flint, Sussex, and Surrey. The most technically advanced of these pioneering efforts was Henry Beighton's *Warwickshire*. Beighton based his map on a trigonometrical survey of the county. This new method gave his work greater accuracy, but his sketches of houses and 'prospects' of churches and windmills still made his map look old fashioned in the eyes of succeeding generations.

The Society of Arts' prize so effectively encouraged surveyors to begin work that during the next twenty-five years almost every county was adequately resurveyed. By 1787 only Norfolk and Cambridgeshire among English counties lacked a reasonably modern-looking, newly surveyed, big-scale map. Not many years separated Bowen's maps from, say, Chapman and André's *Essex* (1777) or John Prior's *Leicestershire* (1779), but they were far behind them in both preparation and presentation. And if you think Moll is a better representative than Bowen of the older cartographers, you can see a similar gulf between, say, Moll's map of Hampshire (1724) and Isaac Taylor's map of the same county just thirty-five years later.

Only about a dozen of the new surveys satisfied the exacting standards which the Society of Arts laid down for its prizewinners. Donn's *Devonshire* was the first in 1765; Burdett's *Derbyshire* the next in 1767. But failure to win the prize does not indicate that a map should be ignored, for all these new maps are well worth studying. They were surveyed on the new triangulation method. The surveyor began with a suitable base line, several miles long, preferably at sea level, and accurately measured with a surveyor's chain. Then, with a theodolite, he sited throughout the county a number of prominent points – the summit of hills, the tops of church spires, or outstanding towers, windmills, or houses. Once sufficient of these were accurately placed on the map, most of the rest of the work could be done by trigonometrical calculations. The map-maker still required the perambulator to measure the roads, and assistants on the ground to determine such details as the exact limits of woodlands or open fields, and the precise position of mill wheels, turnpike gates, or canal locks. But these he could now pinpoint on a mathematically calculated outline. Cartographical skills improved too. Gone were the sugarloaf hills, park palings, prospects, and exaggerated rivers. Instead hatchures indicated heights, different styles of printing separated categories of towns, and neat symbols marked such features as rectories, vicarages, dissenting chapels, toll bars, bridges, and coal pits.

These later eighteenth-century map-makers had a different set of values from their predecessors. Their interest in the details of the changing countryside and the developing towns led them to recognize that England was passing into a new age. Because they each portray their section of the country during the first stages of the Industrial Revolution, their work is particularly precious to those who are primarily interested in the history of the industrial areas. But the detailed evidence of all these maps needs to be handled with care. The historian has constantly to remember that maps were not surveyed in a day – or in a year – and that a decade often elapsed between the first stages of the survey and the publication of the map. And a decade in industrial Britain in the second half of the eighteenth century could easily transform a village into a town or revolutionize a district's communications. No cartographer can help the passage of time giving his map inaccuracies between survey and publication, but these eighteenth-century maps are prone to be patch-work pictures made up of sections of evidence acquired at intervals over a number of years. Most of the surveyors were part-time cartographers. They could not devote all their days to map-making, and frequently difficulties in securing sufficient sponsors held up their work for weeks. Therefore, their maps tend to have one part of the county reasonably up-to-date, another at least three or four years out-of-date, and a third as much as ten or twelve years out-of-date. For anyone content with a telescopic impression of his shire in the late eighteenth century, this hardly matters, but anyone seeking accurate detail will need to check the evidence of the map against such other manuscript sources as may be available. To find a building marked on a map published in 1780 is no convincing argument against a statement elsewhere that it was demolished in 1775: and, conversely, not to find a building marked on a map does not necessarily falsify other evidence that it was built at least five years before the map appeared. Again, despite their comparatively large scale, these new maps were still not big enough to show all details. Therefore, the researcher must interpret such things as the length of a straggling village or the rash of dots representing coalpits as general indications rather than meticulous plotting and enumeration. In non-industrial counties this close, almost pernickety, examination of the map is probably not necessary. The pace of change was not so fast, and therefore the historian can possibly rest content to accept the map's evidence on land utilization, communications, and relative sizes of towns and villages as true in general for the decade in which the map was published.

Most of these later eighteenth-century cartographers enriched their county maps by incorporating some of the recent work done by a number of marine surveyors. During the last twenty years of the previous century, Captain Greenville Collins had chartered several sections of British coastal waters from Shetland to the Channel. Between 1747 and 1786, the two Murdoch Mackenzies, uncle and nephew, produced new charts of the western and south-western waters from Orkney to the Isle of Wight. These were all official admiralty charts. But there were a number of good unofficial charts too, such as that of the approaches to the Thames published by a Frenchman, Jean Bellin, in 1769. They all enabled the cartographers of sea-board counties to plot channels, shallows, and sandbanks off the coast and in the approaches to their rivers. In a similar way, the county map-makers used some of the many excellent town plans which local surveyors periodically produced throughout the eighteenth century either as separate sheets or as illustrations for new books. When they appear as insets they are to be welcomed, but it is always necessary to check the date of the town survey against that of the county map itself. There is sometimes a substantial difference.

The needs of travellers for reliable maps, the general interest in cartography, and the prestige value of possessing collections of county maps all tended to increase rather than decrease as the eighteenth century gave way to the nineteenth. John Cary, who began his career in the late 1780s and died in 1835, was the outstanding map-publisher of his generation. He turned out a formidable array of atlases of county maps, road books, prints, and globes. In his presentation of detail and in his engraving, Cary displayed exceptional care and skill. He revised his maps before he reprinted, and, in those golden days of the stage coach, paid special attention to the mapping of roads. But his revisions were done in the drawing office and not in the field. Once, early in his career and at the bidding of the postmaster general, he surveyed 'the Great Roads, both Direct and Cross', but most of the time he relied for his revisions upon plans in recent directories, estate and enclosure maps, or the deposited plans that accompanied private parliamentary Bills. He did no basic surveying. Yet he was a most successful publisher. His only serious rival for most of his career was Charles Smith, another London-based cartographer and engraver.

But in the difficult years that followed the end of the Napoleonic Wars, Cary and Smith became increasingly aware of the high quality of the work of a young Yorkshire cartographer, Christopher Greenwood. In 1818 Greenwood published a completely new survey of his native county, and followed it with similar maps of Lancashire and Cheshire. From this beginning he went on to survey other counties – Middlesex, Durham, Wiltshire, Warwickshire, Somerset, and Cumberland were among the first – so that by 1834, twenty years after he had begun, Greenwood, with help from his brother John, had published new maps of thirty-five counties. Unfortunately, the Greenwoods never attained their ambition of resurveying every county in England and Wales. It was not through lack of energy. Indeed their constant need to keep their business solvent compelled them to make undue haste in completing their surveys. Even so they lost the struggle, because it was financial troubles that eventually compelled them to abandon their unfinished project.

Christopher Greenwood used triangulations as his predecessors had done, but he had the great advantage of building on foundations recently laid with unusual care by the Board of Ordnance. By the time Greenwood began his work, the Board had already published an outline survey covering the whole of England and Wales. Greenwood had need to supplement this considerably with his own work, but in each county it gave him ready-made a handful of survey points correctly fixed by latitude and longitude and in accurate relation to each other. Greenwood's detailed surveying was good. He traced parish boundaries, carefully defined the limits of urban areas, and with neat symbols, some of which he adopted from the first ordnance survey maps, marked the usual topographical features of both town and countryside. He checked his maps against previous maps of the area and against information in auxiliary publications: 'every description of authentic information, which may be communicated, will be most scrupulously attended to', declared his advance prospectus for his map of Cheshire. Nevertheless, his need for haste betrays itself in the want of such details as the course of some small streams, the generalization of industrial sites, and the lack of information about fields and woodlands remote from roads. To try to keep pace with the ever-changing landscape, the Greenwoods republished revised versions of their maps, reduced in scale, between 1828 and 1834. Of course, revision is the battle which every cartographer, ancient or modern, is bound to lose. But it was not unknown for some of them to gain a temporary victory by intelligent anticipation. Hennet's map of Lancashire, for example, shows both the Liverpool–Manchester railway and the St Helens–Runcorn Gap railway as working concerns. The map was published in 1828; the two railways were opened in 1830 and 1833 respectively. But when Hennet made his map, the railway lines were either in building or planned in detail. It was a fairly safe bet that they would be in action before long.

By the 1830s, however, the day of the private county-map surveyor and publisher was almost over. The official ordnance survey work was growing each year, and private cartographers could not hope to compete in efficiency if they were going to make their business pay. The ordnance survey – so called be-cause it began under the supervision of the master-general of

the ordnance – dates from 1791. The first map, an inch to the
mile map of Kent, appeared in 1801. Four years later the
systematic publication of numbered inch to the mile sheets
began with those of Essex. During the next ten years, the surveyors worked in the counties bordering on the Channel.
The 1830s found them covering the Midlands from East Anglia
to Cardigan Bay; the 1840s busy in the industrial North. The
first survey of England and Wales reached its triumphant
end with the publication of the Isle of Man sheets in 1873.

During the eighty years it spent making this survey, the
Board of Ordnance improved its methods and its skills. Its
surveyors of the early-Victorian period were critical of the
work of their predecessors. They had found from recent
experience in Ireland that they produced more accurate and
satisfactory maps if they drew their basic surveys six inches to
the mile instead of on the usual two-inch scale. Therefore, in the
early 1840s, they began to do this regularly. Number 91 sheet,
covering the Morecambe Bay area, was the first English map
to be based on this more detailed survey. The first section of the
sheet appeared in 1845, but it took another twenty-five years
to survey the rest of England north of the Ribble and the
Humber. The main cause of the delay was the urgent call to
revise the new outdated maps of the southern and midland
counties. There was no denying the need for revision. Maps
made thirty and forty years previously gave little idea of such
areas as the Black Country or the metropolitan area in the 1850s
and 1860s. The revision was competent enough, but since the
revised maps had not entailed new surveys they still carried the
date of the original publication. Nothing could be more
calculated to trap the unwary researcher. There is, however, a
rule of thumb that will save him from error more often than
not. If an ordnance-survey map of any part of England and
Wales south of the Ribble-Humber line shows parish boundaries and has latitude and longitude marked in the margins, it

is almost certainly a revised map issued later than 1840. After 1872 Board of Ordnance surveyors began systematically to survey southern and midland England and Wales on the new scale, and the result was the publication, in 360 sheets, of a second edition of the one inch to the mile maps. This was completed by 1899. Further revision began immediately, and the Board completed its third edition just before the outbreak of the First World War. Since then revision has been continuous, and fortunately better methods of printing have made less laborious the Sisyphean task of trying to keep ordnance survey maps up-to-date.

A very useful by-product of the larger-scale surveying carried out after 1840 was a collection of town plans. The first to be published (in 1844) was that of the rapidly growing township of St Helens in Lancashire. It was on the huge scale of five feet to the mile. Rapidly there followed similar plans not only for most towns in Lancashire and Yorkshire, but for the London districts, Southampton, Windsor, and Kingston-on-Thames. Then, from 1855 to 1894, the Board published nearly 400 English and Welsh town plans on the even larger scale of ten feet to the mile. Some of these were revised versions of earlier surveys, but, since each sheet carries the date of revision and survey, all of them are straightforward historical documents. They are so detailed that they show each separate house and yard, and even the main rooms of the biggest public buildings. They thus preserve a record of many buildings now destroyed, and of areas of towns that bombs or improvers and developers have long since swept away. Unfortunately, none of these plans have been published since 1894.

The town plans are the most detailed surveys the Board has produced, but after 1840 it began to publish the six inch to the mile survey upon which it had based its new one-inch maps. After 1853 it went further, and ventured a new series of twenty-five inch to the mile maps. Before the end of the century, twenty-five inch maps were available for all but the more remote areas of England and Wales. In many ways, these are as useful to the local historian as the town plans. They give all the agricultural, industrial, and topographical information he is likely to want – fields and field names, carefully defined woodland and marsh, quarries and pits, mills, factories, small-holdings and gardens, secular and ecclesiastical boundaries, and paths and rights-of-way however short and insignificant. To make them even more useful, the Board issued booklets to accompany the maps it published between 1855 and 1886. Until 1872 it entitled the booklets *Parish Area Books*; after that year, *Books of Reference*. The chief additional information they give is the area of separate fields and the use to which the farmer was putting them.

It is difficult to imagine the historical interest which is not furthered by a map of one kind or other. Early ordnance survey maps mark archaeological sites many of which have now been destroyed; and eighteenth-century maps occasionally draw 'prospects' of houses, monastic ruins, or castles since over-whelmed by modern needs. A sequence of maps can graphically reveal such varied things as changes in land use, the speed and extent of enclosure and of urban development, the magnetic way a new canal or railway drew industry and housing to-wards it, the encouragement turnpikes gave to ribbon building, the growing network of communications, changing boun-daries, and, with a little interpretation, changing patterns of social life. Maps are lanterns particularly unto the feet of in-dustrial and agricultural historians, and lights unto the paths of industrial archaeologists and historical geographers. But as sources of historical knowledge, maps need allies. To make accurate and full use of them, the researcher must call in the newspapers, directories, prints, photographs, and topogra-phical descriptions which help to supplement and interpret their valuable information.

3. PRINTS, GUIDE-BOOKS, AND TRAVELLERS' TALES

We have seen that successful map-making depended upon the skill of the copper-plate engraver as much as on the scientific accuracy of the surveyor. In the eighteenth and early nineteenth centuries, the educated had a high regard for the work of good engravers and etchers. They looked with a critical eye at the fineness of the engraver's lines, appreciated the half-tone effects achieved by skilful etching, and argued the advantages and disadvantages of lithography. Engravers and etchers were required for all kinds of work. Gentlemen delighted to collect Hogarth prints and engravings of popular paintings. Political groups found cartoons an effective means of discrediting their opponents. James Gillray, who, with Thomas Rowlandson, was the leading cartoonist of the Younger Pitt and Charles James Fox era, was an engraver before he turned political satirist. Book publishers demanded prints in plenty. For guide books they wanted maps and vignettes of streets and public buildings. For travellers' tales they liked to have impressions of mighty mountains and unknown lochs, for works of fiction sketches of incidents and portrayals of characters in action. An outstandingly successful illustrator could delineate a fictional character for all time. Mr Pickwick, Sam Weller, Oliver Twist and many more of the Dickensians are instantly recognizable on the screen or stage, simply because 'Phiz's' or Cruikshank's vision of them has been universally accepted.

Making fine prints and mounting them as single sheets was another side of the engraver's business. Some sold them through booksellers and local agents; others imitated the map-makers and invited subscribers to commit themselves in advance to purchase a series of prints. Nothing was so popular among the aristocracy and landed gentry as prints of country houses.

Interest in architectural styles and in the landscaping of private parks developed into a passion. In the first half of George III's reign, the Adam brothers set the fashion in building, and Lancelot Brown in gardening: in the second half, the lead passed to James Wyatt, John Soane, John Nash, and, in gardening, Humphrey Repton. The well-established aristocratic families were as eager as the new industrial and commercial families to have their house and park in commendable style. Robert Adam, for example, redesigned Syon House for the Duke of Northumberland and Bowood for Lord Lansdowne, as well as Osterley Park for Child the banker and Woolton Hall for Ashton the merchant. In the Regency period, John Nash's and Sir John Soane's work was just as widely distributed, and between them, in their different styles, Capability Brown and Repton must have redesigned almost every sizeable private park in England and Wales.

This enthusiasm for architecture and landscaping bubbled over into print publishing. In the late 1770s, for example, William Watts began planning his *Seats of the Nobility and Gentry*. He published it in parts. Part one appeared in 1779: six years later he was publishing part nineteen despite a succession of serious mishaps such as the bankruptcy of his original publisher and the imprisonment of his letter-press printer. The price of each part to subscribers was 3s. 6d., but it is doubtful if Watts would ever have finished the project if a number of gentlemen had not been willing to pay two or three guineas for the original drawing of their seats and had not ordered a dozen or two extra prints. The drawings, mostly done by local artists, vary considerably in artistic merit. More to the point for the historian, they vary in the degree of truth they convey. There was no sale for an unflattering picture. Patrons wanted their homes to look larger than life and to be given an idealized setting. Artists therefore not only chose the best viewpoint from which to see the property, but they added imaginary amenities and, if necessary, obscured with foliage less worthy parts of the house.

Watts had many followers. J. P. Neale's *Views of the seats of Noblemen and Gentlemen in England, Wales, Scotland, and Ireland* is the late-Regency counterpart of his work, and in the next generation Edward Twycross published *Mansions of England and Wales*. The text in each of these books, as in similar books of the period, is sometimes enlightening, but it was always intended to be subordinate to the prints. Time has not altered this relationship. These publications retain their interest chiefly because, despite their idealization, the prints give us a visual impression of what the buildings and the parks looked like. Little of this kind can be found for earlier days. Cartoons, architectural plans, and landscape paintings have survived from the previous two centuries. 'Prospects' were popular in Anne's and George I's reign, but not until George III's reign do we get these many drawings which give us almost photographic impressions not only of palaces and famous parks, but also of relatively small houses and obscure gardens. We must, of course, make allowances for the artistic liberties and flourishes. It may well be that, despite the evidence of the print, the squire never owned deer, nor the wealthy merchant so fine and large a herd of cattle as the artist shows grazing in his meadow. Certainly such a magnificent coach as that shown in the print infrequently added distinction to the drive of the industrialist's home, and he rarely, if ever, had time to ride with hounds across his park. But the drawings can be accepted as basically truthful. The house must have been in the architectural style depicted – if the drawing was not recognizable, the owner would have no joy in sending copies to his friends – and the carriages, riders' habits, and bystanders' costumes must all be in the current style. The idealization is usually no worse than that of the late-Victorian tradesman photographed in unaccustomed high collar and tall hat, or than that of property advertisements to be found today in estate agents' windows, or pictures of hotel amenities in travel agents' brochures.

With contemporary map and appropriate prints in one hand, the historian 'traveller' must find a matching guide-book for the other, so that he can thoroughly explore the town or area of his choice in the late eighteenth or nineteenth century. He should not have far to seek, especially if his chosen place is one that attracted reasonable attention in the days of the Georges and of Victoria, for the publication of guide-books increased steadily from about the middle of the eighteenth century. The earliest examples are single volumes by local authors. By the end of the eighteenth century a few popular authors were writing one guide-book after another, and, fifty years later still, the uniform series, published by such firms as Black's, Murray's, and Nelson's, dominated the market.

The early guide-books varied considerably in style and quality. They had no fixed pattern, except that they all set out to give the visitor plenty of local information in a small book which he could easily carry about in his pocket. What facts each book provided depended on the interests and outlook of the author. Many began with a history of the town. The influence of William Stukeley is clearly to be seen in most of these potted histories: Roman remains and Gothic architecture usually loom large. Other guide-books gave most of their space to public buildings or to churches: some listed the times of coach and passenger-barge arrivals and departures, the cost of lodgings and local entertainments, and the details of bathing facilities, church services, and postal deliveries and despatches. Nearly all had information about the 'seats' in the area, and about the houses and gardens that the visitor might care to see. None of these earlier guide-books were cheap. The author addressed himself to 'lady' and 'gentleman' visitors, and such readers expected to be shown over a stately home if they presented themselves at the gate. If my lord were not available, the housekeeper would probably admit them. So widespread became this practice of viewing that owners of outstanding houses, such as Chatsworth, Woburn, or Holkham, had, in self-defence, to confine visitors to set hours. The owners made no charge. They seemed content that strangers should wish to call and admire the design of their house, the prospects of their park, the beauty of their pictures, and the elegance of their rooms and furniture.

The 'Gentleman of Oxford' who wrote *The New Oxford Guide or Companion through the University* which was published in 1759 claimed that his book was 'founded on actual observation, and compiled from a real and attentive survey of every particular which it describes'. He did not attempt a history of the city: after five pages of general topographical description, he toured such public buildings as St Mary's, the Ashmolean, the Clarendon Printing House, and 'the Physic Garden'. This is how he described the 'sumptuous pile' of the Radcliffe Camera, which was only fourteen or fifteen years old when he was writing:

The building stands on arcades, which, circularly disposed, enclose a spacious dome in the centre. From hence we pass by a well executed flight of spiral steps into the Library itself. This room, which is a complete pattern of elegance and majesty, rises into a capacious dome, ornamented with fine compartments of stucco ... The room is enclosed by a circular series of arches, beautified with festoons, and supported by pilasters of the Ionic order. Behind these arches are formed two circular galleries, above and below, where the books are disposed in elegant cabinets ... The first stone was laid May 17, A.D. 1737, and the Library was opened April 13, 1745 with great solemnity.

After the public buildings, the author took each college in turn. He spent four or five pages describing the outstanding features of each of them. From the following description of New College Chapel, it is evident that those typical guide and guide-book statistics of doubtful use to any tourist have a long lineage:

We enter the Chapel at the north-west corner. The Chapel exceeds all in the University. The Ante-Chapel, which is supported by four pillars of fine proportion, runs at right angles to the Choir, and is 80 feet long and 36 broad. The Choir, which we enter by a Gothic Screen of beautiful construction, is 100 feet long, 35 broad, and 65 high. From hence the Painting over the altar, done about 60 years ago, by Mr Henry Cook, is seen to the best advantage.

Not unexpectedly, the author devoted his last forty pages to a description of three nearby seats, Blenheim, Ditchley, and Stowe.

The 'Gentleman of Oxford' wrote as objectively as he could, but there were guide-book authors who did not hesitate to express strong opinions or to indulge personal interests in their books. The anonymous author of *The Leominster Guide* of 1803, for example, let his readers know what he thought of the new religious group, the Methodists:

The Methodists are an increasing sect, and formidable as well for their numbers as for their proselyting zeal. Their visits to Leominster are of recent date. At present they possess no established place of worship here, but have hired a malt house in Etnam Street, and have also purchased a house in the Middle Marsh, which is intended to be converted to that purpose. Those who have exhibited their appearance at Leominster profess the religious tenets of the celebrated John Wesley, a man of inflexible resolution, primitive piety, and considerable erudition; whose name and whose exertions will be revered, while lazy and avaricious ecclesiastics will be ingulphed in oblivion.

His views on 'the house of industry' were equally explicit:

[The author] conceives that these asylums of the poor are denominated houses of industry by the same right that a grove is in Latin called *Lucus*, which is derived from *lux*, light; because a grove is impervious to the rays of light ... a house of industry is a place wherein no specimens of industry are displayed.

This guide-book is also one of the type that devotes a section to industry and commerce. Wheat growing and flour milling were flourishing in Leominster in 1803, but cotton spinning and paper manufacture had virtually ceased. The author did not regret this. He recognized that the town had lost wealth, but he thought that it had gained something more valuable by maintaining a higher moral tone. Factories, which he admitted were essential for competitive cotton and paper production, he considered to be morally dangerous and un-desirable:

where a number of poor ignorant people of both sexes, old and young, virtuous and abandoned, associate together, corruption and vice will necessarily diffuse their mischievous influence.

A few early guide-books give so much detail about industry and commerce in their area that they constitute useful sources for industrial archaeologists as well as for economic historians. The revised *Picture of Newcastle upon Tyne*, published in 1812, predictably devoted almost forty pages to the Roman Wall, but, not so predictably, had a considerably longer section full of information about coal mining. Not only did it describe the extent and production of the industry, but it went into detail about the different seams and the various methods of mining and transporting coal. It even had a glossary of technical terms used in the industry:

Winning Head-ways are narrow drifts about two yards wide, in a north and south direction, and are generally the first formation of the workings.

Frame-Dams are made of beams of square fir timber, about three feet long, laid length-ways, closely joined and firmly wedged together. They are used for damming water; and in mines frequently raise it to a great height.

Wastemen: persons that daily examine the state of the workings, and see that they be properly ventilated.

Gin-drivers are boys employed to drive the horses in the gin or engine used in raising coals from pits of moderate depth.

Industrial and commercial information tended to become a commoner feature of guides as the nineteenth century advanced. J. Wodderspoon's *New Guide to Ipswich* (1842), for example, accorded a dozen pages to the story of the planning, building, and recent opening of the wet dock. Local pride inspired every word, and, despite his regret that 'in modern days' Ipswich did not possess 'any particular staple of her own – if, perhaps, we except the making of ladies' stays', Wodderspoon displayed his unshakeable faith in the future prosperity of the town. He listed Ipswich's economic assets: her oil-cake industry, iron foundries, paper mills, 'the largest agricultural implement manufactory in England – and therefore the most extensive in the world', and her malt making, of which he boasted 'perhaps there is no other town of the same magnitude, in which so great a quantity of barley is manufactured into this article as at Ipswich'.

London, of course, had lots of guide-books. During the first third of the nineteenth century, the *Picture of London* alone was reissued in a new edition every year. These handy books, illustrated with engravings, plans, and folded maps, were stuffed with tourist information. Much of it is of historical interest today. We might readily skip the opening historical summary, but different researchers, according to their lines of investigation, will still find useful the details of streets and buildings, the lists of exhibitions, theatres, and inns, the timetables of coaches and canal fly boats, and even the recommended 'twelve days perambulation in London and its environs'.

Guides for spas, bathing places, and the Lake District did not fall far short in number of the London guides. Each revised edition tended to be more compact and selective in detail. Francis Coghlan, one of the most energetic of guide publishers, introduced his 1838 edition of *Brighton and its Environs* with the statement that there was now no need to waste space recounting once again the history 'of this fashionable bathing place, or, to use a modern phrase, *watering-place*'. Instead he proposed to fill his 106 pages with up-to-date information. The visitor could hardly have had a more informative companion. Maps of the environs and a pull-out street map prevented him from getting lost. The list of coaches to London gave him no excuse for being late. It began:

> The *Vivid*, morning at six, from the Spread Eagle
> The *New Times*, morning at seven, from the Red Office

and ended, sixteen lines later,

> The *Times*, evening at 4.30, from the Red Office.
> H.M.R.P. Mail, evening at 11, from the Blue Office.

Details of hotels, boarding houses, hackney coach fares, libraries, riding masters, the hiring of bathing machines, and pier admission charges per day, per week, or per season saved him making numerous inquiries, and a full description of the German Spa, 'an establishment for manufacturing artificial mineral waters', let him know what to expect for his guinea subscription for a week's treatment:

> The patient commences with the water of low temperature, and with two or three glasses of six ounces each, which are increased gradually to six, eight, or ten, and sometimes more, according to the effects; and the warm springs are exchanged for the hotter ones, as the disease seems to require. When the waters do not act upon the bowels, a small quantity of Carlsbad salts are taken with them, or a glass or two of Seidschütz.

There was even news of desirable developments and of delights to come:

Operations have at length commenced upon this long contested railway [Brighton and London Railroad], and it is expected to be completed by 1841. A branch to Shoreham is also in progress which will be opened in 1839. The distance to London will be 50 miles 57 chains.

Cruchley's guides and Kidd's guides competed with Coghlan's in the more popular watering places, but from 1778, when it first appeared, Thomas West's *Guide to the Lakes* was the doyen of numerous books written about the Lake District in the next fifty years. It deserved to be. It coupled practical tourist information with descriptions that induced that poetical, romantic euphoria which every tourist expected to experience. This, for example, is how West taught the sensitive tourist to see Derwentwater:

On the floor of a spacious amphitheatre, of the most picturesque mountains imaginable, an elegant sheet of water is spread out before you, shining like a mirror, and transparent as crystal; variegated with islands adorned with wood, or clothed with the forest verdure, that rise in the most pleasing forms above the watery plane ... no words can describe the surprising pleasure of this scene, on a fine day, when the sun plays on the basin of the lake, and the surrounding mountains are illuminated by his refulgent rays, and their rocky summits invertedly reflected by the surface of the water.

Thomas West's famous book strays part way across the territory that divides the guide-book from the traveller's tale. Travel literature was voluminous in the eighteenth and nineteenth centuries. Numerous *tours*, *itineraries*, *excursions*, *journeys*, and *rides* flowed from the quills of reflective travellers. Everyone, enlarging the tradition of Leland, Camden, Celia Fiennes, and Defoe, burned to record for their own satisfaction and the enlightenment of their contemporaries their experiences, thoughts, and feelings as they walked, rode, or sailed from place to place in these small islands. Some of their books are too slight or too fanciful to be of lasting interest, but others are historical sources which are too often ignored or undervalued. The three different *Tours* of Arthur Young and *The Rural Rides* of William Cobbett are deservedly well known and appreciated, but there are many more that have almost been forgotten. They are all highly personal, but they often convey historical information in interesting and unusual ways. In 1836, four years after Brunel began work on the Clifton suspension bridge, 'Pedestres' described what it was like when his paddle steamer set off down the Gorge towards the Severn estuary.

It was a quarter before seven in the morning when the packet put her kettle of hot water on the fire, and began to bubble, squeak, smoke, groan, splash and flounder down the river like a porpoise. The tide was falling, and a strong current co-operated with the paddle-wheels: but there was no relaxation of steam on our part, and, consequently, by the united efforts of both, we made more knots during the first few miles of our voyage, than we were at all able to do afterwards. We soon glided away from before Clifton; and the serpentine direction of our course very quickly hid the houses from our view. The light grey cliffs stood over us in towering grandeur, and we felt like pigmies creeping round the sides of a mountain. In imagination we saw the intended suspension-bridge stretching across the chasm like a dark band through the heavens, and uniting the rocks from one summit to the other. We would have fancied we heard the hollow rumbling of wheels on the flying road-way so high above our heads; and we would have cherished the idea, that we saw the massive piers rising like towers on each bank and supporting the ponderous chains...

Not all travellers were as imaginative as 'Pedestres'. L. Simond, a French visitor in 1810 and 1811, was a more practical observer. He was distrustful of the design of English stage coaches:

Those made like a vessel are of modern invention, and carry all their passengers inside. I have counted on the top of others as many as seventeen persons. These carriages are not suspended, but rest on steel springs of a flattened oval shape, less easy than the old mode of leathern braces on springs. The consequence of this accumulation of weight on the top is a dangerous tendency to overturn. If a double tier of passengers is necessary, the lower should at least be very near the ground. This has been in part attended to, for some of these stage coaches carry their baggage below the level of the axeltree.

Most of the authors of these travel books were appreciative of the developments that were going on in England and Wales. Some of them in good guide-book style described what they saw. In 1836, for example, Thomas Roscoe set down these facts and this personal impression of the Pontycysyllte aqueduct:

As a work of magnificence and art, this splendid aqueduct is not surpassed by any structure of the kind known in modern times. It impresses the beholder with admiration of the extent of human power and skill, directed by the light of science, and executed by the combination of human energies and wealth. It is situated about four miles from Llangollen, extends 988 feet, consists of 19 arches, each 45 in the span, without including 6 inches of iron-work in continuation at each end . . . The effect of the whole upon the eye is peculiarly striking.

Others also looked deeper and discussed the social and economic advantages that had been derived from technological improvements. In 1780, a mere three years after its completion, Thomas Pennant made these observations about the effect of constructing the Grand Trunk Canal:

Notwithstanding the clamors which were raised against this undertaking, in the places through which it was intended to pass, when it was first projected, we have the pleasure now to see content reign universally on its banks, and plenty attend its progress. The cottage, instead of being half-covered with miserable thatch, is now secured with a substantial covering of tiles or slates, brought from the distant hills of Wales or Cumberland. The fields, which before were barren, are now drained, and, by the assistance of manure, conveyed on the canal toll free, are clothed with a beautiful verdure. Places, which rarely knew the use of coal, are plentifully supplied with that essential article upon reasonable terms: and, what is of still greater public utility, the monopolizers of corn are prevented from exercising their infamous trade; for, by the communication being opened between Liverpool, Bristol, and Hull, and the line of the canal being through countries abundant in grain, it affords a conveyance for corn unknown to past ages. At present, nothing but a general dearth can create a scarcity in any part adjacent to this extensive work.

From such passages we can recapture the hope and optimism that canals, railways, factories, and steam ships brought to the developing industrial Britain. We are not likely to forget the human misery and the inequalities of wealth, but our historical picture will not be complete if we exclude from our understanding of the early days of the Industrial Revolution such men as Pennant, who saw a general good growing out of technical improvement.

4. ENCLOSURE ACTS, TITHE AWARDS, GLEBE TERRIERS, AND LAND TAX RETURNS

There is no lack of auxiliary sources for those who wish to study agricultural history or the man-made features of our landscape. Information is ever likely to be found lurking in such general documents as letters, newspapers, and diaries, but three particular sources – enclosure acts, tithe awards, and glebe terriers – offer details unlikely to be discovered elsewhere. All three are highly specialized documents: in their own narrow field, they often give us more detail than we usually need. But no one studying the history of a parish or a district, rural or urban, in the eighteenth or nineteenth century can afford to ignore any of them.

The corollary of the rapid growth of industrial towns during and after George III's reign was the need to produce considerably more food from British soil. This was achieved partly by new tools and techniques, and partly by enclosing open fields and common lands. Enclosures were nothing new. In the Middle Ages both individual landholders and communities made frequent *assarts* and *encroachments* into the waste and the forest, and neighbouring landholders occasionally sealed agreements to enclose nearby woodlands or to divide and cultivate waste and common pasture between them. In pre-Tudor, Tudor, and Stuart times, manor courts and vestries recorded decisions to fence common land into private enclosures – usually for sheep-rearing – and to subdivide open fields into compact holdings. Many of these changes the lord of the manor or two or three of the richer landholders dictated in order to increase demesne, production, and profits, but just as many occurred because there was mutual agreement between most of the villagers concerned. Outside those areas of Britain where the traditional open three-field system dominated agriculture, it often suited a villager to sell his neighbour his strips in the open field – a factor of diminishing importance in the local economy – and devote all his energy to cultivating and enlarging the holding he had inherited or acquired on the outskirts of the village.

Before George III's reign, enclosure was slow, but in the later eighteenth century it accelerated markedly. The growing towns offered convenient and profitable markets; this ever-increasing incentive to grow better crops and rear more stock insistently drew attention to the inefficiency of the open-field farming and the wastefulness of large, untended commons. The bigger farmers pressed for more enclosure. They argued economic necessity, and used the natural sympathy and fellow-feeling they found in land-owning Lords and Commons to get parliamentary sanction for their schemes. The procedure was the usual one for private Acts – petition for permission to introduce the Bill followed by discussion of the Bill in both Houses. In the reign of Farmer George, Parliament passed more than 3,000 such Acts. It usually appointed commissioners to visit the manor or parish, inspect the proposed enclosures, and arrange compensation for those who could prove they were surrendering land or rights.

The Napoleonic Wars seemed to quicken the demand for enclosures. But the restoration of peace did not slow it down again, because the chief influence on enclosures was not the needs of armies or the commercial consequences of war, but the redistribution of population. By 1815 the industrial towns were growing more rapidly than they had ever done in the eighteenth century, and this growth was to go on unhindered for at least another sixty or seventy years. Consequently, the urge to enclose became more and more insistent. Not surprisingly, a series of nineteenth-century general Acts made enclosure easier and less expensive; in particular the Enclosure Act of 1836 allowed a two-thirds majority of landowners to compel a village or parish to enclose, and the Act of 1845 invested a permanent commission with powers to enclose land wherever it considered action was needed.

The century which followed George III's accession witnessed the enclosure of almost 7,000,000 acres. But by the time Gladstone and Disraeli dominated politics, a reaction was already apparent. Hardly anyone wanted to see open fields preserved, but an increasing number of people were deploring the threatened total disappearance of common land. The Commons Preservation Act of 1876 slowed up the enclosure movement considerably. But by that date, rural England had already been transformed. Hedges, fences, and stone walls divided most of the countryside into private fields. The traditional open fields had virtually disappeared, and there was comparatively little common land left. Man-made features were more prominent than ever in English scenery.

There is no set pattern in enclosure history. Some enclosures brought general benefit to the parish; others profit to the few but misery and gross injustice to the many. Some were achieved naturally with widespread consent, others occasioned bitter strife; some occurred early, others surprisingly late. But at least all the post-1760 enclosures should be sufficiently documented to be capable of being studied in detail. For those enclosures made by private Act, there is both the petition setting out the justification for enclosing, and the Act itself. The *Journal of the Commons*, for example, summarizes the petition presented on 21 February 1798 for the enclosure of Kensworth in Hertfordshire. It is in routine form:

A Petition of the several Persons, whose names are thereunto subscribed, Proprietors of, and Persons interested in, the Open and Common Fields, and other Commonable Lands and Grounds, in the Parish of Kensworth, in the County of Hertford, was presented to the House, and read; Setting forth, That the Lands and Grounds of the several Proprietors, in the said Open and Common Fields, are divided into small Parcels, and lie intermixed with each other, and the same, together with the other Commonable Lands and Grounds aforesaid, are, in their present Situation, incapable of any considerable Improvement; but, if the same were divided and inclosed, and specific Allotments thereof set out to the several Owners and Persons interested therein, according to their respective Rights and Interests, the same might be considerably improved . . .

The Commons accepted this petition. The first reading of the Bill was on 27 April, the second on 4 May. In the committee stage the Bill was amended in some minor details. No one appeared before the Committee to oppose the Bill, but 'the Owners of 122 Acres of Land' refused to sign that they supported it. Since, however, the owners of the other 1,842 acres expressed their approval, the Commons had no hesitation in passing the Bill. On 26 May the Lords returned the Bill with further amendments. The *Journal of the Lords* has this entry dated 25 May:

> The Lord Walsingham reported from the Lords Committees ... That they had considered the said Bill, and examined the Allegations thereof, which were found to be true; that the Parties concerned had given their consents to the Satisfaction of the Committee; and that the Committee had gone through the Bill, and made some Amendments thereto ...
>
> Pr. 46. L.9. After ('Kensworth') insert ('or held in Right of any Church or Chapel')
>
> L.11. After ('Lincoln') insert ('and the Patron or Patrons of the said Vicarage Church or Chapel') ...

There were four such small amendments. The Commons accepted all of them without demur, and the Bill received the royal assent on 1 June. The Act was filed among the Private Acts with the title

> An Act for dividing and allotting, with Powers to inclose, the Open and Common Fields, Common Pastures, Commons, and Waste Lands, within the Parish of Kensworth, in the County of Hertford.

Copies of many enclosure Acts, with their all-important plans, have now found their way to county and other local record offices. The British Museum and the libraries of Cambridge University and London School of Economics have big collections, but the most complete collection is in the House of Lords' Record Office.

Between the original petition and the Act, there was, of course, considerable discussion. Opponents of a Bill were entitled to voice their objections: occasionally, requests were made to enlarge the scope of the proposed enclosure. In February 1807, Thomas Panton sought permission to introduce a Bill to enclose and 'exonerate from great and small Tithes' certain 'Open and Common Fields, Meadows, Commons and Waste Lands' in the parishes of St Andrew the Great, St. Andrew the Less, and St Mary the Less in Cambridge. This roused considerable local feeling. On 23 March, 'the Chancellor, Masters, and Scholars' of the University petitioned that they might be heard, through their counsel, against the Bill. A month later, 'several Inhabitants of the Town of Cambridge' begged leave to speak in favour of the Bill, and 'the Master, Fellows, and Scholars of Christ College' asked the House to insert a clause authorizing Christ College to purchase at least two acres of the common known as Christ Pieces, 'extending the whole length of the Watercourse from the Sluice at Christ College back gate to the ditch at the lower end of the said Pieces'. The college gave good reasons for making this request:

... the said Pieces of Land abut upon the very walls of Christ College, insomuch that a temporary fence has been necessary for the protection of the College windows from the cattle which are turned upon the said Pieces in the summer; and that the said Pieces, being common, it has of late become the practice of the Town's people to lodge their night soil immediately under the College windows, and the Petitioners need not point out to the House how much this evil is likely to be increased when the said Pieces are the only Common Land uninclosed so near the Town ...

The Commons referred these three petitions to the committee of the House which was considering the details of the Bill, and ordered that 'all who come to the Committee are to have voice'. It would appear that the attorney who represented 'the Chancellor, Masters, and Scholars' had the more authoritative or persuasive voice, because neither the *Journal of the Commons* nor the *Journal of the Lords* has anything more to record about this Bill. Presumably, the committee killed it with its adverse vote. Perhaps Thomas Panton would have been more successful if, in cleric-dominated Cambridge, he had not included the clause about being exonerated from tithes, although it had long been common enough for tithe-holders to exchange their rights for a lump sum of money or for a parcel of ground when common land was enclosed.

The General Enclosure Act of 1836 made private Bills unnecessary. Henceforward, a public meeting had power to appoint a commissioner, who would measure, divide, and enclose the common land, and then enrol the agreement with the clerk of the peace of the county. The award was always detailed enough to be a practical document: the plan recorded the square measure of each enclosure, but in style varied from a barely adequate sketch of what the award decreed to a pair of carefully surveyed maps, the first showing the distribution of land before enclosure and the second the new apportionment. Enclosure plans, therefore, cannot be automatically accepted as an exact delineation of the enclosed area. And the commissioners' surveyors varied in skills as well as methods. It is therefore wise to treat these documents as complementary, if not supplementary, to county maps, ordnance survey maps, tithe maps, town plans, estate maps, modern aerial surveys, and any written evidence that might be available.

Nevertheless, enclosure awards and plans must be accepted as nothing less than major historical documents. The simple fact that enclosures revolutionized the system of landholding and farming would be sufficient to put them into that category, but in addition they are the best single source for ascertaining the types of tenure of land in a village, the rents set aside for financing schools and local charities, and details of land draining and customary rights of way. In 1762 Great Harwood Moor near Blackburn was enclosed. Two local arbitrators, 'indifferently elected and chosen', divided the moor between two substantial land-owners; two-thirds went to Sir Thomas Hesketh and one-third to Alexander Nowell. On the plan the arbitrators coloured Hesketh's lands green and Nowell's red. But they also safeguarded access:

And that a way, eight yards wide at the least, shall be laid out and opened through certain closes allotted to the said Alexander Nowell, to be for ever hereafter used as a Highway or Road for all his Majesties liege people, from Rishton Moor to another High Road in Great Harwood aforesaid, the same to be laid and fenced out at the sole expence of the said Alexander Nowell and his Heirs, And the said Alexander Nowell, his Heirs and Assigns shall have an occupation road for the driving of horses, cattle, carts and carriages at all times of the year from the Highway in Great Harwood aforesaid over the East side of a close called the Meadow Hill, allotted to the said Sir Thomas Hesketh, in and to another close of land called the Barnfield, allotted to the said Alexander Nowell.

And the roads described by single Dotted Lines on the said plan are intended to describe footpaths, and the roads described by larger and double Dotted Lines are intended to describe driving Roads for horses, cattle, carts and carriages.

Such details are often evidence in present-day disputes about threats to footpaths and attempted closure of rights of way.

Enclosures encouraged the natural objection many land-owners felt to paying tithes, and hastened the process of tithe commutation. Ever since the Reformation, the assessment and collecting of tithes had tended to become increasingly varied. In most parishes the medieval pattern of paying tithes in kind sooner or later proved grossly inconvenient if not impracticable; assessment, collection, storage, and disposal of tithe goods all presented difficulties. Furthermore, where the great tithes, traditionally the property of the rector, passed into lay hands as a result of the sale of ecclesiastical land after the dissolution of the monasteries, there seemed to remain no valid reason for paying tithes at all. Even in the many parishes where tithes were still part of the stipend of the rector or vicar, dissenters of all kinds failed to understand why they should have to pay tithe to 'maintain error' or finance a 'misguided' church. Many parishes worked out their own system of commuting tithes – a *modus decimandi*, in the language of the lawyers. Some agreed on fixed annual payments; threepence a bushel for wheat, one penny a cow for milk, and a halfpenny for every pig littered would be typical agreements in seventeenth-century parishes where tithes were taken on crops and livestock. Other commuting schemes based payments on the rent of land – 2s. 0d. in the pound was usual – or on rateable value, or, more commonly perhaps, on the area and use of the land – 2s. 6d. an acre for land sown with wheat or barley, twice that for beans, and nothing at all for land lying fallow. Others again, especially as part of an enclosure settlement, put an end to tithes by giving the tithe holder an adequate gift of land, or agreeing to pay him a corn-rent based on the varying price of grain.

Whichever type of settlement the parish made, it needed to have legal sanction if future incumbents were to be prevented from disowning it. By the 1830s, in addition to those enclosure Acts which embodied tithe settlements, there were some 2,000 private Acts concerning tithe alone. The parish of Halifax, for example, secured its settlement in the Spring of 1829. Disputes had arisen, said the petitioners, and therefore they proposed that 'in lieu of Vicarial Tithes . . . Easter offerings and other Vicarial dues and payments . . . a fixed Annual Stipend should be secured to the Vicar'. This they intended to raise by a rate on 'all messuages, corn mills, and arable, meadow, and pasture lands' in the parish. No one offered any opposition. Within two months the royal assent had been given to the Act.

Nevertheless, Halifax was one of the fortunate minority of parishes. Thousands still had no agreed scheme. For this reason, in 1836, Parliament passed the Tithe Commutation Act to negotiate settlements throughout the country. The commissioners were kept busy for the next half century. They drew up about 12,000 'apportionments', and, as experienced professionals in this work, they did the job adequately and consistently. In each parish they prepared a detailed schedule and informative map, showing exact boundaries of fields, gardens, orchards, closes, and buildings, the size of all plots of land, and the names of all the fields. With schedule and map together, the researcher has a large-scale cross-section of the parish in the year the tithe award was made. What is more, he should not have too much difficulty in finding the documents. One copy went to the tithe commissioners, a second to the diocesan registry, and a third to the incumbent of the parish. Tithe-maps are usually too big to store in the parish chest or vestry safe. Accordingly, many incumbents have thankfully deposited them in county record offices for safe keeping. The following is a brief extract from the tithe schedule made at Standish in 1842, now available for study, with its accompanying map, in the Lancashire Record Office. The first column gives the name of the land occupier – the tithe payer; the second the number of the enclosure on the plan; the third the description of the land or premises; the fourth the state of cultivation; the fifth the size of each item in acres, roods and perches; and the last the annual tithe payable to the rector. All the lands listed in the example belonged to Charles Standish, the local squire.

			A.	R.	P.	£	s.	d.
Richard Yates[1]								
725	Dwelling House and Yard				9			2
Peter Parkinson								
735	Out Houses and Garden			3	26		3	3
750	Field	Meadow	3	3	16		13	3
751	Field	Meadow	3	3	35		13	9
752	Garden			1	7		1	0
753	Field	Pasture	2	3	16		9	4
754	Field	Pasture	2	1	24		7	10
835	Field	Pasture	2	1	17		8	4
			16	2	21	2	16	9

1. In the original the name of the land occupier appears in the first column.

	A. R. P.	£ s. d.
Rev. Richard Tyrer		
810 Plantation	9	2
811 Houses and Yards	33	7
812 Garden	35	7
813 Walks and Ornamental Grounds	1 1 20	3 11
	1 3 17	5 3
Stephen Richardson		
800a Site of Standish corn mill	8	
803 Mill Pond and swamp	1 1 27	
	1 1 35	

Tithe commissioners had to find an acceptable compromise between conflicting interests. They satisfied no one fully, but they granted all parties a degree of consolation. The land occupiers still had to pay, but the charge was in the convenient form of a fixed annual sum: the church and lay tithe holders did not like to see the real value of the tithes made vulnerable to future inflation, but at least their rights had been clearly stated and were beyond further dispute. In a large number of parishes, the tithe apportionment allowed the church to put aside its other defensive legal weapon, the glebe terrier. Ever since Elizabethan times, ecclesiastical authorities had used the terrier to keep church endowments and the details of glebe lands 'in perpetual memory'. They felt that periodic revisions of this document were a safeguard against lay encroachments and the constant danger of finding church claims to property challenged in the courts. A canon of 1571 had required that every bishop caused a terrier (*terra* – land) 'to be made of all fields, meadows, gardens, or orchards' belonging to each rectory and vicarage in his diocese; and a second canon of 1604 had enlarged this instruction to include 'houses, stocks, implements, tenements and portions of tithes lying out of their parishes'. By the eighteenth century, some terriers were concerned as much with tithes, church furniture, and the source of the parish clerk's wages as they were with glebe lands, and during the last hundred years terriers have tended to become inventories of church property rather than records of landholding. The distribution of these documents is very patchy. The incumbent, churchwardens, and a small committee of responsible parishioners undertook the task of writing out a terrier only when the bishop on visitation instructed them to do so. Some bishops were apparently content to rely on the terriers their predecessors had filed: others, such as John Fell, bishop of Oxford in James II's reign, and William Nicholson, bishop of Carlisle in Anne's reign, were particularly anxious to have an up-to-date terrier for each of their parishes. Copies were usually kept in the parish chest as well as in the diocesan registry.

If, in times past, the terrier's chief function was to enrol ecclesiastical possessions and rights, today its main value is the historical information it conveys. A single terrier can give us a detailed picture of a church and its endowments in a particular year. Many needed long rolls of parchment to record all the details: others, such as this 1704 terrier of Wigton in Cumberland, were succinct and curt.

The Minister's House is in good Repair. The Glebe-Land is a Close, consisting of one Acre. The Vicar hath onely the Tith-Hay of the Township of Wigton, worth 40s. per Annum and the Tith Piggs. His Salary is £17 6s. 8d. and he has one Tenant, who payes 13s. 4d. a year.

Four or five terriers of the same parish made at intervals over a couple of centuries can usefully illustrate trends and changes in parish prosperity and agricultural methods, and a collection of reasonably contemporary terriers from a diocese or wider area can make a valuable contribution to the history of the region's agriculture, as well as demonstrating sharp inequalities between parish livings and the variety of sources for parsons' stipends.

In 1789 William, bishop of Chester, ordered the minister and chapel wardens of St Peter's, Aston by Sutton, to compile a terrier of 'the Parsonage House and Outhouses, Glebe Lands, Timber, Augmentations, Gifts, Dues, Rights, Furniture, Utensils, Books etc. belonging to the Chapel, Minister, Clerk and Sexton'. The resultant document is typical of terriers in the later-eighteenth and nineteenth centuries, and manifests the kind of historical information they contain. It begins with a description of the parsonage and its outhouses:

IMPRIMIS The Parsonage House consisting of a hall, floor flaged, parlor flaged, kitchen and pantry floors brick, four lodging rooms above floored with bords, inside the walls plastered, the walls brick covered with thatch Item One cow house in breadth 11 feet, length 24 feet, walls brick covered with thatch ... Item One cart-house walls timber covered with thatch ... etc.

There follow details of the glebe lands:

Item One close of meadow land called the Barn Croft containing by measure 1 quarter and 8 perches Item one close of meadow land called the Gighole Croft containing by measure 1 quarter and 3 perches Item one close of arable land, called the pit field containing by measure 1 Acre, 3 quarters and 18 perches – etc.

In addition to its graveyard, the chapel held nine closes altogether – 2 roods (or quarters) and 11 perches of meadow, and 12 acres 1 rood 36 perches of arable, all reckoned by the Cheshire long measurement based on the 24 foot rod or perch, and almost all enclosed by quickset hedges. It also had 'a right of Common pasture', 70 oak trees valued at £15 0s. 0d., an annual rent of £26 16s. 6d. from an estate and meadow outside the chapelry, and three small payments from the lord of the manor, Queen Anne's bounty, and a private trust in the parish of Great Budworth. Among the church goods are listed a communion table with a crimson woollen carpet, and for the time of administering the Lord's Supper, a decent linen cloth, one Chalice of French plate guilt with gold, one small paten of French plate guilt, one large silver paten, one two quart silver flagon, two small boxes to receive the alms of the communicants . . .

There were also inside the chapel the prayer books, bibles and homilies, registers and account books, which one would expect to find, and the usual church necessities – a bell, two ladders, two biers, two palls, two shovels, five planks 'used at funerals', two surplices, and 'one large oak chest in the vestry to keep the register and account books in'. The last paragraph of the terrier records the fees to which the minister and clerk were entitled:

Item, for every marriage by licence, to Minister five shillings, to Clerk one shilling. Item, for every marriage by publication of Banns, to Minister two shillings and sixpence, to Clerk one shilling. Item to Minister for publishing the Banns, one shilling. Item, for churching a woman to Minister, one shilling and fourpence. Item for every burial, the person to be buried being an inhabitant of Aston, Aston Grange, Sutton or Middleton Grange, to Minister, one shilling and fourpence, and to Clerk acting as Sexton also two shillings. Item, for every burial, the person to be buried not being an inhabitant of Aston, Aston Grange, Sutton or Middleton Grange, to Minister two shillings and eightpence, and to Clerk acting as Sexton four shillings. Item, for every tomb erected in the chapel yard, to Minister ten shillings, and for every headstone three shillings and sixpence. Item, the Clerk acting as Sexton wages two pounds a year by custom, paid by the Chapelry.

One usual item which this particular terrier does not mention is the value of the incumbent's Easter offering, but probably this asset at Aston by Sutton passed through the curate's hands into those of the parish priest, the incumbent of Runcorn.

Terriers, therefore, have much in common with enclosure acts and tithe awards. They offer particularly detailed information about one part of the parish, and often supplement the witness of the other two documents. A historian could hardly expect to find three better, mutually supporting and overlapping sources, if his investigation is concerned with the growth of a particular parish, with the development of agriculture and the methods and progress of enclosure, with place and field names, with the social status and worldly rewards of the clergy, with the fabric and furnishings of church buildings, with rights of way, or with land use and the changing appearance of the countryside. It is often possible to impose the extra details of a late terrier on to the parish tithe map. Then with the enclosure map and the large-scale edition of the first ordnance survey map (reinforced if possible by a convenient estate map or, if the relevant year is earlier than 1832, maybe with facts from land tax returns), the local historian has a collection of topographical information which he can use in several ways. If the maps are not too far apart in date, he has ready-made a detailed picture of his parish in an early or mid nineteenth-century decade, and a base on which he can build its subsequent history. He can just as conveniently use the same base for probing further back in time. If enclosure preceded tithe apportionment, he will probably find sufficient evidence in the terrier and the shape of the fields to make reasonable speculations about the divisions and boundaries of the old open fields and common pastures. If enclosure followed tithe apportionment, speculation will be unnecessary; the terrier, tithe map, and possibly, according to its date, the ordnance survey map will establish the details of the pre-enclosed parish, and the enclosure map, supported by later editions of the ordnance survey map, will set out the changes made by enclosure.

The land tax returns mentioned above are voluminous, but they are not as useful a source as they appear to be at first sight. William III's government introduced the tax in 1697. For every county it fixed a quota, and left local assessors to divide each county quota between the parishes, and each parish quota between individual taxpayers. Originally, the assessors took into account movables and salaries as well as real estate, but during the first decades of the eighteenth century, in order to avoid the difficult task of assessing the value of movable property, they concentrated upon the taxpayers' real estate and the easily determined salaries of certain public officers. Furthermore, they made the assessment of real estate very easy by basing it upon a survey of 1692, and virtually never altering it thereafter. Considering the effect of the industrial and agricultural changes of the eighteenth and nineteenth centuries upon the relative values of different estates in various parts of the country, this fixed assessment frequently became unjust and even absurd. By 1800, if not by 1750, agricultural counties such as Suffolk and Sussex were being taxed too heavily, and developing industrial areas such as the Black Country or the West Riding far too little. And inside each county, and even inside each parish, inequalities could not help but occur and increase.

Most county record offices have now acquired land tax returns from some time in the 1770s or 1780s until 1832 at least. From 1779 until the Great Reform Act, the law required duplicate copies of the returns to be sent to the clerk of the peace so that he could check whether would-be voters qualified as 40 shilling freeholders or not. Returns before 1779 and after 1832 may still be found in the parish chest, because the annual assessments had to be posted on the church door, but only the luckiest parish historians are likely to find a substantial run. From 1780 onwards the government insisted upon the returns being made in a regular form to show three things – the owner of the property, the names or number of the tenants, and the tax paid. Gradually it became traditional to levy the tax at 4 shillings in the pound, and in 1798 the law fixed the tax permanently at that sum. The following typical extract is taken from the returns for the parish of Worsley, Lancashire, in 1786

Owner	No. of tenants	Payment		
		£	s.	d.
Worsley:				
The Duke of Bridgewater	60	52	11	5
Rev. Walter Baggot	4	2	1	4
Le Gendre Starkie Esq	—		4	—
Higher Division of Worsley				
Le Gendre Starkie Esq	2	2	6	—
The Duke of Bridgewater	37	18	3	2
Rev. Walter Baggot	3	1	14	8
Swinton Division				
Duke of Bridgewater	17	4	3	5
Rev. Mr Watson	5	1	13	6
Thomas Worsley	3		13	1
Richard Worsley	self		15	8
Feofees of Rivington School	—		14	8
Exors of the late Mr Watson	2	1	9	4
Thomas Bromiley	self	2	4	—
William Martin, officer of excise	—	5	—	—

The last entry is clearly assessed upon income and not on land. The feofees of Rivington School are probably charged on rents derived from endowed lands, just as the two parsons are likely to be assessed upon tithes rather than glebe land. No doubt part of the duke's assessment in all three divisions of the parish is concerned with the canal he built from Worsley to Manchester between 1758 and 1762, for the land tax covered such possessions as canals, quarries, and coalpits.

It is tempting to derive too much information from land tax returns. Like Domesday Survey entries they often pose more queries than they answer. Even within a single parish, it is speculative to assume that the assessment was originally fixed in proportion to the acreage or value of the land held by the different owners, or that a tax return covers all the freehold land in the parish or county. It is even doubtful if owners are always distinguished from occupiers, and after 1798, when it became possible for landowners to free their land from the tax by paying a lump sum, the returns do not necessarily list lands so 'exonerated'. But if their details cannot be the basis of exact statistics, land tax returns can indicate variations and changes in the pattern of landholding. They make it easy to identify squire-dominated villages, clusters of smallholders, and the steady consolidation of land in the hands of a particular family. They are useful auxiliaries to such 'front line' sources as enclosure and tithe awards.

5. DIRECTORIES AND OTHER BUSINESS DOCUMENTS

Directory has several meanings ranging from an ecclesiastical book of rules to a revolutionary French government. Reference libraries offer directories of schools, of museums and art galleries, and of employment opportunities for various categories of workers. But here *directory* means only the commercial directory, which became increasingly available in Britain from the middle of the eighteenth century. It grew to maturity alongside its slightly older sister, the guide-book. In their youth they were often mistaken for one another: the guide-book frequently looked like a directory, and the directory often assumed the features of a guide-book. But in their adult life, especially after 1800, they grew apart, and assumed quite distinct personalities.

The heart of all commercial directories is the list of inhabitants with their addresses, occupations, and businesses. Early directories set out to provide travelling salesmen and other commercial visitors with a readily comprehensible list of potential suppliers, distributors, or customers of or for the particular commodities they were wanting to buy or sell. The first directories printed the list as baldly as possible. The *Liverpool Directory* published in 1766 began

Abbot William, merchant, Cleveland's-square
Adams Samuel, victualler, White Lion, Water-street
Ainsworth Elizabeth, ironmonger, Dale Street

and, nineteen small pages further on, ended

Yates John, watchmaker and corn dealer, Ranelagh-street
Yates Robert, linen draper, James's-street
Young Isaac, watchmaker, John-street

In six pages of appendix, the editor added other details which he thought might be of use to his commercial readers. He listed the names of the mayor, bailiffs, councillors, custom and excise officers, and commissioners of the docks, of the watch, and for the regulation of pilots, and then printed sparse details of stage coaches, wagons and carts, and vessels trading along the coast from the Mersey.

As time went on, however, directories became more complex. The lists of inhabitants grew much longer, because most manufacturers, retailers, and craftsmen made it their business to see that they were included. The editor of the first *Liverpool Directory* confessed himself 'sensible that there may probably be many mistakes, or omissions, in this first attempt', and invited 'his Friends' to inform him of them. By 1800 the alphabetical list had grown to 160 pages, and the appendix to 68 pages. The appendix had some new features – a 'sketch of the town and trade of Liverpool', lists of attorneys, parochial clergy, and parish officers, extracts from Acts of parliament and local by-laws concerning the docks and harbour, details of a number of local charitable institutions, rates of inland and overseas postage, and an alphabetical list of Liverpool streets.

Before long such items as postal charges, street lists, and the addresses of London and provincial banks had become indispensable features of all good directories, and the alphabetical list of householders had been supplemented by a classified list of professions and trades. Maps, often well engraved, appeared as 'throw-outs' or were folded into a pocket inside the cover, and large blocks of advertisements gave later directories much of their extra bulk. *Gore's Directory of Liverpool for 1855* began with 102 pages of advertisements followed by a folded map drawn on the scale of 1 in. = 200 yards. Twenty years later the plan of the same firm's *Directory* was not much altered. The advertisements, 105 pages this time, had been moved from the front of the book to the back, and new features among the extra details included the lengths of the main streets, the distances to a number of inland towns together with carters' rates, and a third list of inhabitants arranged in yet another way, by street and house number. It would be difficult to imagine any other information a buyer or commercial traveller could possibly want before he began working in a strange town.

The development of directory publishing marched step by step with the industrialization of Britain. Outside London, directories began to appear in the early years of George III's reign. In 1763 Samuel Sketchley published the first one for Sheffield and James Sketchley the first one for Birmingham. Three years later, Liverpool's first directory was on sale and Manchester's followed in 1772. As practical aids to promoting industry and commerce, these pocket-sized books immediately proved their worth, so that by the 1770s publishers were investing their capital not only in producing town directories, but county and country-wide directories too. Hampshire and Bedfordshire both had directories by the middle of the decade. In 1781 William Bailey covered the industrial north with his

Northern Directory, and in 1784 published his first *British Directory* in four volumes. Before the nineteenth century was far advanced, directory publishing had become a specialist craft, and the two men who achieved the most notable success in the business were James Pigot and Frederic Kelly.

In 1814 *Pigot's Commercial Directory* covered the main towns in Yorkshire, Lancashire, and Cheshire: the 1815 edition expanded the scope to include Birmingham and Wolverhampton. Outside London, up-to-date, detailed directories of these rapidly growing industrial areas were most in demand. At the end of the 1820s, the firm of Pigot and Company launched a comprehensive national directory in three large volumes. It is still capable of rousing admiration as an enterprising piece of publishing. The first volume, ready in 1827, covered London and the counties of Middlesex, Essex, Hertfordshire, Kent, Surrey, and Sussex; the second volume sixteen more counties; and the third the remaining eighteen English counties together with the southern half of Wales. Frederic Kelly entered this publishing field in 1836, when he took over the post office directories, which hitherto the post office itself had published. His firm, like Pigot's, expanded steadily; and today his name is the first that comes to mind when directories are mentioned.

The primary usefulness of a directory is inevitably short-lived. Even in the brief interval between compilation and publication, people die, established firms close down, and new businesses open up. As the months go by, the need for revision becomes increasingly urgent. Annual directories eventually became the regular practice. But directories have a long-lasting secondary usefulness. Each one is a 'still' picture of its area in a particular year: a series of them can be used as a jerky 'movie' picture of commercial and social life over a decade or a century.

The researcher must, of course, handle this raw material with understanding. Directories were compiled for contemporary businessmen and not for future historians. They were published in haste, and editors had no scholarly scruples about checking their sources, especially if checking threatened to delay publication or if the matter was only of marginal importance to the business community. The previous edition was the essential templet for the new one, so that errors were always liable to be repeated, and deceased householders and defunct businesses to be carried forward into the new lists. Editors made efforts to keep important items such as postal facilities, dock rates, and coach time-tables as accurate as possible, but historical sections were frequently repeated for years without any amendment whatsoever. Fables and fabrications went unchallenged – edition after edition of *Gore's Directory*, for example, had St Patrick sailing from Liverpool for Ireland 200 years after he was dead and 500 years before the first recorded mention of Liverpool. More seriously, recent events were often not added to the local story, and such things as population figures, lists of charitable institutions, and by-laws tended to be transferred from edition to edition without amendment. In 1827 Pigot boasted in his preface to the *London and Provincial New Commercial Directory* that

The historical and descriptive portion of this volume has been observed with the most zealous care ... everything new and pleasing that could be gleaned from authentic sources has been incorporated: nor have exuberant fancy and figurative language been substituted for matters of fact and interest.

But his most pertinent comment was that 'such species of information must of necessity be brief in a work like the present'. He wrote *brief*; if he had been more direct and less fearful of giving offence, he could truthfully have written *unimportant*.

Directories too cannot help but reflect the outlook and values of the commercial world of their day. The lists of charitable institutions, for example, show both the well-intentioned, nibbling attempts they were making in the nineteenth century to fight social evils, and the complacent, condescending attitude adopted by the better-off to the poor and their problems. Since it was unlikely that the reader would wish to know the scope and effect of the work of these institutions, directories said little about them. But printing the names of the committee members prominently in capitals was quite another matter: it would probably increase sales. The list of schools often looked impressive, but such details as the size of classrooms, the regularity of attendance, and the effectiveness of the teaching were not the concern of the directory publishers. Neither were the slums. Public buildings and churches merited space, but the poorer areas of the town were either not mentioned at all, or were dismissed as 'uninteresting' or as 'areas inhabited by the lowest classes'. The publishers saw the need to print coach and rail fares and dock and custom duties, but considered it no business of theirs to give rates of wages. They might quote census figures to illustrate developing prosperity, but never infant mortality rates or deaths from cholera. After all, it was their aim to attract visitors to their town, not to repel them.

Yet with considerations like these always in mind, economic historians can find directories informative about many aspects of commercial and industrial history. Industrial Britain began with large numbers of one-man or family businesses either manufacturing goods, transporting them to where they were required, or selling them at home or overseas. There were no big businesses to begin with, although a few made such rapid progress that before the end of the eighteenth century they were manipulating accumulations of capital and managing hundreds of employees. Bateman and Sherratt (now Mather and Platt), the engineers, and Pickford, the carriers, are examples of these early successes. More pressed quickly forward towards success but, by mismanagement or through hostile circumstances, ended up in bankruptcy. Others set off in one direction, but eventually discovered their fortune lay in another: the Cadbury family began in Birmingham as drapers, and then through tea and coffee found their way to cocoa and chocolate, and Richard and William Pilkington were wine and spirit merchants before they became glass manufacturers. Nineteenth-century self-help and private enterprise offered big prizes to those who successfully navigated the many hazards of industrial and business life. By way of mergers, good management, the failure of competitors, honesty, ruthlessness, sheer good fortune, or a combination of three or four such factors, the successful progressed. Industrial and commercial units steadily grew bigger. But the origin of many well-known and soundly based firms of later years can be traced through a single-line entry or a half-page advertisement in an early directory.

Blundell, Jonathan and Co., sugar bakers, Haymarket
Rathbone, William, timber-merchant, Duke Street

These two items from the *Liverpool Directory* of 1766 indicate the beginnings of what were to become, respectively, one of the biggest colliery [*sic*] companies in Britain and the important shipbuilding and shipowning firm of Rathbone Brothers and Company.

The main sources for business history, however, lie elsewhere. There are two main categories – the national or regional government and public-body reports, accounts, and statistics, and the private minutes, accounts, and correspondence of the businesses themselves. The volume of this material is enormous. Some of it has already been worked on with encouraging results. Much of it awaits examination, and it is very likely there are private archives still to be discovered.

The general indexes to the House of Commons and House of Lords papers are the best guides to what is available in the government collection. Twenty minutes with one of the large volumes summarizing half a century's production of official papers will convince any doubting Thomas of the wealth and variety of information available. In the *Index of House of Commons Papers, 1801–52*, for example, there are, for the brewing industry, numerous reports concerning manufacture in addition to annual figures for excise duty paid and quantities of beer exported; for the copper industry, annual accounts from 1812 to 1852 of copper imported and exported together with the weight of foreign copper imported each year from 1785 to 1827; for the sugar and tea industries, details of annual imports and duties paid; for agriculture, tables of wages, and statistics showing the price and quantities of wheat grown year by year during the twenty years following the 1815 Corn Laws. In addition to such collections of detailed papers on individual industries, there are annual reports galore on imports and exports into and out of the main ports. Under the heading *Bristol*, for example, there are, from 1816 onwards, yearly figures of 'the number of vessels and tonnage entered inwards and cleared outwards at the Port of Bristol, together with the declared value', and under *London* one item concerns 'grain of each kind, distinguishing British, Scottish, Irish, and Foreign', imported into London each year from 1828 to 1841. And to supplement this vast archive, there are the voluminous custom and excise records stored partly in King's Beam House, Mark Lane, London EC 3, and partly in the custom houses at the different ports.

What reports, statistics, and papers a student needs to see depends, of course, on what he is investigating. He must search the indexes first: from the index he passes to his selected documents. Despite the fact that the Lords and Commons papers were printed, individual reports are sometimes difficult to find. Only the biggest reference libraries can make room to store them, and, even so, most of their collections are incomplete. But all papers are available somewhere, and, if proper perspective is to be achieved, it is essential to set the history of a single business enterprise, or the industrial development of a local area, against the background of the appropriate national picture. A graph of a single firm's production figures has much more meaning if it can be imposed on the appropriate graph of national production, and the story of its enterprise can be better appreciated if comparison is made with the activity of other firms in the same business.

Finding the private papers of individual firms is a matter of fortune. Businessmen, as they should be, are far more concerned with current papers than those of past years, so that bundles of old letters and stacks of long-finished account books, minute books, and day books are ever in danger of destruction. Among the dozen or so managers who have held office since the firm began, it only requires one to have once decided 'to make more room', 'have a thorough clear out', or 'contribute to the salvage drive', and the firm's papers have gone beyond recall. Even more frustrating for the firm's would-be historian is to know that the papers still exist, but to find that the firm's policy is to keep them strictly private. Centenaries or, better still, bi-centenaries, often have a surprisingly softening effect on such a policy, but if all the board wants to mark the occasion is a glossy-backed advertisement of the firm's prowess, it would be better for the historian to have nothing to do with the disturbing of the dust. For he must only be concerned with the search for truth. Years of failure are as historically important as years of success, and if there are skeletons in a firm's cupboard they must be revealed and put in perspective in the full story. It is as wrong to highlight them as to hide them away.

Despite the hazards of survival, business records still exist in plenty. Some firms take a pride in their archives and employ their own archivist. Others have willingly handed their earlier papers for safe-keeping and scholarly examination to record offices or public or university libraries. There are several classic stories of unexpected discovery and last-minute rescue. In 1921 George Unwin and Arthur Hulme searched a dilapidated building near the burnt-out shell of a cotton mill in Mellor, Cheshire. They found 'a great number of letters, papers, account books, and other business records of every kind and size, covering the whole floor of a large room and partly hidden from sight by several inches of dust and debris'. Once these papers had been removed and cleaned, Unwin began to examine them. He had discovered a rich cache of ledgers, account books, letters, stocktaking records, wage sheets, pay-tickets, costing books, and memoranda concerning the achievements of the early textile businesses of Samuel Oldknow. The records went back to the 1780s, and they formed the basis of *Samuel Oldknow and the Arkwrights*, published in 1924. In Warrington, a few years later, T. S. Ashton made a similar discovery, which enabled him to write *An Eighteenth-Century Industrialist: Peter Stubs of Warrington, 1756–1806*. Since the last war, the art of business history writing has advanced considerably. It has now become a specialized aspect of historical studies, and, together with its younger contemporary, industrial archaeology, is redressing the balance in our understanding of British economic history in the last two centuries. Reform bills, corn laws, factory acts, Chartists, trade unions, and the fight for free trade, all retain the importance historians have long given them. But individual resource and risk, the development and decline of single businesses, investment and the accumulation of capital, as well as the day-to-day life in factory, counting-house, and manager's office are just as much part of Britain's story. The historian cannot be content to leave these aspects of the industrialization of Britain entirely to the novelist.

Bibliography of Documents 1760–1914: Economic and Topographical

Two volumes of *English Historical Documents* cover part of this period: Vol. 10, ed. A. Aspinall and E. A. Smith (1959), and Vol. 11, ed. G. M. Young and W. D. Handcock (1956).

The story of the first passenger railway is best told in *The Struggle for the Liverpool and Manchester Railway*, by G. S. Veitch (1930). *Lancashire Acts of Parliament, 1415–1800* by R. S. France, was published by Lancashire Record Office in 1950.

The excellent work of J. B. Harley has demonstrated the strength and weakness of maps as a historical source: *Christopher Greenwood, County Map-Maker* (1962); *The Historian's Guide to Ordnance Survey Maps*, with C. W. Phillips (1964); four articles in *Cheshire Round*, Nos. 6, 7, 8, and 9, published by Cheshire Community Council, and articles in *The Amateur Historian, The Local Historian, The Geographical Journal, Imago Mundi*, and other geographical and historical publications. For earlier books on maps and map-makers and for the editions of the maps themselves, see Harley's bibliographical notes, especially in *Cheshire Round*. County record offices and local reference libraries usually have a series of local maps and town plans.

J. E. Vaughan, who kindly made his private collection of guide books available to me, wrote 'Early Guide Books as Sources of Social History', *Amateur Historian*, Vol. 5, No. 6 (1963). Apart from quotations acknowledged in the text, quotations were taken from:

A Pedestrian Tour of 1,347 miles through Wales and England, Pedestres (1836).
Journal of a Tour and Residence in Great Britain . . . in 1810 and 1811, L. Simond (1815).
Wanderings and Excursions in North Wales, Thomas Roscoe (1836).
The Journey from Chester to London, Thomas Pennant (1811).
The Discovery of Britain, by Esther Moir (1964), has a long list of travel books which were published before 1840.

W. E. Tate listed the enclosure acts of many counties: see, for example, Thoroton Society, Record Series Vol. 5 (1935), and Staffordshire Record Society, Vol. 65 (1942). The Great Harwood enclosure agreement is in the Lancashire Record Office. Details of the Halifax tithe settlement will be found in *The Journal of the House of Commons*, February–April 1829. The Wigton terrier is from *Miscellany Accounts of the Diocese of Carlisle*, Cumberland and Westmorland Antiquarian and Archaeological Society, Extra Series, Vol. 1 (1877), and the Aston by Sutton terrier from *Transactions of the Historic Society of Lancashire and Cheshire*, Vol. 102 (1950).

In the last section of this chapter references were made to *The Firm of Cadbury, 1831–1931*, by I. A. Williams (1941) and *Pilkington Brothers and the Glass Industry*, by T. C. Barker (1960). For lists of early directories see *The London Directories, 1677–1855*, by C. W. F. Goss (1932), and *Guide to the National and Provincial Directories of England and Wales, excluding London, published before 1856*, by J. E. Norton (1950).

POLITICAL AND SOCIAL RECORDS

I. OFFICIAL RECORDS: HANSARD, COMMISSIONERS' REPORTS, AND CENSUSES

E. A. Freeman, Regius Professor of Modern History at Oxford from 1884 to 1892, once defined history as 'past politics', and J. R. Seeley, author of the best-selling *Expansion of England* (1883), expressed the same opinion another way by saying it was 'the biography of states'. Not all their contemporaries would have agreed with them. Many who accepted that politics was history's proper domain regarded historical writing primarily as a branch of literature: their delight was Carlyle 'splashing down' what he knew of the French Terror 'in large masses of colour', or Macaulay's resonant Latinized prose describing the Glorious Revolution of 1688 or narrating British achievements overseas. Genealogy and histories of landed families held the interest of antiquarians and cultured amateurs, and a dedicated group of professionals were beginning to explore 'scientifically' the austere territory of constitutional history. Nevertheless, Freeman and Seeley expressed a view readily appreciated and widely accepted in their day.

Memories of history taught at school were of lists of dates – reigns, good and bad; battles, British victories in capitals; and outstanding Acts of parliament, beginning with, by adoption, Magna Carta. Medieval history tended to be nothing but political struggle at court and on the battlefield: more recent history transferred the perpetual conflict to the floor of the House of Commons, the Netherlands, or the Peninsula. Such social history as existed was usually considered food for younger children and, perhaps, for romantic ladies. Stories of Robin Hood,

Elizabeth and Raleigh, or the hard-working but honest chimney sweep adequately covered such topics as medieval hunting, Tudor fashions in dress, or the misery of working-class life in the early nineteenth century. And economic history was not acceptable at all! This narrow concept of history lasted a long time: the cat is deemed to have died in the first years of this present century, but its smile was still visible for the next forty or fifty years.

Political history, of course, still rightfully holds an important place in historical studies. For many people it is still the trunk from which all the branches sprout, since it is the record of events written from the view of the central government. What was royal government in times past gradually became parliamentary government after 1660, and for the period 1760–1914 the essence of political history is government policy at home and abroad, party politics, and parliamentary debate. Reigns are less important than ministries; the years divide more naturally into 'ages' dominated by pairs of politicians – Pitt and Fox, Castlereagh and Canning, Peel and Palmerston, Gladstone and Disraeli, and Asquith and Balfour.

No source for modern political history can therefore surpass the records of parliamentary debate, which, volume on volume, load shelf on shelf of our reference libraries. How detailed the record is, and how it is arranged, depends upon which series is consulted. The *Parliamentary History* covers the earliest years of this period. Indeed it begins, misleadingly, as early as 1066, and sweeps along to 1625 in the first volume. The next five volumes cover the rest of the Stuarts, but it took twenty-two volumes, Volumes 15–36, to record parliamentary business from 1753 to 1803. All the volumes are substantial: they average about 750 quarto pages each. So it is immediately evident that William Cobbett, whose enterprising work this is, succeeded in gathering together considerable material.

During most of George III's reign, parliament had forbidden

the reporting of its debates, but the prohibition had only succeeded in compelling reporters to use devious and underhand methods to try to satisfy the public's hunger for news. They had circulated incomplete and sometimes defective reports of parliamentary business, but frequently had been able to include the full text of a speech which a member had deliberately 'leaked' or sold to them. These were the uneven records that Cobbett preserved in his *Parliamentary History*. The following is a typical report of a routine debate: the occasion was the committee stage, in 1798, of the Bill to impose the new income tax.

Mr *Tierney* reprobated the frequent use of the term 'evasion', and thought a variety of cases of hardship might be put . . . Many men felt themselves so hard pressed by the weight of taxes, that they felt themselves honestly and conscientiously justifiable in trying whether, without violating the letter of the law, they might not avoid a part of the burthen.

Mr *Pitt* said, if hon. gentleman was right in supposing that conscientious men would think themselves justifiable in taking every advantage to evade the tax, it was the more incumbent on him to make the letter of the law so strict that its spirit should not be evaded.

Mr *Wilberforce* dwelt upon evasion . . .

Mr *Tierney* said, it was a common saying, that tricks which were fair in love, were also fair in taxation . . . He might, therefore, suppose that many conscientious men would think themselves justified in taking every advantage of the law; not to evade the letter of it, but its heavy effects . . .

Most of the 'star' speeches Cobbett reported as fully as possible. Fox's speech on the declaration of war against France in 1793, for instance, occupies six full pages, and Burke's on the proposed repeal of the American tea duty in 1774 more than four times that space. Cobbett acknowledged that he had reprinted Burke's speech from 'the original edition printed for J. Dodsley in Pall Mall'.

The printer of the *Parliamentary History* was Thomas, the son of Luke Hansard, who was printing the *Journal of the House of Commons*. Together, from 1803 to 1812, Cobbett and Thomas, or T. C., Hansard shouldered an even more onerous task than compiling the *History*. They began publishing full reports of contemporary debates in both Lords and Commons, together with accounts, schedules, and lists concerned with parliamentary business. This was the beginning of a momentous undertaking. The first volume covered the period from 22 November 1803 to 29 March 1804. By its very nature, this contemporary record had to take precedence over the *History*. Its immediacy was its chief appeal. But the *History* made steady progress nevertheless. In the spring of 1812, Volume 22 of *Cobbett's Parliamentary Debates* advertised Volume 12 of the *History*. That year Cobbett withdrew from the editing of the *Debates*. He left that half of the joint business entirely to Hansard, but pressed on with the *History* so successfully that in 1820 Hansard was able to announce in the preface to the *Debates* the completion of the scheme. 'The Public are therefore now in possession of the only uniform Parliamentary History of the Country that was ever attempted.'

In 1820, on the death of George III and the completion of Volume 41, Hansard closed the first series of *Parliamentary Debates*. His second series, twenty-five volumes, spanned George IV's reign: Volume 21 of this series dropped the usual 'under the superintendance of T. C., (or, later, Mr) Hansard', and boldly assumed the title of *Hansard's Parliamentary Debates*. The third series, 256 volumes covering the long period from 1830 to 1891, was the work of the next generation of Hansards, particularly of Henry, Thomas's nephew. The Hansard method of reporting was to give full summaries of speeches in the third person. But by retaining many of the speaker's phrases, it still allowed his personality, and on occasions his satire, anger, and humour, to shine through the screen of reported speech. The following brief extract is taken from a Commons' debate in June 1886. Henry Labouchere, a prominent back-bencher supporting Gladstone's government, was protesting against the Lords' rejection of a Commons' motion which would have thrown the expenses of electoral returning officers on the rates.

Mr Labouchere said, he was merely pointing out that it had been stated in the newspapers that large sums of money were being subscribed by the opponents of the present Government, and that, in the opinion of those gentlemen, it was most essential that they should have money on their side. This Bill, if those clauses had been retained, would have enabled poor men to send poor men to Parliament; it would have enabled electors to choose Representatives for themselves, instead of having Representatives chosen for them. The House of Lords had chosen to alter that, and he left the country to form an opinion as to their conduct.

From the beginning of 1892 to the end of 1908, several publishers had a hand in recording parliamentary debates. Henry Hansard sold out to the Hansard Publishing Union. This firm quickly failed, however, and no lasting publishing arrangements were made until His Majesty's Stationery Office took over the task in 1909. Nevertheless, there is no gap in the records. Every debate is entered in the 199 volumes, which cover the interim years between the Hansard family bowing out and H.M.S.O. bustling in. The style of reporting varied. The editors still relied on the full summary, but they printed some speeches in the first person and some in the traditional third. But once *Hansard* passed into the hands of H.M.S.O. verbatim, first-person reporting became the rule. The only liberties the editors took, and still take, with the sacred text were to omit repetitions and correct obvious slips of the tongue. Nothing was petty or frivolous enough to be reduced to a summary, still less to be omitted altogether. The early months of 1910 were full of serious issues for Asquith's government. It had been returned in the January election to continue the fight with the Lords over the People's Budget. In February Carson assumed the leadership of the Irish Unionists. The dreadnought controversy was highlighting Anglo-German hostility, and the suffragettes were becoming more belligerent. *Hansard* devoted hundreds of columns to such issues, but it also gave proportionate space to less serious topics. Budgetary and constitutional problems were evidently not the only things on the Chancellor's mind, and chanting 'we want eight and we won't wait' was not the only way of exhibiting anti-German feeling.

LLOYD GEORGE:

Does the hon. Member for Clapham or anyone deny that horse-flesh is consumed in Germany by the working population? Is it denied that they eat black bread? [An Hon. Member: 'It is rye bread'.] Is it not black? ['No'.] Is it not good? Really, hon. Gentlemen, among their other defects, are even colour blind. The Germans themselves call it black bread and that is how you order it . . .

I said in Devonshire, 'You test it; have you any tramps?' They said, 'Yes'. I said, 'The next time tramps come round you keep two or three loaves of this black bread, and every time a tramp calls give him a good chunk of it, and you will get rid of them as effectually as if you had given them rat poison' . . .

Such full reporting inevitably produces bulky records. The H.M.S.O. practice of keeping Lords' business in one series and Commons' business in another helps the searcher a little, but for the post-1909 period he already faces several hundred volumes in each series. Politicians and other directly interested people frequently need to study speeches and parliamentary questions and answers within hours of the event. For their use, H.M.S.O. publishes in paper covers both a daily and a weekly *Hansard*. But the historian finds the bound volumes more convenient for his purpose.

These *Official Reports of Debates*, to give *Hansard* its proper title, represent less than a third of the official sources available to the political historian. Quite apart from such parliamentary business papers as orders of the day or weekly lists of Public Bills, there are, first, the annual *Journal of the Commons* and *Journal of the Lords*, the *Statutes at Large*, *Public General Acts*, *Mirror of Parliament*, and *Index to Parliamentary Papers*, all of which have been mentioned in previous sections; secondly, a large quantity of estimates and accounts; and, thirdly, dozens of reports of royal commissions, of standing, select, and joint committees, of departmental inquiries, and of diplomatic correspondence with foreign powers. Every one of the volumes in this last section is loaded with ore for the historical researcher. Whether he is seeking political, diplomatic, social, economic, or statistical material, he will find it in plenty within the collection. What is more, no seam has yet been fully worked; a few have hardly been prospected. It is always possible to strike something 'new'.

The Industrial Revolution created immense social problems. Most of them grew big and ugly before they attracted national attention. Suddenly influential public opinion realized that they had become dangerously acute, and the government of the day had to attempt to find a solution. No useful precedent ever existed, so the government invariably set up a commission to inquire, establish the facts, and make recommendations. To those who were suffering the hardships, this method must have seemed a time-wasting, delaying substitute for necessary urgent action. In part it was, but governments argued that they could not attempt to cure the social disease until they had a sound diagnosis. Whether these many commissions offered the government good advice or not, they gathered together volumes of evidence both from their own investigations and from the witnesses they summoned before them. They did the job as thoroughly as they could. They were interested in fact rather than theory. They took their evidence from people directly involved, and piled local detail on local detail in order to build up the national picture they eventually presented.

The most difficult social problems grew out of the rapid increase in the size of the industrial towns. Long working days and lack of transport compelled employees to live in the shadow of the new factories, and desperately poor families crowded into old houses or rapidly built, back-to-back terraced cottages. The prevailing maxim of self-help prohibited any welfare schemes beyond the palliatives of charity. Ignorance, chronic poverty, and lack of hope led to bestial living, drunkenness, and crime; shortage of water and primitive sanitation to squalor and disease. Cholera and typhus did not lag far behind. When a cholera epidemic broke out in 1831–2, the government took the emergency action of establishing local boards of health to try to quarantine the victims. This led to the first serious examinations of the basic problem: in 1840 the Select Committee on the Health of Towns published its report; two years later appeared the Report on the Sanitary Condition of the Labouring Population; and two and three years after that, the two Reports of the Commission for Inquiring into the State of Large Towns and Populous Districts. The composite picture was nauseating, documented, and convincing.

The statesmen and officials who had to follow the reports with effective legislation no doubt concentrated upon the summaries and considered opinions of the commissioners:

... defective drainage, neglect of house and street cleansing, ventilation, and imperfect supplies of water contribute to produce atmospheric impurities which affect the general health and physical condition of the population, generating acute, chronic, and ultimately organic disease, especially scrofulous infections and consumption, in addition to the fevers and other forms of disease ...

But social historians find the detailed reports of witnesses the most rewarding parts of these documents. The commissioners appointed to inquire into the state of the large towns took evidence from a number of doctors, surveyors, clergy, and other professional men in different centres in England and Wales. The following extracts are typical of the whole set of reports:

[Dr T. Laycock of York] Water is supplied to the city [York] from wells and cisterns, but principally, for all purposes, from the river Ouse, by a company first established in 1677, and subsequently by Act of Parliament. . . . Iron mains of 11 inches and of 3 inches are laid in the principal streets, and lead service pipes to about 3,000 houses; the total number of houses in the city being nearly 7,000. The greater number of the houses supplied from the water-works have cisterns, but many of the smaller houses have no cisterns, and only taps in the yards.

The annual charge made by the Company appears to be about 9d. or 1s. 0d. in the pound of the rental; it varies according to the class of houses from 4s. 0d. to £5. A six-roomed house at £13 rental, pays from 8s. 0d. to 10s. 0d., a cottage of two rooms, the rental of which is from £4 to £5, pays 4s. 0d. or 5s. 0d. for water supplied to a tap in the yard for a limited time every day, except Sunday . . . some persons complained to the District Visitors that the water was on occasionally for 10 or 15 minutes only. The poor in the neighbourhood of the rivers get their water from thence, otherwise the water-works company have a monopoly of the supply of river-water to the city. Filters are used in private houses of the middle and higher classes, but not often by the poor, who complain of the muddy state of the water . . .

[T. Hawksley, an engineer of Nottingham] With few exceptions the houses of Nottingham and its vicinity are laid out either in narrow streets, or more commonly are built in confined courts and alleys, the entrance to which is usually through a tunnel from 30 to 36 inches wide, about 8 feet high, and from 25 to 30 feet long, so that purification by the direct action of the air and solar light is in the great majority of these cases perfectly impracticable. Upwards of 7,000 houses are erected back to back and side to side . . . Some idea of the extraordinary density occasioned by this arrangement may be inferred from the fact, that in one quarter of the town . . . more than 4,200 people were ascertained to dwell in a square of less than 200 yards on the side.

[Dr W. H. Duncan of Liverpool, quoting from a report made to the Manchester Statistical Society] 'Of the common day-schools in the poorer districts [of Liverpool] it is difficult to convey an adequate idea; so close and offensive is the atmosphere in many of them as to be intolerable to a person entering from the open air, more especially as the hour for quitting school approaches. The dimensions rarely exceed those of the dame-schools, while frequently the number of scholars is more than double. Bad as this is, it is much aggravated by filth and offensive odour arising from other causes...' He notices particularly a school in a garret up three pairs of dark, broken stairs, with forty children in the compass of ten feet by nine; and where, 'on a perch forming a triangle with the corner of the room sat a cock and two hens; under a stump-bed immediately beneath was a dog-kennel, in the occupation of three black terriers... There was only one small window, at which sat the master, obstructing three-fourths of the light it was capable of admitting.'

These reports eventually provoked parliament to legislate. The Public Health Act of 1848 created a central board of health, and gave it powers to set up a local board wherever there was a death rate of over 23 per 1,000 or wherever a tenth of the inhabitants petitioned it to do so. The central board's inspectors visited petitioning townships and parishes, and their reports add further details to our sum of knowledge. Not only did the inspectors describe local conditions in detail, and make practical recommendations for improvement, but they also recorded the objections lodged against the anticipated 'expense', 'centralization', and 'interference' of any change they might advocate. If a local board was established as a result of the petition and inspector's report – and it usually needed a determined group of local reformers to push aside the barriers of indolence and apathy – it had to keep minute books, accounts, and receive reports from its officials. Where such local records still survive, we can see how the Act worked out in practice. Generally, however, the problem was growing in size and difficulty faster than the remedial measures could reduce it. No one seemed willing to spend money on public health; a large section of the British public opposed boards of health on principle, and cheered their virtual end in 1854.

A second cholera epidemic in 1865–6 led directly to another royal commission in 1869. This, in turn, produced the Public Health Act of 1872, which grouped existing sanitary boards and committees into urban or rural sanitary authorities. Each of these new bodies had to appoint medical officers of health. Their periodic, factual reports help us to judge the size of the problem they took over, and to measure the degree of progress they achieved. The medical officer of health for Ramsbottom, for example, made this report in January 1875:

... during the last ten years ... we have had two very severe visitations of Scarlet Fever and one of a milder form. Two of Measles though not to the same extent fatal. One of Typhoid Fever in which the cases were numerous though not of a very severe type and one of Small Pox in which the Mortality was low ... The Small Pox was imported from a Neighbouring Town, and the cases in a few weeks reached a considerable number ... During the year the death rate has been high, there have been no fewer than 116 deaths in the district (26·3 per thousand). Of these 62 occurred in children under five years of age, viz. 32 under 1 year, 17 under 2 years, 13 between 2 and 5 years. Of the children:

4 died from disease of Digestive system.
13 „ „ „ „ Respiratory system.
15 „ „ Fever including Scarlatina, Measles, & Infantile Remittent.
11 „ „ Premature Birth.
5 „ „ Marasmus or general wasting.
6 „ „ Convulsions.
3 „ „ Unclassified causes.
3 „ „ Violent Death necessitating Inquests.
2 „ „ Disease of Brain.

The doctor attributed the 'alarming number' of premature

births to mothers continuing to work up to the last moment before confinement. He hoped that day nurseries would be provided, so that 'the children of women who work in the Factories can be properly looked after and carefully fed and kept clean'. For the high rate of sickness and death, he chiefly blamed 'the filthy condition of the River Irwell'.

Just as the history of public health is to be found in these commissions' reports, local inquiries of national inspectors, and minutes, accounts, and correspondence files of local boards and authorities, so too is the history of the poor law, of National, British, and board school education, of the police, factories, and public transport. During the nineteenth century, government became increasingly complex and top heavy. Successive parliaments created new boards and committees to carry out specialized duties recommended by commissions of inquiry. The sequence of events rarely varied: the 1832 royal commission led to the Poor Law Amendment Act of 1834, which established boards of guardians; the Newcastle and Taunton commissions of the sixties led to Forster's Education Act of 1870, which established school boards; the constabulary commission of 1838–9 led to the Acts of 1839 and 1856, which established local police forces and watch committees. And, of course, the array of available official documents is similar in every case – commissioners' detailed reports, the text of the Bill with the debate reported in *Hansard*, and finally the administrative and financial papers of the local bodies created by the Act.

Eventually, local administration grew so complicated that fundamental change became imperative. As early as 1835, the Municipal Corporations Act had reformed the government of 178 boroughs, but it was not until 1888 that the key change was made. In that year, the County Councils Act replaced over 27,000 local, single-purpose, boards and committees with 62 all-purpose county councils. Five years later these administrative counties were divided into municipal boroughs and urban and rural districts, and in 1899 the complicated problem of Greater London was 'solved' by the federation of metropolitan boroughs under the London County Council. These new authorities steadily took over the duties of such bodies as local sanitary authorities, school boards, burial boards, highway boards, and, eventually in 1929, boards of guardians. They took over their records too. If they have not already put them in the care of the local record office or library – or sent them for salvage – they should still possess them.

Of course, all royal and parliamentary commissions did not lead to action by local authorities. Some commissioners had relatively narrow fields of investigation. Their reports were usually followed by legislation, but the carrying out of the new law did not require the creation of a public board or trust. This does not necessarily diminish the historical importance of their papers. The periodic reports on such matters as factories and trade unions were as significant as any, both to the historian and the politician of the day.

Often the evidence submitted to commissioners vividly reveals aspects of social history that the title of the report hardly leads one to expect. In 1867 the government appointed a commission to 'inquire into the organization and rules of trade unions and other associations'. The commissioners interviewed scores of witnesses and asked thousands of questions. Sir Daniel Gooch put question 10,097 to George Thomas Clark, a trustee of Dowlais Ironworks, Merthyr Tydfil:

You say that you have a benefit fund in your works?

At the request of the men we stop 2d. in the pound of the wages, and we pay that over to a treasurer, and it is divided among the firemen, colliers, and miners funds. Each class of workmen elect a committee. We give them a room to meet in, and they distribute the allowance to the sick according to their own fashion . . .

10,098   Does that include the medical fund?

No, besides that there are two funds for which 2d. more is stopped;

one is for the provision of doctors, and the other of schools. Out of the medical fund we pay the staff of doctors and find the drugs. Out of the school funds we support the schools. We have 2,400 children in our schools ... The company find the school building and playgrounds. We are out of pocket upon those items and upon those items alone, about £500 a year, but everything else is supported either by Government or by the 2d. in the pound stopped, or by 1d., and in the first class 2d., which is paid week by week by each child ... The schools are not voluntary ... We do not give any individual workmen the option of refusing to pay to the school. I wish it was otherwise, but we should get no schools if we did give that option ...

10,101 Do you find cottages for the men employed in your works?
No, we are cottage owners in common with a great number of other persons, but we do not find cottages for them. The ambition of a Welshman, like that of a Cornishman, is to possess a cottage, and when he has saved £50, he builds half a cottage and mortgages it for the other £50.

The *Report of the Royal Commission on Labour* (1893), to take a second example, has detailed information on the administration of cooperative societies, and informative discussions on the causes of strikes and the feasibility of the eight-hour day. Three years later, the *Report from the Select Committee on Distress from Want of Employment* destroyed any complacent beliefs that poverty had been conquered. Among much similar evidence, it described the charitable work of the London Congregational Union, which organized the Self-Help Emigration Society and ran a lodging house in the East End of London. The Union made no charge for the accommodation it offered, but it excluded drunks and tramps and could take no more than 300 men at a time: 'any excess have to leave and fare the best they can'.

... Each man is supplied with half-a-pound of bread and as much water as he likes to drink. There are four drinking fountains in the hall to which the men have ready access. The sleeping accommodation, for which there is no charge, consists of a bunk for each man, a leather-cloth mattress filled with prepared seaweed, a coverlet of the same material, but of double thickness, with an inner lining of felt, and a pillow of the same material . . . Every effort is made to facilitate the men obtaining employment; they may leave at 2 o'clock in the morning if they like, or at 3, 4 or 5; but by 6 o'clock every man must turn out . . .

The total attendance for 1895 was 113,914, and the superintendent estimated that 14,000 different men slept in his bunks during the year. They were the lucky ones.

A third main category of official records for political and social historians is that concerned with censuses. Pushing aside complaints that it was 'subversive to the last remains of English liberty', and bravely disregarding reminders of the wrath of God when David 'numbered Israel from Beersheba to Dan', Addington's government carried out the first British census in 1801, three years after Malthus had published his jeremiad, *Essay on Population*. The census was a simple one. It set out to establish three things – the number and distribution of people living in Great Britain; the number of houses, inhabited and empty; and the numbers of workers engaged in agriculture, in commerce, and in the manufacturing of goods at home or in factories. It did not want any names, only numbers. To avoid unnecessary expense, the parish overseers of the poor were used – at a small fee – as the local enumerators. They visited each house in the parish, and then sent their figures, which they accumulated from answers to oral questions, to the local justice of the peace. The clerk of the peace gathered the lists from the justices, and eventually dispatched the county returns to parliament. That was not quite all. Rickman, the civil servant in charge of the whole operation, was an enthusiastic statistician. He took advantage of the census to arrange for incumbents of churches to compile an abstract from their parish registers. He asked for the numbers of baptisms and burials for every tenth year from 1700 to 1780 and for every year between 1780 and 1800, together with the numbers of marriages each year from 1753 (when Hardwicke's Marriage Act instituted printed forms) to 1800. These returns found their way to parliament, and Rickman's clerks, through the hands of the bishops and privy council.

In 1811, 1821, and 1831 similar censuses were held. In 1841 came change. The combination of the founding of the Royal Statistical Society and the passing of the General Registry Act in 1836 produced a more detailed census, and replaced the overseers, whom the Poor Law Amendment Act had cast aside, by the local registrars and their enumerators. Oral questions were discarded as a thing of the past: theoretically at least, householders now filled in a census form which the enumerator checked with them on the doorstep. There was much grumbling, occasional refusals, and a few ugly incidents, but this method of compiling censuses had come to stay. Succeeding censuses, every tenth year, have asked still more questions, and consequently have recorded more information for the statistician and historian.

Human fallibility has always threatened accuracy in census taking. A few householders inevitably misunderstand the questions or yield to the temptation of reducing their age or elevating their status, and enumerators and registrars are bound to let some mistakes escape their checking eyes. But the margin of error is unlikely to be big enough to invalidate totals and statistical schedules. To these decennial reports we can go in confidence to study the overall increase in the population of Great Britain, the development of industrial and market towns, and the movements of people from countryside to terraced streets, from the upper to the lower industrial valleys as the steam engine superseded the waterwheel, and from the city centre to the suburbs. The recording of birthplaces in and after 1851 has made the perplexing study of migration easier and more rewarding, and for genealogists tracing the history of families has frequently forged the vital link between the post-1837, Somerset House records and the particular parish registers, which record the baptisms and burials of earlier generations. The requirement in and after 1841 to state 'profession, trade, employment or of independent means' has encouraged a number of useful historical exercises, from compiling distribution maps of different industries in successive decades, or tracing the transition from small unit to big unit industry, to graphing the slow improvement in the employment conditions of young children, or establishing, as a social factor, the waxing and waning of the numbers of domestic servants. Census figures concerning schools, ministers of religion, and places of worship have obvious, specialized historical uses, and details of age, blindness, dumbness, and mental deficiency help to establish reliable figures about expectation of life, occupational mortality, and the incidence of physical and mental handicaps.

Census documents are not difficult to find. At the end of the section entitled 'Social and Economic History', the Victoria County Histories carry useful summaries of their own county returns. They give the figures for each census under townships and chapelries grouped into hundreds or boroughs. At a glance it is easy to see in Sussex, for example, the comparative stability of places like Arundel and Steyning, and the contrasting rapid growth of nearby Brighton or, in the second half of the nineteenth century, the sudden increase in the size of Bexhill. Difficulties arise when boundaries have changed since 1801, and when towns have not only incorporated neighbouring units, but have also spread into more than one county division. To get a true picture of Birmingham's growth, we must include Aston and Edgbaston before, as well as after, they became part of the city, and to calculate the increasing population of Chester-le-Street, we must add Lambton and Lumley, which were in Easington Ward, to the main part of the town in Chester Ward. The problems are usually easy enough to solve, especially with the help of the first edition of the ordnance survey map.

For those who wish to study the national picture, there are the printed reports on all censuses. The first census produced three volumes. One published the figures for England and Wales, another the figures for Scotland, and the third the findings of the parish register inquiry. The official returns from 1841 onwards have ever grown more voluminous, but the summary volumes serve as efficient guides, and often supply the student with the facts he is seeking. The editor of the 1851 summary rightly considered that he had been 'engaged in a work of utility', and that 'much valuable information connected with the general results of the Census, now brought within a small compass, would find its way into the hands of many to whom it would otherwise be inaccessible'. The 'compass' was not as small as he inferred. The first half of his closely printed book consisted of short but thoughtful observations on what the census revealed about population distribution, ages, marriage, occupations, birthplaces, infirmities, and public institutions. The following short passages illustrate the style and scope of his comment.

Mr Rickman noticed that in 1821 and 1831 the number of males under twenty years of age and upwards were nearly equal ... The Census of 1851 reveals a very different state of things; for even if the army, navy, and merchant seamen abroad are omitted, the males in Great Britain of twenty years of age and upwards (5,475,540) exceed the males under twenty years of age (4,779,313) by 696,227 ...

The following are the most remarkable results: of the 14,422,801 people living in 1821, 6,981,068 were under twenty years of age, and 7,441,733 were twenty years of age and upwards; while of the 21,185,010 living in 1851, the numbers under twenty years of age were 9,558,114 and the numbers of the age of twenty years and upwards were 11,626,896 ... The males at the soldier's age of twenty to forty amounted to 1,966,664 in 1821, and to 3,193,496 in 1851: the increase in the thirty years is equivalent in number to a vast army of more than *twelve hundred thousand men* (1,226,832).

It has been generally considered ... that crowded dwellings and other circumstances attendant upon dense populations ... have caused a greater amount of blindness in towns than in rural localities ... But ... it is clear from the returns that a much larger proportion of blind persons is found in agricultural than in manufacturing and mining counties. For example in Wilts, Dorset, Devon, Cornwall, and Somerset there is an average of 1 blind in every 758 inhabitants; in Essex, Suffolk, and Norfolk 1 in 888 ...

In striking contrast with these are the following manufacturing or mining counties:

Yorkshire, West Riding	1 blind in every			1,231	inhabitants
Cheshire and Lancashire	1	„	„	„ 1,167	„
Durham	1	„	„	„ 1,163	„
Staffordshire	1	„	„	„ 1,082	„

Conclusions unfavourable to the rural districts should not, however, be deduced from a mere comparison ... an examination of the *ages of the Blind* shows that nearly one-half of the persons deprived of sight are above sixty years of age ... In the great seats of manufacturing industry the population generally is much younger than in most of the agricultural counties where ... persons in large numbers, and especially females, are living, in circumstances favourable to longevity, at very advanced ages ...

In the second and longer half of the book, the editor printed fifty-eight statistical tables. Some of them were quite short. Table II, in half a page, listed the number of houses (inhabited, uninhabited, and building) and the population (persons, males and females) in Great Britain, England and Wales, Scotland, and Islands in the British Seas for all six censuses from 1801 to 1851; and Table VII, in two pages, showed the distribution of the 1851 figures for houses and population 'in the Counties and Parliamentary Divisions of Counties, including and excluding Represented Cities and Boroughs, with the Number of Members returned'. On the other hand, succinct as all the tables are, it took twenty-one full pages to list, in alphabetical order, the occupations of the people, and twenty-six pages (two counties to a page) to summarize the census statistics for each county in England and Wales. But there is hardly a general calculation that has been missed: these tables disclose such varied facts as that out of the 491,720 people living in Dorset in 1851, 4,940 had been born in Ireland; that of the 164 candlestick-makers in Great Britain, all but fourteen were males; that 39,631 Europeans, including women and children, were in the service of the East India Company; that in England and Wales there were just about twice as many widows (661,894) as widowers (333,926), and that out of 223,271 farms 142,358 were less than 100 acres in extent. To complete this comprehensive summary, the editor included a folding map showing in considerable detail the distribution of occupations throughout Great Britain.

For each succeeding census there was a similar digest or summary volume. The statistical tables grew more comprehensive as the list of census questions grew longer: by 1911, for example, they occupied over 400 folio pages. In addition, each census produced specialized volumes summarizing the information on such subjects as schools, religious worship, and health. If these concise volumes do not satisfy a researcher's needs, then he will have to consult the full printed *Official Returns of the Census* published by the registrar general during the decade following each census. If even these are not full enough – and many genealogical and local inquiries require more detail still – there are the enumerators' books. For the censuses of 1841, 1851, and 1861, these 'grass root' papers are available for study in the Public Record Office. For later censuses they are still stored in the recesses of Somerset House. It is not possible for students to examine them there, but it is always possible to purchase a photograph of pages required.

2. PRIVATE WITNESS: POLITICAL AND SOCIAL
LETTERS, DIARIES, REMINISCENCES AND AUTO-
BIOGRAPHIES

The first aim of the political historian is to relate a sequence of events. This apparently straightforward task is not always as easy as it seems. One witness's evidence of time or place or happening can conflict with that of another, and the discovery of new facts, or a re-examination of old ones, is always likely to modify or reject the official or traditional version of what happened. But when a historian goes a stage further and asks why events took the course they did, he is facing more difficult problems still. To find his answer he has to probe beneath the surface of the story he is telling. He has to concern himself with thoughts that were uppermost in men's minds, with a particular generation's view of life, with changes that were taking place in the distribution of wealth or in the pattern of political power, and with the battles the reformers of the age were fighting, and the future the prophets were foretelling. Diligence and patience might lead him to an answer which satisfies himself. It is certain, however, he will never find an answer that will satisfy every-one.

The first stage in this fascinating pursuit of 'why?' is to under-stand the thinking that produced the action. *Hansard* helps to enlighten us about political thought and argument, but we can never be sure that on the floor of the House, or on any public occasion, politicians are being entirely honest. They are on stage, often striking a pose, always to some extent saying what their colleagues and the public expect them to say. In major debates most speeches, especially the leading ones, are predict-able. They present the considered, official opinion of either the government or opposition. To find out how that opinion was reached, how strongly it is held, or what reservations and modifications the speaker nourishes at the back of his mind, it is necessary to ask him questions in private and to promise to treat his answer in confidence. A close friend or a reputable journalist can do that: a historian cannot. The best he can do is to seek out such documents as letters and diaries, which were once private or even secret, and study the reminiscences and autobiographies, which the politicians and others wrote later in life when the issues they were concerned with had been settled. For the period 1760–1914, there is plenty of such material both in print and in manuscript. The historian's difficulty is not to find it, but to interpret it.

Letters and diaries have the advantage over reminiscences and autobiographies that they were written nearer the events they describe. But to be good historical material, they must be honest to the point of imprudence. If the letter is in any degree formal, if it has been written circumspectly, or if its chief object is to bolster a political or literary reputation, then it is no more use to the historian than a speech in the Commons or a letter to the press. To get behind the public front of a politician, the historian must find him off guard. He is likely to do that when he reads what he said in anger or in moments of frustration or joy, or when he discovers letters he sent to intimate friends, or when he turns the pages of the politician's private journal. Such sources help the historian to follow the build-up of an incident, to trace the origin and development of a particular political policy, to study the interaction of personalities, and to assess the amounts of principle, expediency, personal dislike, self-interest, and self-deception that combined to make an individual take the stand he did, or the political group adopt the programme it advocated in the Commons or on the hustings. The public statement is usually the outcome of considerable thought and argument: in the private letter or *aide-mémoire* lies the historian's best chance of finding out how thought evolved and how decision was reached – in other words, of answering the question 'Why?'.

It is well known that Lord Melbourne's Whig government resumed office in 1839 and limped on for another two years, simply because the queen and Sir Robert Peel disagreed about which ladies should be appointed ladies of the bedchamber. The official records merely outline the events: Melbourne's offer of resignation; Wellington's decision not to accept the invitation to form a government; Peel's attempt to do so; Victoria's refusal to make required changes in her household; the decision of Melbourne's government to withdraw its offer of resignation, and to continue in office. But in the unofficial records – especially the letters and journal of Victoria herself – lie the clues which may explain why the apparently trifling disagreement between Peel and the queen led to so serious an outcome. Of the several reasons that soon appear, Victoria's dread of losing Melbourne as her private minister is the most obvious. The third-person formality of this letter oddly matches the emotion she felt on receiving the news of his impending resignation:

The Queen thinks Lord Melbourne may possibly wish to know how she is this morning; the Queen is somewhat calmer; she was in a wretched state till nine o'clock last night, when she tried to occupy herself and try to think less gloomily of this dreadful change, and she succeeded in calming herself till she went to bed at twelve, and she slept well; but on waking this morning, all – all that had happened in one short eventful day came more forcibly to her mind, and brought back her grief . . .

An hour or two later, Wellington's decision deepened her disappointment, so that Peel, 'who came after two', encountered the queen's hostility almost as soon as he entered the audience chamber. Victoria began by telling him he must find a post for Wellington, and by talking of 'her great friendship for, and gratitude to Lord Melbourne'. Intentionally or not, she made it crystal clear that, if she had had her way, she would never have asked Peel to form a government. Little wonder that in her eyes he appeared 'embarrassed and put out', 'a cold, odd man . . . not happy and sanguine'. Reading between the lines, however, Peel appears to have acquitted himself well in the audience. He mollified the queen a little by sympathetic nods and grunts, showed no eagerness to assume responsibility – 'he felt unequal to the task . . . he quite approved that the Duke should take office' – yet managed to slip in at least one condition of his acceptance. 'He would require me,' Victoria reported to Melbourne, 'to demonstrate (*a certain* degree, if *any* I can only feel) confidence in the Government, and that my Household would be one of the marks of that.'

The queen wrote this letter to her prime minister as soon as Peel had left the palace in the afternoon of 8 May. The household matter was then a secondary affair. Her personal agitation was uppermost: it confused her narrative of events, and destroyed the formality of her letter:

The Queen then mentioned [to Wellington] her intention to prove her great *fairness* to her new Government in telling them . . . that I meant to see you often as a friend as I owed so much to you . . . The Queen don't like his [Peel's] manner after – oh! how different, how dreadfully different, to that frank, open, natural and most kind warm manner of Lord Melbourne. The Duke I like by far better to Peel . . .

But very quickly, Peel's insistence on household changes grew in her mind. She picked out of Melbourne's reply the part she wanted – 'this matter of the Household is so personal to yourself, that it was best to give an intimation of your feelings upon it in the first instance' – and apparently failed to notice the rest of his advice – 'if Sir Robert is unable to concede it, it will not do to refuse and to put off the negotiation upon it. Lord Melbourne would strongly advise your Majesty to do everything to facilitate the formation of the Government.' The next morning the issue had assumed the guise of a principle at stake. The first letter Victoria wrote to Melbourne that day informed him,

Sir Robert Peel has behaved very ill, and has insisted on my giving up my Ladies, to which I replied that I never would consent, and I never saw a man so frightened . . .

The second showed the issue growing bigger still:

. . . the Queen felt this was an attempt to see whether she could be led and managed like a child; if it should lead to Sir Robert Peel's refusing to undertake the formation of the Government, which would be absurd, the Queen will feel satisfied that she has only been defending her own rights, on a point which so nearly concerned her person, and which, if they had succeeded in, would have led to every sort of unfair attempt at power . . .

Later that evening, in a long extract in her private journal, the queen justified her part in the day's events. She gave herself considerable credit for not objecting to the ministers Peel proposed to appoint – 'though I said I might have my personal feelings about Lord Lyndhurst and Lord Aberdeen' – and then recorded her firm stand on the question of the household:

. . . Soon after this Sir Robert said: 'Now, about the Ladies', upon which I said I could *not* give up *any* of my Ladies, and never had imagined such a thing. He asked if I meant to retain *all*. '*All*', I said. 'The Mistress of the Robes and the Ladies of the Bedchamber?' I replied, '*All*', – for he said they were the wives of the opponents of the Government, mentioning Lady Normanby in particular as one of the late Ministers' wives. I said that would not interfere . . .

The queen's version of the facts caused Melbourne's cabinet to advise Victoria to stick to her guns: only during the week following did members begin to realize that Peel had been more moderate and reasonable in his demands than they had first been led to believe. The queen unburdened herself to the Grand Duke of Russia, who happened to be in London, and to Leopold of Belgium. Both, of course, gave her the moral support she was obviously seeking. For some weeks she seems to have seen herself as a royal heroine upholding the rights of all crowned heads against unjustified encroachment, but her real satisfaction was in Melbourne's return to office. Time steadily reduced the incident's importance in the queen's mind. She was wise enough not to risk a second collision with Peel two years later, when the Whigs could continue no longer. Prince Albert as well as Melbourne advised against such a course. Officially, the issue did not arise, because the three ladies to whom Peel chiefly objected all 'resigned' before he became prime minister.

Victoria's letters and journals let us see how the 'crisis' developed. Wellington's comments, written and reported, Peel's terse observations, and the writings of other contemporaries such as Croker and Greville fill out the story still further. Each such source gives a personal view. Not one of them has a monopoly of truth, any more than one historian can claim he has made a flawless interpretation of the evidence he has examined. A private letter does not attain a greater degree of truth just because it is private. Each one the historian must judge on its merits, and, of course, to make truth more elusive still, there will be many occasions when historians will differ considerably in their judgements. There would seem to be little doubt, for example – though some readers may disagree – that Captain James Watson's report to his admiral about his experience in the Nore mutiny of 1797 was a fair, factual description of what happened to him.

... Next morning [31 May], I found the fleet in the utmost disorder. I was surrounded by armed vessels, and told if I did not hoist the red flag the tender would be sunk. The contagion spread like fire among the volunteers, who, stimulated by some deserters and other villains then on board, made an attempt to take possession of the vessel, without success ... How I felt afterwards at seeing every possibility of escaping rendered impracticable by the 5 men of war I passed in Yarmouth Roads coming fast up, all in a state of mutiny, is not easy to be described; I had no resource but to bring the ship to, in the midst of the fleet. I was dragged like a culprit before their infernal tribunal ...

On the other hand, it is a matter of personal judgement if Lord Aberdeen was correct or exaggerating when he informed Princess Lieven in June 1835 that Palmerston had put the Melbourne administration in jeopardy by allowing British subjects to enlist on Queen Isabella's side in the Spanish civil war.

This is a new kind of intervention, which, we may presume, is not to be called war ... Call it what they may, it is a disgraceful, and a barbarous thing, that an independent nation should be delivered up to the ravages of foreign mercenaries ...

Our ministers are not much disturbed in Parliament, but they know the instability of their position, and do not disguise it. The moment of their overthrow is not yet come; but it depends on Peel to hasten, or to delay it. He could destroy them whenever he pleased; but the difficulty is to retain possession of the Government, when it is obtained. This, we have shown, that we were not able to do; and there must be some change in a portion of the House of Commons, before it could be safely attempted again ...

Right or wrong, keen assessment or wishful thinking, this letter appears to express honestly held opinions. The fact that Melbourne's government continued in office for another six years does not prove Aberdeen a liar: it does not necessarily diminish the quality of his political judgement. His is a different case altogether from Disraeli's assessment of Palmerston in a letter to Lady Londonderry in February 1855. Just as Aberdeen was furious with Palmerston over his Spanish policy, so Disraeli, twenty years later, was furious with him for having outwitted Derby and accepted the queen's invitation to form a government. Frustration and anger completely upset his judgement:

... he is really an impostor, utterly exhausted, and at the best only ginger beer and not champaign [sic], and now an old painted Pantaloon, very deaf, very blind, and with false teeth, which would fall out of his mouth, when speaking, if he did not hesitate and halt so in his talk . . .

During the next ten years Palmerston showed remarkable vigour and leadership for so infirm a man!

Most of the letters written between 1760 and 1914 which have found their way into print were written by people prominent in party politics. If they have not been gathered together and published as collections of letters, such as the three volumes of *Correspondence of John, fourth Duke of Bedford* or the two volumes of *The Queen and Mr Gladstone*, they have been quoted freely in such long biographies as Monypenny and Buckle's *Disraeli* (6 volumes) or Garvin and Amery's *Joseph Chamberlain* (6 volumes). Indeed, judging from the ease with which biographers have discovered bundles of private letters, it would seem that parents and friends, as well as the aspiring politicians and future men of affairs themselves, had their eye on posterity from the beginning. No doubt the widespread practice of keeping letter books helped to preserve the unofficial, and often trifling, letters as well as the official or particularly important ones. In addition, many people in public life kept journals. Some of them are little more than a bare record of activities – a readily consulted index of a political career – but others, often from secondary figures in political life, are well-informed commentaries on people, policies, and occasions. Undoubtedly, some of these diarists and commentators have been conscious of future generations looking over their shoulders as they were writing: they have carefully recorded episodes they were privileged to witness, in much the same way as, in time of war, generals and others have made daily jottings as a basis for a future *apologia*. But they are not merely journalists; they are participators, not observers, small-part actors on the stage, not critics sitting in the stalls. Charles Greville's aristocratic eyes studied English politics and politicians from the vantage point of the clerkship of the privy council. During the 1820s, '30s, and '40s they missed very little of what was going on behind the scenes, and *The Greville Diary* is therefore a well-informed, if jumbled, spasmodic and idiosyncratic commentary on both politics and London society. Greville's point of view is his own, often violently opposed to that which was, and still is, commonly accepted. Lord Durham is usually appreciatively remembered for the wise, forward-looking report he made on Canada's problems in 1840. To Greville he appeared to be 'the most ill-conditioned, ill-behaved coxcomb that ever was suffered to swagger and bully in a Cabinet'. Of Dr Kay's Poor Law School at Norwood – seen as a progressive experiment by most social historians – Greville wrote:

As I looked at the class to whom a lesson was then being read, all the urchins from eight to eleven or twelve years old, I thought I had never seen a congregation of more unpromising and ungainly heads, and accordingly they are the worst and lowest specimens of humanity; starved, ill-used children of poor and vicious parents, generally arriving at the school weak and squalid, with a tendency to every vice . . .

He had the grace to acknowledge that, 'under able and zealous teachers', Kay's system acted 'with rapid and beneficial effect on these rude materials', and went on

to reflect with shame and sorrow . . . on the imperfect and defective education which is given to the highest and richest class of society, who are brought up thus stupidly at an enormous expense, acquiring little knowledge, and what they do acquire, so loosely and incompletely as to be of the smallest possible use.

An older observer admired by Greville was Thomas Creevey, who was in and out of parliament during and after the Napoleonic Wars, when his party, the Whigs, was in the political wilderness. At the beginning of his political career he gained the patronage of the Duke of Norfolk, and throughout his life enjoyed the support and friendship of the Earl of Sefton. He married Mrs Ord, a fairly wealthy widow, and she enabled him to lead a busy, if financially unprofitable, life in political society. His letters were carefully preserved, and frequently copied, by his step-daughter, Elizabeth Ord: Creevey himself suggested that she should do this – 'in future times the Creevey Papers may form a curious collection'. They form more than that. Since Maxwell edited two volumes of *The Creevey Papers* in 1903, they have been everywhere accepted as important source material for the political and social history of his day. They do not consist only of letters and journal entries by Creevey himself: among the other papers are letters written by his wife, Henry Brougham, Lord Grey, Lady Holland, Mrs Fitzherbert, Sir John Moore, and several other prominent contemporaries.

One of Creevey's acquaintances was the Rev. Sydney Smith, another unusual, illuminating letter-writer. In 1812 he wrote to Creevey that in a Yorkshire election he had voted for Wilberforce

on account of his good conduct in Africa, a place returning no members to parliament, but still, from the extraordinary resemblance its inhabitants bear to human creatures, of some consequence. An election at Westminster is sad work – at the moment of the greatest ferment, York was, in the two great points of ebriety and pugnacity, as quiet as average London at about 3 o'clock in the morning.

Smith was no party man. He could not believe that 'the salvation of several planets depended upon the adoption of Mr Johnson and the rejection of Mr Jackson'. He was interested in the material welfare of all mankind, and many of the career politicians who heard him talk construed his common sense as cynicism and his satirical wit as amusing nonsense. They laughed and declared him 'diverting', but probably with Creevey privately considered him 'too much of a buffoon'. They understood John Wilson Croker much better. He thought and behaved more conventionally for he was an orthodox politician, the Tory equivalent of Creevey, and unashamedly proud of his friendship with Wellington and Peel. He served as secretary to the admiralty from 1809 to 1830, but his claim to fame is the collection of private papers, *The Croker Papers*, published in 1884.

Lord Shaftesbury was another politician-recorder. He was a Tory, in the Commons from 1828 and the Lords from 1851 to his death in 1885. He upheld 'authority' in the state and, even more strongly, in the church. He rejected liberty and equality as desirable political aims, but he so hated unnecessary suffering that he became the champion of the depressed classes. 'The greatest Jacobin in your Majesty's dominions', Melbourne is reported to have told Victoria. In a political sense, nothing could have been more ludicrous; but the mixture of political comment and social concern in Shaftesbury's diary makes it easy to understand why Melbourne described him as a revolutionary.

I shall have no ease or pleasure in the recess, should these poor children [the sweeps] be despised by the Lords, and tossed to the mercy of their savage purchasers. I find that Evangelical religionists are not those on whom I can rely. The Factory Question, and every question for what is called 'humanity', receive as much support from the 'men of the world' as from the men who say they will have nothing to do with it . . .

Men are talking, they know not why, and they do not reflect *how*, of *this* slight concession and *that;* of an 'enlargement of the franchise', and other vagaries. No one, except the Chartists, has asked for it . . . A Sanitary Bill would, in five years, confer more blessing and obliterate more Chartism than universal suffrage in half a century; but the world, when ill at ease, flies always to politics, and omits the statistics of the chimney corner, where all a man's comfort or discomfort lies.

There are many more of these inner windows we can open to examine the political world during the years 1760–1914. The papers of George Grenville, first lord of the treasury from 1763 to 1765, and *The Works and Correspondence of Edmund*

Burke look out on to the beginning of this period. George III's letters are as available as Queen Victoria's, and both aristocratic William Windham, Foxite and, later, Pittite, secretary for war from 1794 to 1801 and again in the Ministry of All the Talents, and George Rose, minor office holder under Pitt and member of Perceval's cabinet, have left dull utilitarian diaries behind them. Thomas Raikes, a Yorkshireman living in fashionable and political society in London's West End, wrote a far livelier and thoughtful diary, which enables us to understand Tory hopes and fears during the 1830s and 1840s. His comments upon the Reform Bill of 1832 are a typical illustration of his viewpoint and his perspicacity. On Saturday, 19 May, a private meeting of Tory peers decided not to vote when the Bill reached the Lords. That ensured that the Bill would soon become law. Raikes's immediate comment was:

> The die is cast; to go back is impossible; the tide of innovation has set in, and who shall say where it will carry us? From this day dates a new era for England. Placards are streaming about the streets with 'Glory and honour to the people'. And what is the people? What has the people always been? The most capricious, the most cruel, the most ungrateful and selfish class of society . . . This is the real evil; it is not the disfranchising rotten boroughs, and the enfranchising other places, it is the reckless agitation of the whole country, caused by an unprincipled set of men, to keep themselves in place, which we have now to deplore.

Eight volumes of *Despatches, Correspondence, and Memoranda of the Duke of Wellington* were published between 1867 and 1880. Many selections of ministers' letters, including those of Melbourne, Peel, and Russell, have long been in print, and almost every prominent politician and office holder in Victoria's reign was deemed worthy of a full-length biography, if not before he died, then shortly afterwards. These nineteenth-century biographers, apparently untroubled by costs of book production, did not always write good biographies, but they all compiled handy and rich collections of primary sources for later historians. Their historical judgements may be jejune and their style wearisome to eye and ear, but their books are worth library shelf space if only for the first-hand material which they quote and so make readily available.

Cultivated society had, of course, other aspects beside party politics. The letters and journals of such authors as Fanny Burney, John Keats, George Eliot, and Lord Macaulay, as well as the writings of 'literary observers' like Caroline Fox, Henry Crabb Robinson, and Dorothy Wordsworth, all enrich our knowledge of the literary world. The diaries of Cardinal Manning and Bishop Wilberforce, Fanny Kemble and Charles Macready, illuminate ecclesiastical and theatrical society, and the letters of Charles Darwin and T. H. Huxley as well as Samuel Butler's and Benjamin Jowett's note books – hardly diaries – shed restricted light on the activities of intellectuals and academics.

As we descend the social ladder, letters and diaries are not so numerous. In the work-a-day world there was usually less incentive, or need, and far less time and opportunity, to write letters and keep diaries. But those that have survived have a particular value. They show us the country and its political and social problems from unusual angles. The writers were not daily rubbing shoulders with the legislators. Nor were they looking out on 'the people' from a privileged seat in Westminster or the bow window of a political club in Piccadilly. They were not the rulers but the ruled, enduring or enjoying earning their living. Some of them, such as William Cobbett or the two parsons, Benjamin Newton of Yorkshire and Francis Kilvert of the Welsh Marches, knew something of comfort, but they lived entirely outside fashionable society. Cobbett battled his way into political life and eventually into the Commons, but he was never fully integrated into party politics. He was not a politician, as his contemporaries understood the term. Both the parsons lived provincial lives. Both seem to have enjoyed themselves, Newton in a rapidly changing north country at the beginning of the nineteenth century, and Kilvert in rural Radnorshire and Herefordshire in the 1850s and 1870s. But there were other diarists and letter writers who lived much harder lives. Ellen Weeton kept the household together by running a dame's school; Private Wheeler served in the ranks throughout the Peninsular War and the Waterloo campaign; and John O'Neil, a Lancashire weaver, struggled to make his trade union effective, and managed with great difficulty to survive the years of the cotton famine. Comments such as these, from O'Neil's diary, allow us to see a little of the darker side of political life – darker in two senses, first because it was clouded with poverty and discomfort, and secondly because, unlike the parliamentary activity of the time, it does not enjoy the illumination afforded by the letters and diaries of many participants.

15 December 1860. I left my work [at Low Moor, Clitheroe] at noon to go to Colne, as there was a [union] executive meeting which I must attend, I got there by half past four and got my tea and lodgings at the Red Lion. After we got tea we had a walk through the town and market and then had a look into the Cloth Hall where there was a meeting of the operatives. It is a large place and there would be about 1,600 people in it . . .

16 December. . . . We then went to the Committee room and commenced business. There was a great deal to do, as the Colne Masters are bringing a great deal of families from Coventry, where there is a great deal of distress upon account of the ribband trade being slack; and they say they will fill all the looms with Coventry people if the Colne workers will not go to work. But at the meeting last night in the Cloth Hall they were determined to remain firm to the last . . .

17 April 1864. I have had another weary week of bad work. I have just earned 7s. 3½d. off three looms and there are plenty as bad off as me, and if any one complains to the Master of bad work [i.e. working with poor quality Surat cotton] he says, if you don't like it you can leave.

He wants no one to stop that does not like it, and that is all the satisfaction we can get ...

A person's motives for putting pen to paper is one of the factors historians have always to keep in mind. As O'Neil was writing his daily entries in his marble-boarded cash book, it is most unlikely that he felt he was compiling a social or trade union record. Ellen Weeton tells us – and we can believe her – that she wrote her long letters and kept her journal in order to while away many a lonely hour, and busy men of affairs, dashing off letters day after day, have little time to think of anything but the matters in hand. Similarly, the political pamphleteer and the writer of the open letter or election squib has no consideration but his immediate purpose. This directness and simplicity of aim give these writings value. Historians have little difficulty in assessing their worth, and it is fortunate that, in addition to letters and diaries, copies of hundreds of ephemeral political publications still survive in the remoter recesses of our reference libraries and record offices.

It is quite different when we have to evaluate an autobiography or a collection of political memoirs. These were usually written at leisure with time enough for reconsideration and revision. The authors were writing for publication: they were aware that their own and future generations would be critical of what they said, and would judge them by the evidence they gave. Consequently, they acted as their own editors and their own censors. How they exercised these powers differed with each writer, but the historian who uses such writings as primary sources has always to be on his guard against self-justification, favourable exaggeration, suppression of damaging details, distortion of facts, and the blowing of trumpets. This is not to attribute base motives to autobiographers nor to dismiss such books with contempt. The evidence of a first-class witness cannot help but carry weight, but memory is just as fallible as human nature. 'I remember' or 'I was present' must always make us prick up our ears. At best it can be the beginning of a sober, authoritative description of events, clearly recalled with significant detail, and partial only in the sense that it is the evidence of one pair of eyes. At the worst it can be the prelude to a tall story, a persuasive self-defence, or a catalogue of self-pitying excuses. Most autobiographies and political memoirs lie between these two extremes: the value of their witness has to be estimated in the light of the other evidence available. Nevertheless, our historical sources would be much poorer if politicians such as Lord Holland (the nephew of Charles James Fox), Sir Robert Peel, and Lord Brougham had not written their political memoirs, if such different ladies as Elizabeth Ham, Gwen Raverat, Margot Asquith, and Beatrice Webb had not given us their own account of their lives and the society they knew, and if Samuel Bamford, Francis Place, William Lovett, Thomas Cooper, James Sexton, and other radicals and revolutionaries had not sat down comparatively late in life and told us of their earlier struggles to improve the lot of working men and women.

3. OUTSIDE OBSERVATION AND COMMENT: VERSE, CONTEMPORARY WRITINGS, NOVELS, AND NEWS-PAPERS

> ... Blush ye not
> To boast your equal laws, your just restraints,
> Your rights defin'd, your liberties secur'd,
> Whilst with an iron hand ye crush to earth
> The helpless African; and bid him drink
> That cup of sorrow, which yourselves have dash'd
> Indignant, from oppressions' fainting grasp?

This was the theme of William Roscoe's *The Wrongs of Africa*, published in 1787. At that time Roscoe was not yet actively engaged in party politics, but the slave trade had outraged his moral sense and feeling for justice. Writing this poem was his way of rebuking his fellow citizens in Liverpool for inflicting misery on other human beings. It had a marked effect. It roused debate, and gained support for the abolition movement. Thirty years later, as Whig member for Liverpool, Roscoe had the deep satisfaction of voting in favour of the abolition of the slave trade.

Poems, squibs, and jingles were commonly used in the eighteenth and nineteenth centuries to make political comment. They had the advantage of being easy to memorize and pithy to quote. Some, such as *The Wrongs of Africa*, were long and well argued: they required time and concentration to read and master. But others made no attempt to put forward a serious argument. They praised their heroes, poked fun at their opponents, or attacked a particular policy or politician. Some used a rapier, but most preferred a bludgeon. The gifted poets were as ready as the jingle-writers to contribute to the continuous political commentary.

> O for the coming of that glorious time
>   When, prizing knowledge as her noblest wealth
> And best protection, this imperial Realm
>   While she exacts allegiance, shall admit
> An obligation on her part to *teach*
>   Them who are born to serve her and obey.

So wrote Wordsworth in 1814. He was half way along his personal road of political belief, which in forty years led him from such revolutionary heights as unconditional acceptance of the French Revolution – 'Blest was it in that dawn to be alive' – to the reactionary lowlands of opposition to parliamentary reform and alarm at the social consequences of the spread of mechanics' institutes. Coleridge, Tennyson, and Matthew Arnold also commented upon the political ideals of their day, but more immediately effective political verses came from

Byron and Shelley. They were not content to express their opinion in philosophical poetry or to wrap political criticism in imagery or metaphor. They hit out in words that men could readily understand and remember. Byron had no love of George III or any other crowned head. Southey's *Ode on the Death of George III* provoked him to write the scurrilous *Vision of Judgment:* he explained in his preface that for Southey 'to attempt to canonize a monarch, who, whatever were his household virtues, was neither a successful nor a patriot king ... necessarily begets opposition'. Byron more than counter-balanced Southey's praise.

> ... A better farmer ne'er brush'd dew from lawn
>   A worse king never left a realm undone!
> He died – but left his subjects still behind,
>   One half as mad – and t'other no less blind.
>   ... Of all
> The fools who flock'd to swell or see the show,
>   Who cared about the corpse? The funeral
> Made the attraction, and the black the woe.
>   There throbbed not there a thought which pierced the pall;
> And when the gorgeous coffin was laid low,
>   It seemed the mockery of hell to fold
> The rottenness of eighty years in gold. ...

Shelley could be just as bitter in his attacks. In 1817 he censured Lord Eldon, the lord chancellor:

> Thy country's curse is on thee! Justice sold,
>   Truth trampled, Nature's landmarks overthrown.
> And heaps of fraud-accumulated gold ...

And he could be as rousingly revolutionary as the most enthusiastic Chartist or Luddite:

> Men of England, wherefore plough
>   For the Lords who lay ye low? ...
> Wherefore feed, and clothe, and save,

From the cradle to the grave,
Those ungrateful drones who would
Drain your sweat – nay, drink your blood?

The political ballad-monger produced his flimsy sheets of verse whenever a controversial issue sharply divided opinion, and whenever an election roused party feeling. The poems were all strongly partisan, little more than caricatures in verse. Most of them had the scathing cruelty, and occasionally the scatological imagery, of a Rowlandson or Gillray cartoon. The best of them were redeemed by humour, the most successful had verse forms that fitted popular tunes. The following three stanzas come from a Tory song in favour of Canning and against Brougham, who were opponents in the Liverpool election of 1812. The tune is 'Yankee Doodle'. In their heavy humour and lack of argument these verses are typical of popular, election comment. Their theme is Brougham making a whistle-stop tour of the borough in a carriage. Pink was the Whig colour.

At length arrived at Dale Street top,
    A spot long famed for speeches,
When Brougham did out his visage pop,
    And again began his twitches.
            Yankee Doodle, etc.

At this some ladies decked in pink,
    And perfumed sweet as roses,
Looked all askew as though a stink
    Had just assailed their noses.
            Yankee Doodle, etc.

Oh la! that sure can ne'er be he,
    'Bout whom they've made such pother;
But now he's not the man for me,
    So I'll support another.
            Yankee Doodle, etc.

As historical sources such political verses have limited value. In no sense can they be accepted as fair comment – still less as contributions to political argument – but they do recall the atmosphere of past elections and controversies. They are social documents rather than political documents. They illustrate old styles of popular humour, and help us to appreciate contemporary views of political issues and personalities. Political cartoons do a similar job. Gillray's cartoons of the 1780s and 1790s, Cruikshank's and those of the *Punch* caricaturists of the early Victorian period, Beerbohm's and Spy's of the Edwardian age, all had cogent political influence in their day. They helped to shape people's opinions, not by logical, stage-by-stage argument, but by presenting their interpretation of a political issue so compactly and pointedly that it stuck in the reader's mind. As historical documents, their chief use is to illustrate contemporary opinion, and to show us politicians and others in public life as their friends and opponents saw them at different stages in their career. Their social comment, often unintentional, is sometimes most revealing. So is that of the picture postcard, which came into its own at the turn of the twentieth century.

More serious, well-developed, political and social comment also exists in plenty. Each generation during this period produced its quota of thoughtful commentators. Some set out merely to describe what they saw around them; others plunged straight into constructive and destructive criticism, and a few argued their way towards new and more successful policies. These categories of commentators are not exclusive. Writers like Malthus, Engels, and Charles Booth would claim that they were only stating facts as they saw them. But *An Essay on the Principle of Population* discussed likely consequences as well as making acute observations, and *The Condition of the Working Class in England in 1844* gathered together facts chiefly to base on them the theory – unwarrantable as it proved – that the middle class was already losing its lead in developing Britain.

In *Labour and Life of the People* (1891), Charles Booth made a social survey of London without any obvious political axe to grind. His work is more akin to a commissioner's report than to Engel's book half a century earlier. But all three books instigated thought on social–political problems, and must be classed as significant historical documents. So must the writings of such authors as Burke, Tom Paine, Adam Smith, Bentham, Gibbon Wakefield, J. S. Mill, Samuel Smiles, and the Fabian essayists, all of whom wrote to point out 'errors' in current thinking and to bring policy back on to the 'right' lines. Several of them were well ahead of their times. *The Wealth of Nations* was published in 1776, but half a century had to elapse before its free-trade doctrines began to be seriously considered by those in government; Jeremy Bentham's long life ended in 1832, on the eve of the period when his followers achieved their best results; and the writings of such Fabian socialists as Sidney Webb, Annie Besant, and Bernard Shaw had more practical effect after the First World War than before it. And of course not all political teachers and prophets succeeded in winning sufficient pupils and followers to be widely influential. Thomas Carlyle thundered away against the evils of unrestricted competition without noticeable results, and John Ruskin's eloquent attacks on the economists did not significantly diminish the lasting influence of Mill's *Principles of Political Economy*. Even the sensitive writings of social reformers such as F. D. Maurice, Charles Kingsley, and William Morris had nothing like the immediate impact of such books as Samuel Smiles's *Self-help* or John Seeley's *Expansion of England*, which, instead of re-examining problems, put into words the popular thought of their day. Yet all these writings help the historian to understand the past. Failure to influence other men's thinking is as eloquent a fact as the ready acceptance of a new theory: the fierce opposition roused by *The Origin of Species* and *The Descent of Man* is as important a historical happening as the immediate popularity of

Burke's *Reflections on the French Revolution* or the reading public's open-armed approval of the Waverley novels, with their veneration of tradition.

Fiction has historical significance too. Some novels express political opinion as directly as a speech in the Commons; Disraeli's and Wells's novels do, and Scott's and Kingsley's sometimes get near it. But it would be difficult to imagine a novel not having social comment, either explicit or implicit. The comment can be avowedly approving, as in George Meredith's descriptions of life in the English country house, or G. A. Henty's stories of Empire heroes; or it may be neutral or gently ironic, as in Jane Austen's or Trollope's novels; or it may be sharply disapproving as in Dickens's *Oliver Twist*, Kingsley's *Alton Locke*, or Mrs Gaskell's *North and South*. Most novelists pose as observers, rather than conscious critics, of society. In the telling of their tales, they describe the society they know, and are content to allow their readers to approve or disapprove. But the personal views of the best novelists show through the veil of their stories. Their own opinions influence their descriptions. Personal disapprobation is quite clear in Charlotte Brontë's 'objective' description of Lowood School in *Jane Eyre*. It was not an imagined school: she was describing the Clergy Daughters' School which she and her sisters had attended in the 1820s at Cowan Bridge near Kirkby Lonsdale.

... we came upon the hum of many voices, and presently entered a wide, long room, with great deal tables, two at each end, on each of which burnt a pair of candles, and seated all round on benches a congregation of girls of every age, from nine or ten to twenty. Seen by the dim light of their dips, their number to me appeared countless, though not in reality exceeding eighty; they were uniformly dressed in brown stuff frocks of quaint fashion, and long holland pinafores. It was the hour of study; they were engaged in conning over tomorrow's task, and the hum I had heard was the combined result of their whispered repetitions.

Miss Miller signed to me to sit on a bench near the door, then walking up to the top of the long room, she cried out,

'Monitors, collect the lesson-books and put them away!'

Four tall girls arose from different tables, and going round, gathered the books and removed them. Miss Miller again gave the word of command,

'Monitors, fetch the supper-trays! . . .'

For the girls at Cowan Bridge, school life was probably no harder than for the new boys at Rugby. But Thomas Hughes, looking back in *Tom Brown's Schooldays* on his own experiences just as Charlotte Brontë was recalling hers, obviously approved, at least in retrospect, the ordeals they had to endure:

The sixth-form boys had not yet appeared, so to fill up the gap, an interesting and time-honoured ceremony was gone through. Each new boy was placed on the table in turn, and made to sing a solo, under the penalty of drinking a large mug of salt and water if he resisted or broke down. However, the new boys all sing like nightingales tonight, and the salt water is not in requisition . . . And at the half-hour down come the sixth- and fifth-form boys, and take their places at the tables, which are filled up by the next biggest boys, the rest, for whom there is no room at table, standing round about . . .

Augustus Hare was at Harrow a few years later than Hughes was at Rugby. He saw the relationship between senior and junior boys as nothing but cruel bullying. In *The Story of my Life*, he wrote:

How terrible the bullying was in our time . . . little boys were constantly sent in the evening . . . to bring back porter under their greatcoats, certain to be flogged by the headmaster if they were caught, and to be 'warped' by the sixth form boys if they did not go . . . If they did not 'keep up' at football, they were made to cut large thorn sticks out of the hedges, and flogged with them till the blood poured down outside their jerseys . . .

The explanation of the contrast between these two pictures of public school life lies not in the differences between Rugby and Harrow, but in the different outlooks of Hughes and Hare.

It is a moot point whether a novelist or dramatist reflects current opinion more than he leads and strengthens it. Would Dickens ever have written such a novel as *The Old Curiosity Shop* or Mrs Gaskell *Mary Barton* if, in the late 1830s and 1840s, a sizable section of the public had not already been concerned with the cruelty of life under industrial conditions? The answer is 'Probably not'. But it is equally true that both these novels helped to centre more public attention on this problem, and to increase sympathy for the victims. A historian goes to a novelist to study both the social scene of his generation, and to find out what his contemporaries were concerned about, what they took a pride in, and what they despised. He cannot of course assume that the novelist's judgement or scale of values is universal for his generation, but, to be accepted and successful, a novelist or a playwright must express the thought and opinion of at least a considerable minority of his fellows. He might be ahead of the majority, but he cannot be running entirely counter. To read Kipling's *Plain Tales from the Hills*, or even his *Stalky and Co.*, would rightly convince the reader that in the last two decades of Victoria's reign most Britishers took a solemn pride in, and were enthusiastic for, the Empire, just as to read or see Shaw's *The Devil's Disciple*, first produced in 1895, would lead him to think that, at the height of imperial fervour, there were at least a few Britishers critical of it.

Although the work of poets, novelists, dramatists, sociologists, economists, cartoonists, and photographers can all be plundered for contemporary political and social comment, the historian's most reliable and voluminous commentator is the journalist. The files of old journals and newspapers are stuffed with facts and current opinion on all kinds of subjects. Politics, however, is the newspaper's most consistent theme. We have already seen that the *raison d'être* of most of the eighteenth-century newssheets was to bring reports of parliamentary debates to their readers. The *Morning Chronicle*, first published in 1770, owed its spectacular early success to the excellent parliamentary reporting of William Woodfull. In the next two decades, however, James Perry's *Gazette* brought the *Morning Chronicle* to the verge of bankruptcy, simply because, by an ingenious deployment of a team of reporters, it managed to give its readers even more detailed reports of what went on in the Commons. The anti-authoritarian papers of the early nineteenth century – *Black Dwarf, Gorgon, Political Register,* and *The Poor Man's Guardian* – were almost entirely concerned with political news and comment, and throughout its long life, *The Times,* which began in 1785 as the *Daily and Universal Register,* has given political news priority. Even the sensational Sunday papers, which go back to the birth of *News of the World, Reynold's News,* and *Lloyd's Weekly News* in 1836, allotted considerable space to politics, and most of the nineteenth-century dailies, London or provincial, were founded to support one or other political party or to advocate a particular political policy. The *Evening Standard,* founded in 1827 primarily to oppose Catholic Emancipation, remained Tory in outlook. The Whig *Manchester Guardian* (1821) soon begot a Tory rival, the *Manchester Courier,* which began publication in 1825. And in 1886 a group of Yorkshire Tories founded the *Yorkshire Post* to counterbalance the radicalism of the *Leeds Mercury.* The first issue of the *Daily News,* dated 21 January 1846, carried four articles pressing for the repeal of the Corn Laws as well as a full report of a recent speech by Cobden at Ipswich. It continued to support the Liberal cause until twentieth-century competition forced it, first to combine with its political ally, the *Daily Chronicle,* distinguished in pre-1914 days for its support of the socially oppressed, and secondly, to cease publication altogether.

The style, size, and distribution of newspapers all changed dramatically during the course of the nineteenth century.

Under its first editor, John Walter, *The Times* was a single sheet folded across to form four pages. It was printed by hand, 'solid' in columns, and sold about a thousand copies of each edition. By the 1820s, it had more than doubled its newsprint and was distributing about 15,000 copies a day. *The Times* was exceptionally successful. The other dailies did not enjoy the support it received from the commercial middle class, and so did not reach anything like this circulation. It is true that in 1816 Cobbett's *Political Register* was printing over 40,000 copies of each number, but the *Register* was a weekly, and at that time it was avoiding stamp duty – and therefore selling cheaply at 2d. a copy – by printing no news, only comment. Each number consisted of a political letter, nominally addressed to such groups as 'The Journeymen and Labourers of England, Wales, Scotland, and Ireland', 'The Luddites', 'The Men of Bristol', or 'The Weaver Boys of Lancashire', but eagerly read by all who could lay hands on a copy, either to drink in the words with the eagerness of devoted disciples or to explode with wrath at Cobbett's latest enormity. The influential quarterlies – *Quarterly Review*, *Edinburgh Review*, and *Blackwood's* – were in similar style. Their political views were different from Cobbett's and they were not as single-mindedly political as the *Register*, but, like the *Register*, they carried no news. The Great Reform Bill became law in June 1832, but the next number of *The Edinburgh Review*, published in July, contained not a word about it in all its 286 pages. The political articles of that volume discussed the politics of the Italian states, the 'present state' of Spain, the taxation of insurance policies, British manufacturing industry, and 'corn-law rhymes'.

Three things were chiefly responsible for the nineteenth-century revolution in the newspaper world – the invention of automatic printing machines, the effect of the telegraph and the railway on communications and the speed and ease of distribution, and, in 1836, the reduction of the newspaper stamp duty from 4d. to 1d. a copy, followed by its total abolition twenty years later. These combined improvements meant that newspapers had a fuller, wider, and quicker coverage of news, that London could support an increased number of vigorous dailies, and that every important provincial centre could sustain at least one daily paper that both mirrored local opinion and exerted a strong political influence in its area. No longer had the local newspaper to be content with adding snippets of local news to political clippings from the London papers of the previous week.

For the historian, this radical change means that from the middle of the nineteenth century he can go to the newspaper files for much more material. As well as parliamentary reports (which he can find more handily in *Hansard*) and leader comment, he can look for detailed descriptions of events and occasions of all kinds, both national and local. These newspaper reports frequently constitute the best source available, for they have the authority of eyewitnesses and record immediate reactions and comment. As he turns the yellowing and crackling pages, the researcher's eye moves from general elections to murder trials, society scandals to scientific inventions, obituaries to sports reports. In the files of the national newspapers, he can also find lengthy descriptions of British activities overseas. The telegraph made possible the foreign and the war correspondent. Editors valued good correspondents for their scoops and the beneficial effect they had on circulation, but the historian looks not for speed of dispatch but for reliability and quality of descriptive reporting. W. H. Russell's dispatches to *The Times* from famine-stricken Ireland in 1845 and 1846 and from the battlefields in the Crimea are as valuable as historical sources as they were politically influential in the mid nineteenth century. Archibald Forbes sent the *Daily News* remarkable accounts of the progress of the siege of Paris in 1870–71 and of incidents in the first Boer War ten years later, and Henri

Blowitz, one of the many distinguished foreign correspondents of *The Times*, wrote colourful and well-informed accounts of such different events as the Congress of Berlin in 1878 and the repercussions of the Dreyfus case in the 1890s. And, of course, for the description and the atmosphere of such domestic, politically emotional issues as the Parnell scandal or the constitutional crisis of 1910–11, or for accounts of state occasions such as the jubilees or the coronations, or for the appreciation of national feeling about such controversial matters as the dockers' tanner, the pro-Boers, or votes for women, the columns of the newspapers of the day are the most reliable and most detailed sources.

Searching newspaper files is a tedious, if ultimately rewarding, job. If the researcher is not merely browsing but making a purposeful search for information on a particular topic, the nuggets he wants seem to be deeply buried in masses of irrelevant matter. Some libraries have been helpful by compiling indexes of their more important files, but where there is no index, there is no alternative to turning over page after page. The British Museum has the most comprehensive collection of British newspapers, both national and local. For newspapers before 1800 it is necessary to go to the Reading Room in Bloomsbury, but nineteenth- and twentieth-century newspaper files are at the special Newspaper Reading Room at Colindale, Hendon. All large reference libraries have substantial runs of some national and local newspapers, and more and more of them are supplementing their stock with microfilmed copies of missing numbers. Local historians are rightly making more use of the local newspaper files which they are discovering in 'the reserve stock' of town libraries or in the archives of newspaper offices. They find copies of newspapers they never knew existed, for every town or locality boasted two or three rival local newspapers, especially in the second half of the nineteenth century. Some of them only lived a few years or even a few months, but the weakest of them can add its tiny quota to the sum of historical information. In recent years, local groups of The Library Association have prepared lists of newspapers published before 1900. They not only give the titles and dates of newspapers published, but also guide the reader to where he will find the files available. From *Newspapers First Published before 1900 in Lancashire, Cheshire and The Isle of Man*, the booklet issued by the North-western group, the following, for Congleton and Manx papers, are two typical entries:

Congleton Advertiser. 4A [indicating that the copy is to be found in the Congleton Chronicle office] (Jul. 24, 1858, Special Sheet, 1858).

Congleton and Macclesfield Mercury. 4A (Jul. 10, 1858, Sep. 20, 1862, June 17 and Jul. 1, 1871, Sep. 6, 1873, Dec. 5, 1874, Jan. 3, 1880, Jul. 12 and Sep. 6, 1884, Ap. 19, 1890, Dec. 21 and 28, 1895).

Congleton Chronicle. 4A (Oct. 1893 –).

Congleton, Crewe and Sandbach Free Press and Macclesfield, Leek and Biddulph Observer. 4A (Oct. 13, 1883).

Congleton Guardian. 68A [i.e. in Nantwich Guardian office] (1902, one issue only).

Congleton, Sandbach and Crewe Advertiser and South Cheshire Record. 4A (Mar. 19, 1864).

Congleton Weekly. 4A (Ap. 15 and 29, 1893).

Isle of Man Examiner. 55 [i.e. in Douglas Public Library] (1880–87, 1894 –).

Isle of Man Times (Isle of Man Weekly Times). 55 (1867–1883, 1888–9, 1891–3, 1895–9, 1901 –).

Manx Advertiser. 55 (1802–6, 1811–22, 1825–6, 1828–31, 1837).

Manx Patriot. 55 (Oct. 1906–Nov. 1909).

Manx Reformer. 55 (Nov. 1902–Oct. 1904).

Manx Sun. 55 (1837–40, 1845–84, 1892–1906).

Manxman. 55. (1896–1900).

Mona's Herald. 55 (1838–40, 1843–6, 1850–80, 1891 –).

Local newspapers are particularly valuable for tracing the stages in the growth of the town, for finding out how reform legislation such as the Poor Law Amendment Act or Forster's

Education Act worked out in practice, for studying local reaction to such political upheavals as Chartism, the public health Acts, or the trade union movement, and for filling in the background to terse official reports of town councils or of local industrial, commercial, or cultured bodies and organizations.

From the beginning, newspapers have carried advertisements. Many newspapers have included the word *Advertiser* in their titles, and advertisements have always been a major factor in keeping down the cost and extending the distribution of newspapers. Advertisements have obvious uses for the social historian. A nineteenth-century private school announcing its syllabus, diet, and fees; a hotel stating its charges and amenities; a bookseller's list; the appearance of such new mechanical aids as sewing machines, bicycles, and horseless carriages; notices of auctions or property sales; the advertisements of clothing, furniture, patent medicines, sports gear, and food – all these and others like them help to give the social scene significant detail. Nineteenth-century advertising was relatively cheap. This allowed advertisers to print more information than they would feel justified in doing today, or to fill their allotted space with illustrations of their commodities. There is no need to imagine from verbal description what 'the patent mangle', 'thermal bath cabinet', 'pedestal combination closet', or 'Sawyer's velocipede' looked like. The picture in the appropriate advertisement is good enough to answer every reasonable question.

The invention of the camera and sensitized plate created another, increasingly fruitful source for the historian. Long before Scott-Archer, Madox, Bennett, and the other pioneers of the mid-Victorian era succeeded in quickening photographic processes and making them practical, newspaper editors knew the attractive power of illustration. They employed artists to make the drawings, and then reproduced their work by means of woodcuts. This method produced some striking results. The *Observer*, for example, carried excellent pictures of the coronations of William IV and Victoria, and from 1842 the *Illustrated London News* has supplied its readers with a weekly batch of pictures of contemporary happenings. The *Graphic* and the *Sphere*, with their fashionable offspring *Bystander and Tatler*, joined the ranks of the illustrated weeklies before the end of the century. They continued to use the traditional method of printing pictures, largely because of the cost and difficulty of making half-tone blocks. During Victoria's last years, photographic technicians forged ahead, but it was only in Edward VII's day that press photographers came into their own and editors began to print good photographs in every edition. Fortunately, the historian is not dependent on the newspapers or weekly journals for photographs from the last decades of the last century. There were many professional photographers and enthusiastic, competent amateurs. Most public libraries and record offices have built up local collections of their work, many firms have useful files of industrial and commercial photographs, local authorities keep their own records and private enthusiasts their own collections, and professional agencies, the chief of which is now the amalgamated Radio Times Hulton Picture Library, are constantly supplying old photographs of countless subjects to illustrate history books or press articles. Thanks to the photograph, we have an undimmed vision of the personalities, dress, homes, public buildings, transport, and political, military, social, and sporting occasions of the fifty years before 1914. We have nothing like this for any previous age. How far this extra faculty of clear visual impression helps the historian to understand and rightly interpret the age he is studying, it is still too early to determine.

Bibliography of Documents 1760 – 1914: Political and Social

All the reports of commissioners have been published either by royal command or by order of parliament. The official census returns are published by authority of the registrar general. For help in interpreting censuses see *Guide to Official Sources No. 2, Census Reports of Great Britain, 1801–1931* (1951) and 'The Taking of the Census, 1801–1951', by A. J. Taylor in *British Medical Journal* (7 April 1951). The report of Ramsbottom's medical officer quoted in the text is in the Lancashire Record Office.

Quotations have been taken from the following:

Queen Victoria's Letters, ed. A. C. Benson, Lord Esher and G. E. Buckle (1907 and 1926).

The Naval Miscellany, Vol. 2, Navy Records Society, Vol. 40 (1912).

The Correspondence of Lord Aberdeen and Princess Lieven, ed. E. Jones Parry, Camden Third Series, Vols. 60 and 62 (1938–9).

Disraeli, Robert Blake (1966).

The Greville Diary, ed. P. Whitwell Wilson (1927).

Creevey, John Gore (1948).

The Life and Works of the Seventh Earl of Shaftesbury, Edwin Hodder (1887).

A Portion of the Journal of Thomas Raikes (1856–7).

'The Diary of John Ward [O'Neil]', ed. R. S. France in *Transactions of the Historic Society of Lancashire and Cheshire*, Vol. 105 (1953).

Miss Weeton: Journal of a Governess, ed. Edward Hall (1969).

Details of the other diaries, letters, memoirs, and autobiographies mentioned in the text will be easily found in such classified bibliographies as those at the end of the appropriate volumes of *The Oxford History of England*.

Roscoe's poems have been collected in *William Roscoe, 1753–1831*, by G. Chandler (1953), and the election song is from *Addresses, Songs, Squibs etc. published during the Election of Members of Parliament for the Borough of Liverpool, October 1812* (1812).

Apart from the files of journals and newspapers themselves, there are a number of full texts or extracts printed in book form. The following are among the most useful to the historian:

Selections from Cobbett's Political Works, J. M. and J. P. Cobbett.

The Poor Man's Guardian, 1831–35, ed. Patricia Hollis (1969).

The Edinburgh Review, two quarterly issues bound together in each volume.

BIBLIOGRAPHY

The History of The Times (1935–1954).

The Victorian Scene, Nicolas Bentley (1968), is an attractive collection of pictorial illustrations of English life in the nineteenth century.

Throughout this period 1760–1914, *The Annual Register* provides a summary of the events of each year. It is principally concerned with political events, and its degree of impartiality varies as one editor succeeds another.

Cornucopia, a favourite image of minor poets, seems to be the word best fitted to describe the primary sources available to the historian studying the twentieth century. It is hard to think of anything he lacks: out of his horn of plenty flows an endless stream of records, the envy of all historians engaged on the study of more distant generations.

To begin with, he has everything that his 'nineteenth-century' colleague has, but in clearer detail and greater quantity. His copies of *Hansard* quote every word. Central government and administration has become increasingly complex, so that in and around Whitehall, daily piling up their papers, there are several new ministries, Labour and Health among them, in addition to the Home Office, the Board of Trade, and the rest of the well-established departments of government. To these must be added the nationalized industries and public corporations, each of which already has bulky stores of records. It is true that in this century the number of newspapers, national and local, has declined considerably, but single copies are much bigger – consider the Sunday papers! – more periodicals are being published, and the relevance of the foreign press, even to British domestic issues, has significantly increased since the end of the First World War. Fortunately, there are now two or three guides offering to help researchers find their way through the press jungle. *The Times* publishes an annual index to its files. Since 1931, *Keesing's Contemporary Archives* has been recording world events and collecting and summarizing press comment. *The Survey of International Affairs*, the annual publication of Chatham House, dates from 1925, and even more general guides such as *Dod's Parliamentary Companion* and *Who's Who* can often save much newspaper searching. And, of course, since the beginning of the twentieth century, the files of newspaper offices and press agencies have become the richest source for photographs. At least since 1914, the press photographer has played Jonathan to David, the press reporter.

More books are being published than ever before, so that, even for the study of short periods, there are shelves of pertinent social comment, economic inquiry, on-the-spot reporting, political argument, autobiography and reminiscence that no conscientious historian can ignore. Moreover, since the books have been recently published, there is no scarcity of available copies. Twentieth-century census returns outpace their predecessors both in size – population has continued to increase – and in the number of questions they pose and answer. Maps, directories, and illustrated topographical descriptions abound. Nor is the contemporary historian short of statistics. Quite apart from many special statistical studies that have been published both annually by government departments and irregularly by individual economists, he has the official, annual summaries, which before the Second World War were entitled *Statistical Abstract of the United Kingdom*, and since 1946 *Annual Abstract of Statistics*. On many occasions, however, such compilations as *Whitaker's Almanack* or *The Statesman's Year-Book* will satisfy his statistical needs. And then there is the vast field of local government, where the voluminous records of the committees and departments of county and county borough councils have replaced such lesser, obsolete sources as the minutes of school boards or improvement commissioners and the annual accounts of guardians or turnpike trusts.

On top of this untold wealth, there are the auditory and visual records that no previous century was capable of producing. The gramophone disc and the magnetic tape allow us to hear the twentieth-century past still talking: the film and video tape to see and hear it in action. 'Let's have that again', says the sports commentator, and on our television screens, with time to examine and judge, we have a second opportunity to see whether the batsman's leg was really obstructing the wicket, or by how much the tennis ball dropped outside the court. In a similar way, the archives of the film libraries and of the broadcasting and cinema companies make it possible for historians of the most recent past to study events by 'having them again'. Cornucopia indeed!

But among the many items flowing from the horn, some are sealed and some are marked private. These are not yet available for historical research. All official records are subject to the so-called 'thirty years rule', so that the contemporary historian cannot freely examine the basic material when, for example, he is studying government policy. Instead of being able to handle and read the mass of minutes, telegrams, and memoranda for himself, he has to be satisfied with press reports, official 'handouts', and such documents as other people have chosen, when writing their memoirs, or when compiling a commissioned selection of papers, or preparing an official history. Sir Herbert Samuel and Winston Churchill, to take but two examples, quoted plenty of primary documents in their autobiographical works. The *Correspondence between the Chairman of the Council of Ministers of the U.S.S.R. and the Presidents of the U.S.A. and the Prime Ministers of Great Britain during the Great Patriotic War of 1941–45*, and *Documents on British Foreign Policy, 1919–1939* are among the many published compilations of documents, and C. F. Aspinall-Oglander's *Gallipoli* and Sir Charles Webster and Noble Frankland's *The Strategic Air Offensive against Germany 1939–1945* are examples of official histories. All such books – and there are many of them – are welcome grist to the historian's mill, but they are an unsatisfactory substitute for a free and personal choice from all the documents potentially available. Again, the rich archives of television companies and press agencies are not open for research. Newspapers and commercial photographers usually respond helpfully to specific requests for photographs. A few selected broadcast programmes can be bought through commercial recording companies, and outstanding new films can be hired from educational film companies, the National Film Library, and the Imperial War Museum. But, once again, the historian has not the free choice he would like to have.

Another restriction on the contemporary historian's use of his material is the human mind's limited power to grasp and comprehend. Three factors chiefly contribute to this restriction. First, the contemporary historian cannot help but be emotionally involved in many of the issues he is writing about. His hatred of a particular policy, his admiration for a certain man or cause, his indifference to some problems, and his conviction that the best hope for the future is to do this and that – all these characteristics of a thinking, committed citizen and human being make it difficult for him to study the immediate past impartially and calmly. He cannot see the years of his own lifetime 'steadily'. Secondly, to continue Wordsworth's phrase, it is just as difficult for him to see them 'whole'. His face is too near the canvas of events. Parts of the panorama appear big, others distorted, and some are hardly visible, and yet it is impossible for him to step back to view it all in perspective. Thirdly, the section of the contemporary picture which is in his focus is so crowded with events, personalities, arguments, causes, issues, and interests jostling all together that he finds great difficulty in sorting out those things which are important and progressive. Of course, time will eventually make the picture more comprehensible: it will both improve the perspective by carrying the viewer farther away from the picture, and emphasize all that is fundamental, sincere, and significant, and diminish the evanescent, the shallow, and the trivial. But time is a provokingly slow worker. Most of us will be dead before it has done this job.

The archivist finds time just as frustrating as the historian does. He faces the big problem of which contemporary papers to preserve and which to destroy. Concerning records before the twentieth century, he has a very confident answer: *Hold fast to all that remain*. For good or ill, time and accident have already made their selections. Often they have been too drastic, so that, as we have already seen, historians are frequently left to create their jig-saw pictures from insufficient pieces. They have to guess what originally filled the gaps. But the archivist has no such obvious policy when faced with the mass of official and unofficial papers of today. Each single sheet is a record of the twentieth century: in the future, many of them will be eloquent about our way of life. Since it is not possible to preserve them all, the archivist has to decide which documents future historians will prize and which belittle. Time alone safeguards the answer, but, when it eventually reveals it, the irrevocable decision will have been taken. Just like present-day and all other historians, future historians of the twentieth century will have to fashion their interpretation of the past from the primary sources which they find themselves fortunate enough to inherit. They will not grumble. Historical study which did not involve perplexing and controversial problems of interpretation would be dull indeed.

INDEX

Dates following names of kings and queens are dates of their reign. Dates following other names are of birth and death, or death alone, or period when most active.

MORE ABOUT PENGUINS
AND PELICANS

Penguinews, which appears every month, contains details of all the new books issued by Penguins as they are published. From time to time it is supplemented by *Penguins in Print*, which is a complete list of all books published by Penguins which are in print. (There are well over three thousand of these.)

A specimen copy of *Penguinews* will be sent to you free on request, and you can become a subscriber for the price of the postage. For a year's issues (including the complete lists) please send 25p if you live in the United Kingdom, or 50p if you live elsewhere. Just write to Dept EP, Penguin Books Ltd, Harmondsworth, Middlesex, enclosing a cheque or postal order, and your name will be added to the mailing list.

Some other books published by Penguins are described on the following pages.

Note: *Penguinews* and *Penguins in Print* are not available in the U.S.A. or Canada

THE PELICAN HISTORY OF THE CHURCH

1. THE EARLY CHURCH
Henry Chadwick

The story of the early Christian church from the death of Christ to the Papacy of Gregory the Great. Professor Henry Chadwick makes use of the latest research to explain the astonishing expansion of Christianity throughout the Roman Empire.

2. WESTERN SOCIETY AND THE CHURCH IN THE MIDDLE AGES
R. W. Southern

In the period between the eighth and the sixteenth centuries the Church and State were more nearly one than ever before or after. In this new book Professor Southern discusses how this was achieved and what stresses it caused.

3. THE REFORMATION
Owen Chadwick

In this volume Professor Owen Chadwick deals with the formative work of Erasmus, Luther, Zwingli, Calvin, with the special circumstances of the English Reformation, and with the Counter-Reformation.

4. THE CHURCH AND THE AGE OF REASON
G. R. Cragg

This span in the history of the Christian church stretches from the age of religious and civil strife before the middle of the seventeenth century to the age of industrialism and republicanism which followed the French Revolution.

5. THE CHURCH IN AN AGE OF REVOLUTION
Alec R. Vidler

'A most readable and provocative volume and a notable addition to this promising and distinguished series' – *Guardian*

6. A HISTORY OF CHRISTIAN MISSIONS
Stephen Neill

This volume of *The Pelican History of the Church* represents the first attempt in English to provide a readable history of the worldwide expansion of all the Christian denominations – Roman Catholic, Orthodox, Anglican, and Protestant.

THE PELICAN HISTORY OF ENGLAND

While each volume is complete in itself, the whole series has been planned to provide an intelligent and consecutive guide to the development of English society in all its aspects. The nine volumes are:

'As a portent in the broadening of popular culture the influence of this wonderful series has yet to receive full recognition and precise assessment. No venture could be more enterprising or show more confidence in the public's willingness to purchase thoughtful books . . .' – *Listener*

ENGLAND IN TRANSITION

Dorothy George

This is a social history of England in the period from about 1690 to 1815. Dr George gives us a vivid picture of what is so often called 'the golden age', immediately before the Industrial Revolution. It is true that she shows us that the gold was strongly mixed with alloy, but the attraction remains. Apparently optimism has always been a feature of the English character. In the late seventeenth century, when more than half the population was said to be on the verge of pauperism, there was current a ballad which began 'Hang care, the parish is bound to save us'.

Dr George deals with England as it appeared to and was described by Defoe. She discusses the situation immediately prior to the dawn of the Machine Age; the coming of industrialism; the village in transition; and shows how old were some of the evils often supposed to be due to the Industrial Revolution. Her book is a delightful survey of a very interesting period in English history. It is illustrated by reproductions of contemporary prints.

A HISTORY OF LONDON LIFE

R. J. Mitchell and M. D. R. Leys

We have all heard of the Great Fire of 1666, but how many of us know of the Great Stink of 1858? The 'Blind Beak', Bartholomew Fair, public executions, the street vendors of birds' nests, groundsel, and lavender – these and many other curiosities are all described in this intriguing chronicle of the lives of London's inhabitants, ranging in time from pre-Roman days to the formation of the L.C.C. The authors, both distinguished historians, have drawn on varied contemporary sources such as unpublished letters, official documents, cartoons, and advertisements, to present an unusual and entertaining survey. Each of the chapters is linked with the name of a famous Londoner representative of his age, and through the eyes of such as Chaucer, the Chippendales, and Charles Dickens a fascinating composite picture of the metropolis emerges.

'Provides much welcome information, and is equipped with model footnotes to indicate sources. Sections cover every possible interest' – *Daily Telegraph*

A HISTORY OF BRITISH TRADE UNIONISM

Henry Pelling

'A genuine and worthwhile addition to the growing literature on trade unionism' – George Woodcock in the *Sunday Times*

Today trade unionism plays a more important part in the nation's economy than ever before, and its problems of internal reform and its relations with the government and the public are constantly under discussion. But its present structure can only be understood in relation to its long history.

Henry Pelling, a Fellow of St. John's College, Cambridge, and author of *The Origins of the Labour Party*, leads the reader through a vivid story of struggle and development covering more than four centuries: from the medieval guilds and early craftsmen's and labourers' associations to the dramatic growth of trade unionism in Britain in the nineteenth and twentieth centuries.

He shows how powerful personalities such as Robert Applegarth, Henry Broadhurst, Tom Mann, Ernest Bevin, and Walter Citrine have helped to shape the pattern of present-day unionism; and also how the problems of today's leaders stem from the need to adapt attitudes and structure moulded in the conflicts of earlier generations.

'Readable and intelligent' – *The Times Educational Supplement*

A DOCUMENTARY HISTORY OF ENGLAND
VOLUME I (1066–1540)

J. J. Bagley and P. B. Rowley

Since Magna Carta, and before, the development of English society has been marked by a progression of key conflicts and advances. These advances have been recorded in, or made possible by, a series of vital documents – religious, political, constitutional, and social – which moulded the course of our history, sometimes even to our own day. The names of most of these documents are household words, but how many people have ever had the opportunity to read them?

In the two volumes of this *Documentary History of England* the authors present the essential passages of the most important of these documents. To many readers the clarity and interest behind the dry names of Acts of Parliament and the like will come as a revelation. In addition each document had been introduced and placed in its historial context so that the general reader, as well as the student of history, can grasp its full significance.

This first volume studies fourteen key documents, from the Coronation of Henry I (1100) to the Act for the Dissolution of the Greater Monasteries 1539, and includes such crucial documents as the Magna Carta, the Cosmology of John Holywood and the Poor Law of 1388.

A *Documentary History of England: Volume 2 (1559–1931)*, by E. N. Williams, is already available in Pelicans.